Principles Of Software Engineering

Eric Frick

Copyright

For additional resources, hands-on labs, and course materials, visit: Destin Learning Lab at https://labs.destinlearning.com

Preface

Software development is about far more than writing code.

Learning to program is an important step toward becoming a software developer, but knowing how to write functions, create classes, work with databases, or build a web application is only part of the profession. In real-world software development, the code itself exists within a much larger process. Successful software must solve the right problem, satisfy the needs of its users, be designed thoughtfully, remain maintainable over time, operate securely and reliably, and evolve as requirements and technologies change.

That broader perspective is the focus of **Principles of Software Engineering**.

Software engineering is the discipline of applying structured methods, proven principles, and sound judgment to the creation and maintenance of software systems. It asks questions that go well beyond *How do I write this code?* A software engineer must also ask:

- What problem are we trying to solve?
- Who are the users and stakeholders?
- What are the actual requirements?
- How should the system be designed?
- How should the application be divided into components?
- How will those components communicate?
- How can the software be tested effectively?
- How will developers collaborate on the codebase?

- How will the system be secured?
- How will it be deployed, monitored, and maintained?
- What happens when requirements change?
- How can the system evolve without requiring us to start over?

These questions become increasingly important as software grows in size and complexity. A small program written by one developer may contain hundreds of lines of code. A production application can contain thousands, hundreds of thousands, or even millions of lines of code developed and maintained by teams over many years. At that scale, simply knowing how to program is not enough.

From Programmer to Software Engineer

One of the goals of this book is to help you begin making the transition from thinking primarily as a **programmer** to thinking as a **software engineer**.

A programmer naturally focuses on making code work. A software engineer must think about what happens after the code works.

Can another developer understand it?

Can it be tested?

Can it be changed safely?

Can the application handle additional users?

What happens when a component fails?

Can a security vulnerability in one part of the system compromise another?

Can a new developer join the team and understand how the application is structured?

Can the software still be maintained five years from now?

These concerns influence virtually every decision made during professional software development.

Throughout this book, you will explore the principles and practices that help engineering teams answer these questions. You will examine requirements engineering, software design, modeling, object-oriented design, SOLID principles, design patterns, software architecture, source control, maintainable code, testing, security, DevOps, software maintenance, cloud-native development, and distributed systems. The book also examines the growing role of artificial intelligence in software engineering and how AI tools can assist developers while preserving the need for human judgment and engineering discipline.

Software Development Is a Team Activity

Professional software development is also rarely an individual activity.

Software engineers work with other developers, architects, testers, project managers, product owners, business analysts, operations teams, security professionals, customers, and other stakeholders. The ability to communicate clearly and collaborate effectively can be every bit as important as technical ability.

Requirements must be discussed. Designs must be explained. Code must be reviewed. Tradeoffs must be evaluated. Problems must be documented. Production incidents must be investigated. Developers must frequently work on code written by someone else —and eventually, someone else will have to work on the code they write.

For this reason, good software engineering is as much about **people, processes, communication, and decision-making** as it is about programming.

Good Software Is Designed to Change

Another important theme of this book is that software is rarely finished.

Business requirements change. Users request new features. Security vulnerabilities are discovered. Technologies evolve. Systems need to scale. Dependencies must be updated. New developers join the team. Old components eventually need to be replaced.

A well-engineered system anticipates this reality.

Principles such as modularity, abstraction, encapsulation, separation of concerns, low coupling, high cohesion, automated testing, continuous integration, and clearly defined interfaces are not academic exercises. They help us create software that can change without becoming increasingly fragile.

The objective is not to create a perfect architecture or predict every future requirement. In fact, attempting to do so often creates unnecessary complexity. Instead, good software engineering seeks an appropriate balance between today's requirements and tomorrow's uncertainty.

Learning Software Engineering by Doing

Software engineering cannot be mastered by reading about it alone.

For that reason, this book emphasizes practical application. The concepts presented throughout the chapters are reinforced through hands-on exercises and labs that allow you to work with requirements, designs, source control, testing, refactoring, architecture, security, containers, continuous integration, cloud-native concepts, and AI-assisted development.

The goal is not simply to memorize terms such as *SOLID*, *dependency injection*, *microservices*, or *continuous integration*. The goal is to understand **why these ideas exist, what problems they solve, and when they should—or should not—be used**.

As you progress, try to approach each exercise as an engineer rather than simply as a programmer. Do not ask only whether your solution works. Ask whether it is understandable, maintainable, testable, secure, and appropriate for the problem being solved.

The Changing Role of the Software Engineer

Software engineering is entering another major period of change.

Artificial intelligence can now generate code, explain unfamiliar applications, create tests, identify potential defects, assist with requirements, suggest architectures, produce documentation, and help developers refactor existing systems. These capabilities will continue to improve.

This does not make software engineering principles less important. It makes them **more important**.

Generating code is becoming easier. Determining whether that code is correct, secure, maintainable, appropriate, and aligned with business requirements remains an engineering responsibility.

AI can suggest a solution. A software engineer must understand the problem.

AI can generate an architecture. A software engineer must evaluate the tradeoffs.

AI can generate tests. A software engineer must determine whether the right things are being tested.

AI can produce code quickly. A software engineer remains responsible for the software that ultimately reaches users.

The value of the modern software engineer increasingly lies not simply in the ability to type code, but in the ability to **understand systems, solve problems, evaluate alternatives, make sound technical decisions, and use powerful tools responsibly**.

More Than Code

If there is one idea I hope you carry throughout this book, it is this:

Software engineering is about building solutions—not simply writing code.

Code is the raw material from which software is constructed, but engineering provides the discipline that turns that code into a dependable system.

A successful software engineer learns to see the entire lifecycle: from an initial business problem to requirements, design, implementation, testing, deployment, operation, maintenance, and eventually modernization or replacement.

Developing that perspective takes time and experience. This book is intended to help you begin that journey.

Welcome to **Principles of Software Engineering**.

Eric Frick
Destin Learning

Table of Contents

Chapter 1: Introduction to Software Engineering and Development Processes

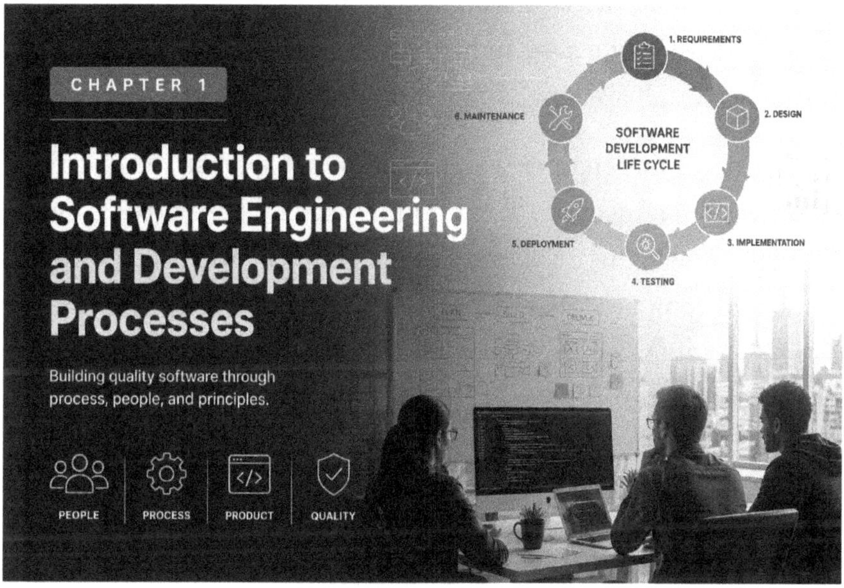

Software runs the modern world. The apps on your phone, the systems that route airline traffic, the machines that keep hospital patients alive, and the platforms that move trillions of dollars each day are all built from code. But writing code that works once, on your own machine, is very different from building software that thousands or millions of people can rely on day after day. That gap — between a clever program and a dependable product — is what this book is about.

In this chapter, you will learn what **software engineering** actually is and how it differs from the act of programming you may already know. You will explore how professional teams organize their work through the software development life cycle, who does what on those teams, and why so many software projects still fail despite decades of hard-won lessons. You will also survey the major process models the industry uses to build software, from the classic Waterfall approach to modern Agile and DevOps practices.

By the end of this chapter, you will be able to explain the discipline of software engineering, describe the phases every project moves through, weigh the risks and responsibilities that come with the work, and compare the leading development methodologies so you can reason about which one fits a given situation. These ideas form the foundation for everything that follows, so it is worth taking the time to understand them well.

1.1 What Is Software Engineering?

Before you can practice software engineering, you need a clear picture of what it is. Many people use the words *programming* and *software engineering* as though they mean the same thing. They do not. Programming is one activity inside a much larger discipline, and confusing the two leads to poor decisions, missed deadlines, and fragile systems.

In this section, you will learn a working definition of software engineering, see how it differs from programming, and understand what separates high-quality software from code that merely runs. These distinctions will shape how you think about your own work for the rest of your career.

What Is Software Engineering?

Software engineering is the systematic, disciplined application of engineering principles to the design, development, testing, deployment, and maintenance of software. The key word is *systematic*. Rather than relying on individual cleverness or last-minute heroics, software engineering brings repeatable processes, measurement, and accountability to the creation of software.

Think about how a bridge gets built. No one just starts pouring concrete. Engineers study the site, calculate the loads the bridge must carry, produce detailed plans, review those plans, build in a controlled way, and inspect the result before anyone drives across it. Software engineering applies that same mindset to software. The goal is to produce systems that are reliable, safe, and maintainable — not just programs that happen to work today.

The term itself dates back to the late 1960s, when the industry faced what became known as the **software crisis**. Projects were routinely late, over budget, and riddled with defects. Practitioners realized that building large software systems required more than talented individuals writing code; it required an engineering discipline. That realization is the root of everything in this book.

Software Engineering vs. Programming

Programming is the act of writing code that instructs a computer to perform a task. It is a craft, and it is an essential part of software engineering — but it is not the whole of it. A single programmer can write a working script in an afternoon. Building a payroll system that must handle tax law across fifty states, protect sensitive data, and run correctly every two weeks for a decade is a different kind of problem entirely.

Consider the difference in a simple example.

```
def calculate_total(prices):
    total = 0
    for price in prices:
        total += price
    return total

print(calculate_total([19.99, 5.49, 3.25]))
```

This code works. It correctly sums a list of prices and prints `28.73`. As a piece of *programming*, it is complete. But a software engineer immediately asks harder questions. What happens if the list is empty, or contains a string, or a negative number? Should the result be rounded to two decimal places for currency? Who else will use this function, and how will they know how to call it? Is it tested? Will the next developer understand it in a year?

A more engineered version might look like this:

```
def calculate_total(prices):
    """Return the sum of a list of item prices, rounded to cents.

    Args:
        prices: A list of non-negative numeric prices.

    Returns:
        The total as a float rounded to two decimal places.
    """
    if not prices:
        return 0.0
    total = sum(prices)
    return round(total, 2)
```

The logic is barely more complex, but the intent has changed. This version documents its behavior, handles the empty case explicitly, uses a clearer built-in, and rounds appropriately for money. The difference between the two versions is exactly the difference between programming and software engineering. Programming asks "does it work?" Engineering asks "will it keep working, for everyone, under all the conditions we care about?"

Characteristics of High-Quality Software

If the goal of software engineering is high-quality software, you need to know what "quality" actually means. It is not a vague feeling — it is a set of measurable, describable attributes.

- **Correctness:** The software does what it is supposed to do, according to its requirements.

- **Reliability:** It behaves consistently over time and recovers gracefully from errors rather than crashing.
- **Usability:** People can actually use it to accomplish their goals without confusion or frustration.
- **Maintainability:** Other developers can read, understand, and safely change the code later.
- **Efficiency:** It uses resources — time, memory, network, battery — sensibly for the job it does.
- **Security:** It protects data and resists misuse or attack.
- **Portability and scalability:** It can run in different environments and handle growth in users or data.

Notice that only some of these — correctness and efficiency, for instance — are visible when you run the program once. Others, like maintainability and reliability, only reveal themselves over months and years of real use. This is why quality cannot be bolted on at the end. It has to be built in from the start through deliberate engineering choices, which is the theme we will return to throughout this book.

Summary

- Software engineering is the systematic, disciplined application of engineering principles across the entire life of a software system, not just the coding phase.
- The concept arose from the 1960s software crisis, when the industry learned that large systems need an engineering discipline, not just talented individuals.
- Programming is writing working code; software engineering asks whether that code will keep working reliably for everyone under all expected conditions.
- High-quality software is defined by measurable attributes such as correctness, reliability, usability, maintainability, efficiency, security, and scalability.
- Many quality attributes only appear over time, which is why quality must be engineered in from the beginning rather than added at the end.

1.2 The Software Development Life Cycle and Development Teams

Building software is a journey with recognizable stages. Whether a project takes two weeks or two years, it moves through the same fundamental activities: figuring out what to build, designing it, building it, checking that it works, releasing it, and keeping it running. Understanding these stages gives you a mental map of any project you join.

In this section, you will learn the phases of the software development life cycle, why software engineering counts as a genuine engineering discipline, and the roles that make up a professional development team. Even if you plan to write code, knowing how the whole machine works will make you far more effective within it.

The Software Development Life Cycle

The **software development life cycle (SDLC)** is the sequence of phases a software product passes through from its first idea to its eventual retirement. Different organizations describe it with slightly different names, but the core phases are consistent:

1. **Requirements:** Discover and document what the software must do and the constraints it must satisfy.
2. **Design:** Decide how the system will be structured to meet those requirements — its architecture, data, and interfaces.
3. **Implementation:** Write the actual code that realizes the design.

4. **Testing:** Verify that the software meets its requirements and find defects before users do.
5. **Deployment:** Release the software into the environment where real users will use it.
6. **Maintenance:** Fix defects, adapt to changing needs, and improve the system over its operational life.

It is tempting to think of implementation — the coding — as the "real" work and everything else as overhead. In practice, the opposite is often true. Studies of long-lived systems consistently show that **maintenance** consumes the majority of a product's total cost, frequently more than half. The decisions you make in requirements and design ripple through every later phase. The SDLC is not bureaucracy; it is the structure that keeps those decisions from turning into expensive surprises.

Software Engineering as a Discipline

What makes software engineering a genuine *engineering discipline* rather than an art or a trade? Engineering disciplines share several traits: they rest on a body of established knowledge, they apply repeatable processes, they measure their work, and they hold practitioners accountable to standards. Software engineering has grown to include all of these.

The nature of the ripple effect makes this discipline especially valuable. A mistake caught early is cheap to fix; the same mistake caught late can be enormously expensive.

This relationship is one of the most important ideas in the entire field. A requirement misunderstood during planning might cost an hour to correct if you catch it then. If it slips through design, coding, and testing and only surfaces after release, correcting it may mean redesigning components, rewriting code, retesting the system, and issuing an emergency update to every customer. Engineering discipline pays off precisely because it front-loads the cheap corrections.

Roles on a Software Development Team

Modern software is built by teams, and teams are made up of specialized roles. You will rarely do all of these jobs yourself, but you will work alongside people who do. Understanding their responsibilities helps you collaborate effectively.

- **Product owner / product manager:** Decides *what* the product should do and in what priority, representing the users and the business.
- **Business analyst:** Bridges business needs and technical teams, often gathering and clarifying requirements.
- **Software engineer / developer:** Designs and writes the code that implements features.
- **Software architect:** Defines the high-level structure and key technical decisions that shape the whole system.
- **Quality assurance (QA) engineer:** Designs tests and verifies that the software meets its requirements.
- **UX/UI designer:** Designs how the product looks and how people interact with it.

- **DevOps / release engineer:** Automates building, testing, and deploying the software reliably.
- **Project manager / Scrum master:** Coordinates the team's work, removes obstacles, and keeps the effort on track.

These roles are not rigid walls. On a small team, one person may wear several hats; a startup founder might be product owner, developer, and DevOps engineer all at once. On a large team, each role may be filled by dozens of people. What matters is that all of these responsibilities exist on every serious project, whether or not there is a separate person for each one. Good engineers understand the whole picture and communicate across these boundaries.

Summary

- The software development life cycle organizes any project into recognizable phases: requirements, design, implementation, testing, deployment, and maintenance.
- Maintenance typically consumes the majority of a system's total cost, so coding is only one part of a much larger effort.
- Software engineering qualifies as an engineering discipline because it applies established knowledge, repeatable processes, measurement, and professional accountability.
- The cost of fixing a defect grows dramatically the later it is discovered, which is why engineering front-loads careful decisions.
- Professional software is built by teams of specialized roles, and understanding each role helps you collaborate even when one person wears several hats.

1.3 Risk, Failure, and Professional Responsibility

Software engineering is not a neutral technical exercise. The systems you build affect real people, sometimes in ways that are difficult to reverse. A defect in a game is an annoyance; a defect in a medical device or a financial system can cost fortunes or even lives. To engineer software responsibly, you have to take its risks seriously.

In this section, you will learn why software defects are so costly, why so many projects fail even with skilled people involved, and what professional and ethical responsibilities come with the job. You will also see how the role of the modern software engineer has expanded far beyond writing code.

The Cost of Software Defects

A **defect**, or bug, is any flaw in software that causes it to behave incorrectly. The cost of a defect is rarely limited to the effort of fixing the code. There is the cost of discovering it, diagnosing it, retesting the system, redeploying, and dealing with whatever damage it caused in the meantime — lost revenue, damaged reputation, or harm to users.

History offers sobering examples. In 1996, the Ariane 5 rocket exploded seconds after launch because of a software conversion error, destroying hundreds of millions of dollars of equipment. The Therac-25 radiation therapy machine delivered fatal overdoses in the 1980s due to software defects. More routinely, a single bad deployment can take a major online service offline for hours, costing companies millions. These are not stories about careless programmers. They are stories about the immense leverage software has, for good and for ill.

Why Software Projects Fail

If the industry has known about the software crisis for over fifty years, why do projects still fail so often? Failure here means being cancelled, drastically over budget, delivered far too late, or unusable once delivered. The causes are remarkably consistent across decades of research:

- **Unclear or changing requirements:** The team builds the wrong thing because no one clearly defined the right thing.
- **Poor communication:** Stakeholders, managers, and engineers misunderstand one another.
- **Unrealistic schedules and estimates:** Deadlines are set by wishful thinking rather than evidence.
- **Inadequate risk management:** Known dangers are ignored until they become emergencies.
- **Scope creep:** The project keeps growing as new features are added without adjusting time or resources.
- **Weak technical practices:** Little testing, no version control, or fragile design.

Notice how few of these are purely technical. Most software failures are failures of communication, planning, and expectations. This is a crucial insight for a beginning engineer:

your ability to listen, clarify, and manage expectations matters as much as your ability to write clever code.

Professional and Ethical Responsibilities

Because software has such reach, engineers carry real responsibilities. Professional bodies such as the ACM and IEEE have published codes of ethics that spell these out. At their heart, they ask you to act in the public interest, to be honest about what your software can and cannot do, to protect user privacy and security, and to maintain your own competence.

In everyday terms, this means you do not ship code you know to be dangerously broken. You do not quietly collect user data you were not authorized to collect. You raise concerns when you are asked to cut corners on safety. You give honest estimates rather than telling managers what they want to hear. These may sound simple, but they can be genuinely hard when a deadline looms or a boss is unhappy. Ethics in engineering is mostly about doing the right thing when it is inconvenient.

The Modern Software Engineer

The role of the software engineer has broadened dramatically. Not long ago, a developer might write code and hand it to a separate team to test and yet another team to deploy. Today, engineers are increasingly expected to own their software across its whole life — writing it, testing it, deploying it, monitoring it in production, and responding when it breaks.

This "you build it, you run it" philosophy means that modern engineers must understand testing, security, deployment automation, and operations, not just their programming language. They collaborate constantly, work in short feedback cycles, and treat quality as their own responsibility rather than someone else's checkpoint. The rest of this book will prepare you for exactly this kind of well-rounded, responsible engineering.

Summary

- The true cost of a software defect includes discovery, diagnosis, retesting, redeployment, and real-world damage — not just the code fix.
- High-profile failures like Ariane 5 and Therac-25 show the immense leverage software carries and why reliability matters.
- Most project failures stem from non-technical causes such as unclear requirements, poor communication, unrealistic schedules, and scope creep.
- Professional codes of ethics call on engineers to act in the public interest, be honest, protect users, and maintain their competence, especially when it is inconvenient.
- The modern engineer owns software across its whole life cycle, embracing a "you build it, you run it" mindset that spans testing, deployment, and operations.

1.4 Classic and Iterative Process Models

Knowing the phases of the SDLC tells you *what* activities happen. A **process model** tells you *how* to arrange those activities in time — in what order, how often, and with how much overlap. Choosing a process model is one of the most consequential decisions a team makes, because it shapes how the project responds to change, risk, and discovery.

In this section, you will learn what a software development process is, then study three foundational models: the sequential Waterfall model, the family of iterative and incremental approaches, and the risk-driven Spiral model. These classic models are the ancestors of everything that came later, including Agile.

Understanding the Software Development Process

A **software development process** is the particular way a team applies the SDLC phases to build a product. Two teams can both perform requirements, design, coding, and testing yet organize them completely differently. One might insist on finishing all requirements before any coding begins. Another might build a little, test it, show it to users, and repeat.

There is no single correct process. Each model makes trade-offs between predictability and flexibility, between up-front planning and rapid feedback. The right choice depends on the project's risk, the stability of its requirements, and the environment the team works in. Learning several models gives you the vocabulary and judgment to pick well.

The Waterfall Model

The **Waterfall model** is the classic sequential approach. The project flows downward through the phases in strict order: complete all requirements, then all design, then all implementation, then all testing, then deployment. Each phase must finish before the next begins, and each produces a formal document that feeds the phase after it.

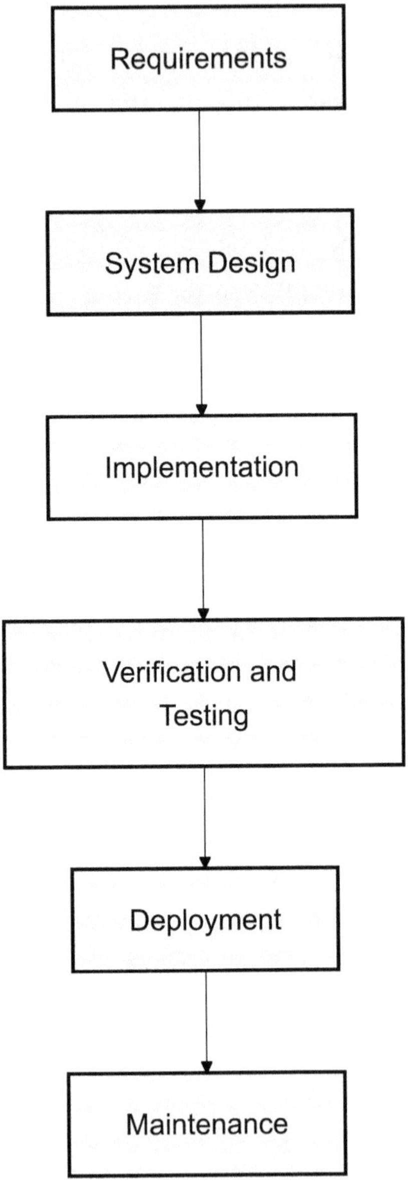

Waterfall's greatest strength is discipline and predictability. Because everything is documented and each phase is signed off, the project is easy to plan, budget, and audit. This makes Waterfall a reasonable fit for projects with stable, well-understood requirements — for instance, systems governed by fixed regulations or contracts.

Its great weakness is rigidity. Waterfall assumes you can know all the requirements up front and that they will not change. In reality, users often do not know exactly what they want until they see something working, and requirements shift as the world changes. In Waterfall, testing happens near the very end, which is precisely where defects are most expensive to fix. A misunderstanding baked into the requirements may not be discovered until months of work have been built on top of it.

Iterative and Incremental Development

The response to Waterfall's rigidity is to stop trying to do everything once, in order, and instead work in repeated cycles. **Iterative development** means building the system in successive versions, refining it a bit more each time. **Incremental development** means delivering the system in pieces, adding functional chunks one at a time. In practice the two ideas are usually combined.

Imagine building a shopping app. Instead of specifying, designing, and building the entire app before anyone sees it, you build a small working slice — say, browsing products — then show it, gather feedback, and build the next slice, like the shopping cart. Each cycle passes through requirements, design, coding, and testing for that slice. This approach surfaces misunderstandings early, when they are cheap to fix, and delivers usable value long before the whole system is complete. The cost is that it requires more coordination and is harder to plan as a single fixed schedule.

The Spiral Model

The **Spiral model**, introduced by Barry Boehm, combines iterative development with a strong focus on **risk**. The project proceeds through repeated loops, and each loop is divided into four activities: identifying objectives, evaluating alternatives and analyzing risks, developing and testing that cycle's product, and planning the next loop.

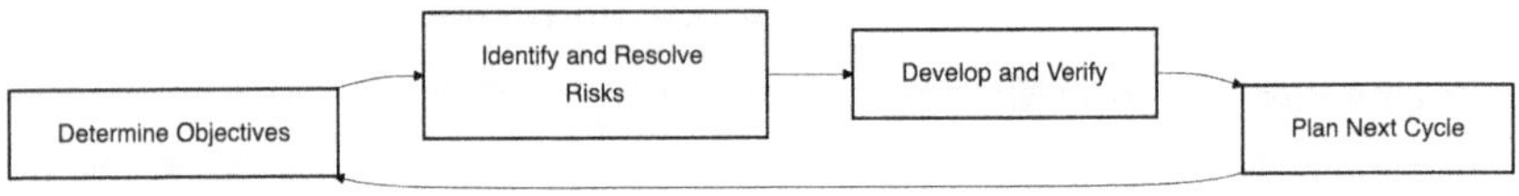

The defining idea of the Spiral model is that the biggest risks are tackled first. Early loops might produce nothing more than a paper design or a throwaway prototype whose only purpose is to answer a scary question — Can this technology even do what we need? Is this algorithm fast enough? Only once the major uncertainties have been reduced does the team invest in building tested, production-quality code in later loops.

This makes the Spiral model especially suitable for large, expensive, high-risk projects where an unexamined assumption could sink the whole effort. Its downside is complexity: it demands genuine risk-assessment expertise and can be overkill for small, low-risk projects where the constant risk analysis is more overhead than benefit.

Summary

- A software development process is the specific way a team arranges the SDLC phases in time; there is no single correct choice.
- The Waterfall model runs the phases in strict sequence with formal documents between them, offering predictability but little flexibility for change.
- Iterative and incremental development build the system in repeated cycles and functional slices, surfacing problems early and delivering value sooner.
- The Spiral model wraps iterative development around explicit risk analysis, tackling the biggest uncertainties first through prototypes before committing to full production.
- Each model trades off up-front planning against adaptability, and the best fit depends on the project's risk and requirement stability.

1.5 Agile Software Development

By the 1990s, many teams had grown frustrated with heavy, document-driven processes that struggled to cope with change. Requirements shifted faster than plans could keep up, and rigid processes produced software that satisfied the specification but not the customer. Out of this frustration grew a movement that reshaped the industry: **Agile**.

In this section, you will learn the values and principles behind Agile software development, then study its two most popular frameworks — Scrum and Kanban. Agile is not a single method but a mindset, and understanding that mindset is essential for working on almost any modern software team.

Agile Software Development and the Agile Manifesto

In 2001, seventeen software practitioners met and wrote the **Agile Manifesto**, a short statement of shared values. It expresses four preferences:

- **Individuals and interactions** over processes and tools
- **Working software** over comprehensive documentation
- **Customer collaboration** over contract negotiation
- **Responding to change** over following a plan

The manifesto is careful to say that the items on the right still have value; the items on the left simply have *more*. Agile does not mean "no documentation" or "no planning." It means valuing real, working software and real human collaboration above paperwork and rigid adherence to a plan that may already be out of date.

Underneath these values lie twelve principles, but the spirit is captured in a few ideas: deliver working software frequently, welcome changing requirements even late in development, build projects around motivated individuals, and reflect regularly on how to improve. Agile embraces the reality that you cannot know everything up front, so it builds constant feedback and adaptation into the process itself.

Scrum

Scrum is the most widely used Agile framework. It organizes work into short, fixed-length cycles called **Sprints**, typically one to four weeks long. The goal of each Sprint is to produce a *potentially shippable increment* — a piece of genuinely working software.

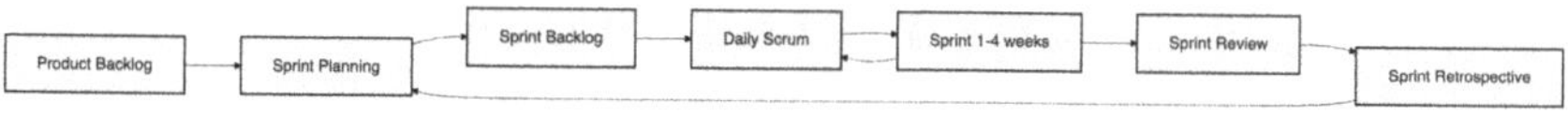

Scrum defines a small set of roles, artifacts, and events. The **Product Owner** owns and prioritizes the **Product Backlog**, the master list of everything the product might need. The **Scrum Master** helps the team follow the process and removes obstacles. The **Development Team** does the building. At the start of each Sprint, the team pulls the highest-priority items into a **Sprint Backlog** during Sprint Planning. Each day they hold a brief **Daily Scrum** to synchronize. At the end they demonstrate the increment in a **Sprint Review** and reflect on their process in a **Sprint Retrospective**.

The power of Scrum lies in its rhythm. Every few weeks, the team delivers something real, gets feedback, and adjusts. Priorities can change between Sprints without derailing the project, because only the current Sprint's work is committed. This steady cadence of build-inspect-adapt is what makes Scrum so responsive to change compared to the classic models.

Kanban

Kanban takes a different approach to agility. Rather than organizing work into fixed time boxes, it focuses on visualizing the flow of work and managing it continuously. The heart of Kanban is the **Kanban board**, a set of columns representing the stages work passes through — for example, *To Do*, *In Progress*, *Testing*, and *Done*. Each task is a card that moves across the board.

The defining rule of Kanban is the **work-in-progress (WIP) limit**: each column may only hold a set maximum number of cards at once. This sounds minor but is transformative. By limiting how much can be in progress simultaneously, Kanban forces the team to finish work before starting new work, which exposes bottlenecks and improves the overall flow. Kanban has no Sprints and no prescribed roles; work is pulled continuously as capacity frees up. This makes it a strong fit for teams with a steady stream of incoming requests, such as support or maintenance teams, where the workload does not divide neatly into fixed cycles.

Summary

- Agile is a mindset expressed by the Agile Manifesto, which values individuals, working software, customer collaboration, and responding to change.
- Agile does not reject documentation or planning; it simply values working software and adaptation more highly than paperwork and rigid plans.
- Scrum organizes work into fixed-length Sprints that each produce a potentially shippable increment, using defined roles, artifacts, and events to sustain a build-inspect-adapt rhythm.
- Kanban visualizes work as cards flowing across a board and uses work-in-progress limits to expose bottlenecks and improve continuous flow.
- Scrum suits work that divides into fixed cycles, while Kanban suits a continuous stream of incoming tasks.

1.6 DevOps and Choosing a Methodology

Agile solved much of the problem of building the right software quickly, but a gap remained. Development teams could produce working software rapidly, yet handing that software off to a separate operations team to deploy and run often created delays, friction, and finger-pointing. **DevOps** emerged to close that gap and complete the modern picture of software delivery.

In this final section, you will learn what DevOps is and the practices that support it, and then step back to consider how to choose among all the methodologies you have studied. The goal is not to crown one winner but to help you reason about which approach fits a given situation.

DevOps and Modern Development Practices

DevOps is a culture and set of practices that unite software **Dev**elopment and IT **Op**erations so that software can be built, tested, released, and operated smoothly and continuously. It grew directly out of the Agile mindset, extending the principles of collaboration and fast feedback beyond development into deployment and operations.

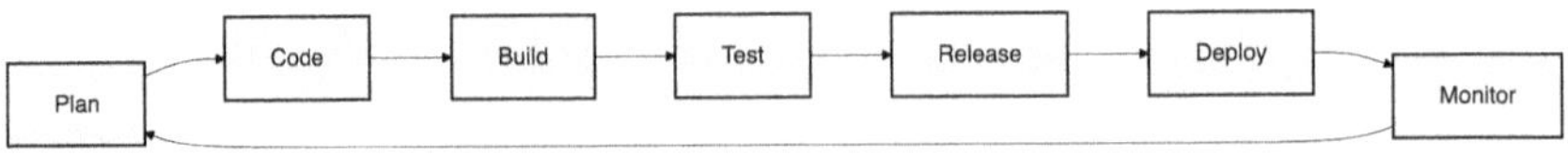

DevOps rests on several key practices. **Continuous Integration (CI)** means developers merge their code into a shared repository frequently, where automated builds and tests run against every change. **Continuous Delivery (CD)** extends this so that software is always in a releasable state, with deployments automated and repeatable. **Infrastructure as Code** treats servers and environments as configuration files that can be versioned and recreated reliably. **Monitoring and observability** feed real production data back to the team so they learn quickly when something goes wrong.

Together these practices turn releasing software from a rare, stressful event into a routine, low-risk activity. Some organizations deploy to production many times a day with confidence, because automation and testing catch problems long before users do. The cultural core of DevOps is shared ownership: developers and operations succeed or fail together, and quality is everyone's job.

Choosing a Development Methodology

You have now seen a spectrum of approaches, from the highly structured Waterfall model to the flexible flow of Kanban and the continuous delivery of DevOps. A natural question follows: which one should you use? The honest answer is that it depends, and a good engineer learns to reason about the trade-offs rather than following fashion.

Consider a few guiding questions when evaluating an approach:

- **How stable are the requirements?** Stable, well-understood requirements favor more sequential approaches; uncertain or evolving requirements favor Agile.
- **How high is the risk?** Large, high-risk projects benefit from risk-driven models like Spiral or from delivering small, testable increments.

- **How much does the customer need to be involved?** Frequent feedback favors iterative and Agile methods.
- **How quickly must you release and update?** Fast, frequent releases point strongly toward Agile combined with DevOps automation.
- **What are the team and organization ready for?** A methodology only works if the people and culture can actually support it.

In practice, most modern teams do not pick a single pure model from a textbook. They blend ideas — running Scrum for planning, using Kanban boards to visualize flow, and adopting DevOps automation to deliver continuously. What matters is understanding *why* each practice exists and *what problem it solves,* so you can assemble a process that genuinely fits your project rather than cargo-culting someone else's. That judgment is the mark of a real software engineer, and developing it is the work of your entire career.

Summary

- DevOps unites development and operations through culture and automation so software can be built, released, and operated continuously and reliably.
- Core DevOps practices include continuous integration, continuous delivery, infrastructure as code, and monitoring, which together make releasing routine and low-risk.
- The cultural heart of DevOps is shared ownership, where developers and operations succeed together and quality is everyone's responsibility.
- No single methodology is universally best; the right choice depends on requirement stability, risk, customer involvement, release frequency, and organizational readiness.
- Most modern teams blend Scrum, Kanban, and DevOps practices, and the mark of a good engineer is understanding why each practice exists rather than following it blindly.

Chapter Summary

This chapter laid the foundation for everything that follows by answering a deceptively simple question: what does it mean to build software well? You began by distinguishing software engineering from programming, learning that engineering is the systematic, disciplined pursuit of software that is not merely working but correct, reliable, maintainable, and safe over its entire life. From there you saw how that discipline plays out across the software development life cycle and across the specialized roles of a real development team.

The chapter then confronted the stakes of the work. Because software carries enormous leverage, its defects can be catastrophically expensive, and most project failures trace back not to weak code but to weak communication, planning, and expectations. Those realities give rise to genuine professional and ethical responsibilities and to the modern expectation that engineers own their software from idea through operation. To meet those responsibilities, teams organize their work using process models — and you surveyed the whole landscape, from sequential Waterfall through iterative, incremental, and Spiral approaches, into the Agile frameworks of Scrum and Kanban, and finally into the continuous, automated world of DevOps.

Taken together, these ideas give you a map of the profession. You can now describe what software engineering is, explain how projects move from concept to retirement, recognize the risks that derail them, and compare the major methodologies teams use to manage that journey. Every later chapter — on requirements, design, coding practices, testing, and delivery — builds on this map, filling in the concrete skills that turn these principles into working, dependable software.

Chapter Lab: Comparing Development Methodologies for a Real Project

In this lab, you will step into the role of a technical lead evaluating how to run a software project. Given a project scenario with its own requirements, risks, and constraints, you will analyze the situation and recommend a development methodology, justifying your choice using the trade-offs explored in this chapter. You will apply your understanding of the SDLC, the classic and Agile process models, and DevOps practices to make and defend a real engineering decision.

Chapter 2: Requirements Engineering

Every successful software project begins not with code, but with understanding. Before a single line is written, someone must answer a deceptively simple question: what should this software actually do? **Requirements engineering** is the discipline of discovering, documenting, and managing the answer to that question. It sits at the very front of the software lifecycle, and the decisions made here ripple through every phase that follows.

In this chapter, you will learn why requirements matter so much, and what happens when teams get them wrong. Studies consistently show that the most expensive defects are not coding mistakes but misunderstandings about what the software was supposed to do in the first place. A requirement misunderstood in week one can cost a hundred times more to fix after release than it would have cost to clarify up front. By the end of this chapter, you will be able to distinguish between different kinds of requirements, gather them from the people who matter, express them in clear and testable ways, and manage them as they inevitably change over time.

Building on the software development lifecycle concepts from Chapter 1, we now zoom in on that critical first phase. You already understand that software moves through distinct stages. Here you will see how the quality of your requirements work determines the quality of everything downstream. Think of requirements as the foundation of a building: no amount of skilled construction can save a house built on a cracked foundation.

2.1 Understanding Software Requirements

Before you can gather or manage requirements, you need to understand what a requirement actually is and what forms it can take. This foundational understanding shapes how you think about every project you work on. In this section, you will learn what requirements are, who they come from, and how to classify them into two essential categories.

The distinctions you learn here are not academic hair-splitting. They directly affect how you plan, estimate, design, and test software. A team that cannot tell the difference between what a system must do and how well it must do it will struggle to build software that satisfies anyone.

What Is a Software Requirement?

A **software requirement** is a statement that describes a capability or condition the software must provide or satisfy. In plain terms, a requirement expresses something the system needs to do or a quality it must have. Requirements are the bridge between the fuzzy world of human needs and the precise world of software behavior.

Consider a real-world analogy. When you order a custom cake, you might say, "I want a chocolate cake for twelve people that says 'Happy Birthday' and is ready by Saturday." Each of those phrases is a requirement. The baker cannot start without them, and if any is misunderstood, the result disappoints. Software works the same way, only the stakes and the complexity are usually higher.

Good requirements share several qualities. They are **clear**, meaning only one reasonable interpretation exists. They are **complete**, capturing everything needed without gaps. They are **consistent**, not contradicting one another. And critically, they are **verifiable**, meaning you can objectively confirm whether the finished software satisfies them. A requirement you cannot test is a wish, not a requirement.

Stakeholders and Business Needs

Requirements do not appear out of thin air. They originate from **stakeholders**, which are the people and groups who have an interest in the software or are affected by it. Identifying your stakeholders early is one of the most important steps in requirements engineering, because a requirement you never hear about is a requirement you cannot satisfy.

Stakeholders fall into several groups. There are **end users**, who interact with the software directly. There are **business owners**, who fund the project and expect it to deliver value. There are **domain experts**, who understand the specialized rules of the field. And there are often others: legal teams, security officers, operations staff, and external partners. Each group sees the system through a different lens, and each brings its own needs.

Behind every requirement lies a **business need**, which is the underlying reason the software is being built at all. Your job as an engineer is to trace requirements back to these needs. When a stakeholder asks for a specific feature, the more valuable question is often "why?" Understanding the need behind the request lets you propose solutions the stakeholder may not have imagined, and it protects you from building the wrong thing well.

Functional Requirements

Functional requirements describe what the system must do. They specify behaviors, features, and functions: the actions the software performs in response to inputs and conditions. Most people, when they imagine requirements, are thinking of functional requirements.

Here is a simple way to model functional requirements in code, treating each one as a discrete, checkable behavior.

```
class FunctionalRequirement:
    def __init__(self, req_id, description, actor, action):
        self.req_id = req_id
        self.description = description
        self.actor = actor
        self.action = action

    def summary(self):
        return f"{self.req_id}: {self.actor} shall {self.action}"


login = FunctionalRequirement(
    req_id="FR-01",
    description="Registered users can access their account",
    actor="registered user",
    action="log in using email and password",
)

print(login.summary())
```

This code produces the output `FR-01: registered user shall log in using email and password`. Notice the structure of the requirement itself: an **actor** performs an **action**. This "actor-action" pattern is a reliable template for writing functional requirements clearly. The word "shall" is a convention in requirements writing that signals a mandatory behavior, removing ambiguity about whether the feature is optional.

Functional requirements are usually the easiest to identify because stakeholders naturally think in terms of features. "The system should let me search for products." "Managers should be able to approve expense reports." Each is a discrete capability you can build and test.

Nonfunctional Requirements

If functional requirements describe what the system does, **nonfunctional requirements** describe how well it does it. These are the quality attributes: performance, security, reliability, usability, and more. They are often invisible in casual conversation, yet they frequently determine whether users actually love or abandon your software.

Consider two systems that both "let users log in." One responds instantly and never loses data; the other takes ten seconds and occasionally locks people out. They satisfy the same functional requirement but differ enormously in their nonfunctional qualities. That difference is what separates a professional product from a frustrating one.

```python
nonfunctional_requirements = [
    {"id": "NFR-01", "type": "performance",
     "statement": "Login must complete within 2 seconds for 95% of requests"},
    {"id": "NFR-02", "type": "security",
     "statement": "Passwords must be stored using a salted hash"},
    {"id": "NFR-03", "type": "availability",
     "statement": "The system must be available 99.9% of each month"},
]

for nfr in nonfunctional_requirements:
    print(f"[{nfr['type'].upper()}] {nfr['id']}: {nfr['statement']}")
```

This snippet lists three nonfunctional requirements, each tied to a measurable target. The key detail is the presence of numbers: "within 2 seconds," "99.9%," and a specific security technique. Vague nonfunctional requirements like "the system should be fast" are worthless because no one can verify them. Attaching concrete, measurable criteria turns a preference into a testable requirement. Nonfunctional requirements are notoriously easy to overlook, so make a habit of asking about performance, security, and reliability on every project.

Summary

- A **software requirement** is a clear, verifiable statement of what the system must do or what quality it must have.
- **Stakeholders** are the people affected by the software, and every requirement should trace back to a genuine **business need**.
- **Functional requirements** describe system behaviors, often following an actor-action pattern.
- **Nonfunctional requirements** describe quality attributes like performance and security, and must include measurable targets to be verifiable.

2.2 Gathering and Expressing Requirements

Knowing what requirements are is only the beginning. The harder work is coaxing them out of stakeholders who may not fully know what they want, and then writing them down in a form your team can build and test. This section teaches you the practical techniques professionals use to gather and express requirements.

You will learn how to gather requirements through structured conversation, and how to capture them using two industry-standard formats: **user stories** and **use cases**. You will also learn how to attach **acceptance criteria** that make a requirement testable. Together, these tools turn vague conversations into a shared, actionable understanding.

Requirements Gathering

Requirements gathering, sometimes called requirements elicitation, is the process of discovering what stakeholders need. The word "elicitation" is telling: you rarely just receive requirements as a neat list. You have to draw them out, because stakeholders often know their problems better than their solutions.

Several techniques help you gather requirements effectively:

- **Interviews:** One-on-one conversations that dig deep into a stakeholder's needs and frustrations.
- **Workshops:** Group sessions where stakeholders collaborate, surfacing disagreements early.

- **Observation:** Watching users do their actual work, which reveals needs they would never think to mention.
- **Document analysis:** Studying existing systems, forms, and reports to understand current processes.
- **Prototyping:** Building quick mockups so stakeholders can react to something concrete.

The most important skill in gathering requirements is not talking but listening, and asking "why." When a user says they need a button that exports data to a spreadsheet, the real need might be that they must report figures to their manager every Friday. Understanding that underlying need might lead you to a better solution, such as automated reports, that the user never requested.

User Stories

A **user story** is a short, simple description of a feature told from the perspective of the person who wants it. User stories became popular with agile development because they keep the focus on user value rather than technical detail. They are intentionally brief, meant to spark a conversation rather than replace one.

The classic user story template has three parts: a role, a goal, and a benefit.

```python
def user_story(role, goal, benefit):
    return (f"As a {role},\n"
            f"I want to {goal},\n"
            f"so that {benefit}.")


story = user_story(
    role="frequent shopper",
    goal="save items to a wishlist",
    benefit="I can quickly find them when I am ready to buy",
)

print(story)
```

This function assembles a well-formed user story from its three parts. The output reads: "As a frequent shopper, I want to save items to a wishlist, so that I can quickly find them when I am ready to buy." The power of this format lies in the third clause. The "so that" phrase forces you to state the benefit, which is really the business need in disguise. If you cannot articulate the benefit, you should question whether the feature is worth building at all.

User stories deliberately avoid technical implementation details. They do not say how the wishlist is stored or what the button looks like. That freedom lets the development team choose the best technical approach while keeping everyone anchored to the user's actual goal.

Use Cases

Where user stories are brief, **use cases** are detailed. A use case describes a complete interaction between an actor and the system to achieve a goal, including the step-by-step flow and the alternative paths when things go differently than expected. Use cases shine when a process is complex and you need to capture exactly how it should unfold.

```
withdraw_cash_use_case = {
    "name": "Withdraw Cash",
    "actor": "Bank Customer",
    "precondition": "Customer has a valid, activated card",
    "main_flow": [
        "Customer inserts card and enters PIN",
        "System validates the PIN",
        "Customer selects a withdrawal amount",
        "System verifies sufficient funds",
        "System dispenses cash and prints a receipt",
    ],
    "alternate_flows": {
        "Invalid PIN": "System prompts for re-entry, up to 3 attempts",
        "Insufficient funds": "System displays an error and cancels",
    },
}

print(f"Use Case: {withdraw_cash_use_case['name']}")
for step_number, step in enumerate(withdraw_cash_use_case["main_flow"], start=1):
    print(f"  {step_number}. {step}")
```

This dictionary captures a use case for withdrawing cash from an ATM. The loop prints the numbered main flow, which represents the ideal path where everything goes right. The **precondition** states what must be true before the use case begins, and the **alternate flows** capture what happens when reality deviates, such as an invalid PIN or insufficient funds. Those alternate flows are where use cases earn their value, because real systems must handle failure gracefully, not just success.

Choose the right tool for the job. Reach for user stories when you want lightweight, conversation-driven features. Reach for use cases when a process is intricate enough that the details of every branch truly matter, such as financial transactions or regulated workflows.

Acceptance Criteria

A user story or use case tells you what to build, but **acceptance criteria** tell you when you are done. Acceptance criteria are the specific, testable conditions that must be true for a requirement to be considered satisfied. Without them, "done" becomes a matter of opinion, and opinions cause endless arguments.

A popular format for writing acceptance criteria is the **Given-When-Then** pattern, which describes a starting context, an action, and an expected outcome.

```
def acceptance_criterion(given, when, then):
    return f"GIVEN {given}\nWHEN {when}\nTHEN {then}"


criterion = acceptance_criterion(
    given="a shopper is viewing a product page",
    when="they click the 'Add to Wishlist' button",
    then="the item appears in their wishlist and a confirmation message is shown",
)

print(criterion)
```

This function formats a single acceptance criterion using Given-When-Then. The output spells out exactly what a tester or developer should check: starting from a product page, clicking the button must add the item and show a confirmation. Because each clause is concrete, there is no room for disagreement about whether the story is finished. A single story usually needs several such criteria to cover its important scenarios, including error cases. When you write acceptance criteria before development starts, you effectively define your tests up front, which is one of the most powerful habits in professional software engineering.

Summary

- **Requirements gathering** is an active process of eliciting needs through interviews, workshops, observation, and prototyping.
- **User stories** capture features briefly in a role-goal-benefit format that keeps the focus on user value.
- **Use cases** provide detailed, step-by-step interactions including alternate flows, ideal for complex processes.
- **Acceptance criteria**, often written in Given-When-Then form, define the testable conditions that mark a requirement as complete.

2.3 Managing Requirements Over Time

Requirements are not carved in stone. Markets shift, stakeholders change their minds, and new information emerges as the project unfolds. A requirement that made perfect sense in month one may be obsolete by month six. Learning to manage requirements over their lifetime is what separates teams that stay in control from teams that drown in chaos.

In this section, you will learn how to prioritize requirements when you cannot build everything at once, how to validate that requirements are correct before you invest in building them, how to trace requirements through your project's artifacts, and how to handle the constant reality of change. These are the disciplines that keep large projects coherent over months and years.

Requirements Prioritization

No team has unlimited time or budget, so you must decide which requirements to build first. **Requirements prioritization** is the process of ranking requirements by their importance and urgency so that the most valuable work happens first. Done well, it ensures that even if the project runs short on time, the essential features are already delivered.

A widely used prioritization technique is **MoSCoW**, which sorts requirements into four buckets: Must have, Should have, Could have, and Won't have this time.

```
requirements = {
    "User login": "Must",
    "Password reset via email": "Should",
    "Dark mode theme": "Could",
    "Social media integration": "Won't",
}

priority_order = {"Must": 1, "Should": 2, "Could": 3, "Won't": 4}
ranked = sorted(requirements.items(), key=lambda item: priority_order[item[1]])

for feature, priority in ranked:
    print(f"[{priority:5}] {feature}")
```

This code stores each requirement with its MoSCoW category, then sorts them so the highest priorities appear first. The `priority_order` dictionary translates the category labels into numbers the `sorted` function can rank. The output places "User login" at the top as a Must-have and "Social media integration" at the bottom as something explicitly deferred. That last category matters more than it seems: writing down what you will *not* build prevents scope creep and keeps stakeholders honest about trade-offs.

Prioritization is fundamentally a conversation about value versus cost. A feature that delivers huge value at low cost is an obvious Must. A feature that costs a fortune for marginal benefit belongs far down the list. Making these trade-offs explicit turns prioritization from a guessing game into a rational, defensible decision.

Requirements Validation

Requirements validation is the process of confirming that the requirements you have gathered are correct, complete, and actually reflect what stakeholders need. It answers the question, "Are we building the right thing?" This is distinct from verification, which asks, "Are we building the thing right?" Validation happens early, before you invest heavily in construction, precisely because that is when fixing mistakes is cheapest.

Validation techniques include reviews, where stakeholders read and confirm the requirements; prototyping, where they interact with a mockup; and walkthroughs, where the team traces scenarios through the requirements to spot gaps. The goal is to catch misunderstandings and contradictions while they are still cheap to fix. A requirement that is ambiguous, untestable, or in conflict with another requirement should be flagged and resolved now, not discovered during testing.

The most valuable validation question you can ask a stakeholder is simply, "If I built exactly this, would it solve your problem?" Their hesitation, if any, tells you where the requirement is weak. Validation is your last, cheapest chance to change course before the cost of change climbs steeply.

Requirements Traceability

As a project grows, a single requirement can influence design decisions, several code modules, and multiple test cases. **Requirements traceability** is the practice of maintaining links between a requirement and every artifact that implements or verifies it. Traceability lets you answer critical questions: Which code satisfies this requirement? Which tests prove it works? If this requirement changes, what else is affected?

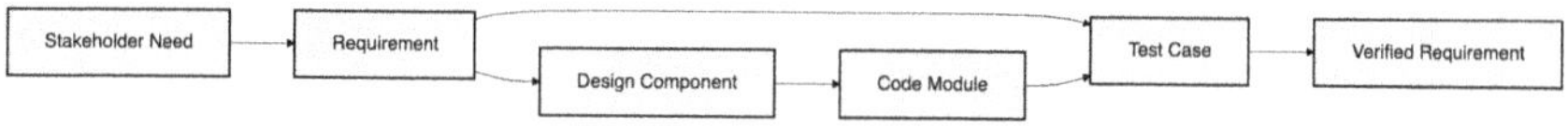

These links connect each stakeholder need to its design decisions, its code, and its tests, forming a chain you can follow in either direction. Trace forward from a requirement to find everything built to satisfy it. Trace backward from a piece of code to discover which requirement justifies its existence. A common tool for organizing these links is a **traceability matrix**.

```
traceability = {
    "FR-01 (User login)": {
        "design": "AuthModule design doc",
        "code": ["auth/login.py", "auth/session.py"],
        "tests": ["test_login_success", "test_login_invalid_password"],
    },
    "FR-02 (Password reset)": {
        "design": "AuthModule design doc",
        "code": ["auth/reset.py"],
        "tests": ["test_reset_email_sent"],
    },
}

for requirement, artifacts in traceability.items():
    print(f"{requirement}")
    print(f"  Design: {artifacts['design']}")
    print(f"  Code:   {', '.join(artifacts['code'])}")
    print(f"  Tests:  {', '.join(artifacts['tests'])}")
```

This code models a small traceability matrix as a nested dictionary. Each requirement maps to the design document, code files, and tests that fulfill and verify it. The loop prints a readable report of these links. In real projects, this structure is invaluable: when a stakeholder proposes changing the login requirement, you can instantly see that `auth/login.py`, `auth/session.py`, and two specific tests must be revisited. Traceability turns the frightening question "what will this change break?" into a question you can actually answer.

Managing Changing Requirements

Change is inevitable, so the goal is not to prevent it but to control it. **Change management** is the disciplined process of evaluating, approving, and incorporating changes to requirements. Uncontrolled change leads to **scope creep**, the gradual, unmanaged expansion of a project until deadlines and budgets collapse under the weight of "just one more feature."

A healthy change process follows a clear sequence:

1. A change request is submitted with a description of what should change and why.
2. The team assesses the impact, using traceability to identify affected code, tests, and other requirements.
3. Stakeholders weigh the value of the change against its cost and risk.
4. The change is approved, deferred, or rejected, and the decision is recorded.
5. If approved, the requirement, its traceability links, and its acceptance criteria are all updated.

Notice how the earlier concepts come together here. Traceability tells you the impact of a change. Prioritization tells you whether the change is worth doing now. Acceptance criteria must be revised so the updated requirement stays testable. Managing change is not a separate activity bolted on at the end; it is where every skill in this chapter is exercised at once. The teams that thrive are not the ones that avoid change, but the ones that absorb it gracefully.

Summary

- **Requirements prioritization**, using techniques like MoSCoW, ensures the most valuable work is done first and defers or rejects the rest explicitly.
- **Requirements validation** confirms early that you are building the right thing, catching problems while they are cheap to fix.
- **Requirements traceability** links each requirement to its design, code, and tests, so you can assess impact in either direction.
- **Change management** provides a disciplined process for evaluating and incorporating change while preventing scope creep.

Chapter Summary

This chapter took you through the full life of a requirement, from its first appearance in a stakeholder's mind to its ongoing management across a project. You began by learning what requirements are and how to classify them, distinguishing the functional behaviors a system must perform from the nonfunctional qualities that determine how well it performs them. That classification is the vocabulary on which everything else depends.

From there you moved from understanding requirements to actively producing them. You learned to elicit needs through interviews, observation, and prototyping, and to express what you discover in the forms your team can act on: user stories for lightweight value-focused features, use cases for detailed complex interactions, and acceptance criteria that make any requirement objectively testable. These formats transform vague desires into a shared, buildable plan.

Finally, you saw that requirements live and change over time, and that managing them is an ongoing discipline rather than a one-time task. Prioritization, validation, traceability, and change management work together to keep a project coherent as reality intrudes on the original plan. You can now do something you could not do before this chapter: take a fuzzy idea from a stakeholder and turn it into clear, prioritized, testable, and traceable requirements that a team can build with confidence. This foundation is what everything in the rest of the software engineering process is built upon.

Chapter Lab: Requirements, User Stories, and Acceptance Criteria for the Course Project

In this lab, you will apply the requirements engineering skills from this chapter to your ongoing course project. You will identify stakeholders and business needs, capture functional and nonfunctional requirements, express key features as user stories, and attach Given-When-Then acceptance criteria that make each story testable. The exercise brings together elicitation, expression, and prioritization so that you leave with a concrete, well-structured requirements set to guide the rest of your project work.

Chapter 3: Principles of Good Software Design and Modeling

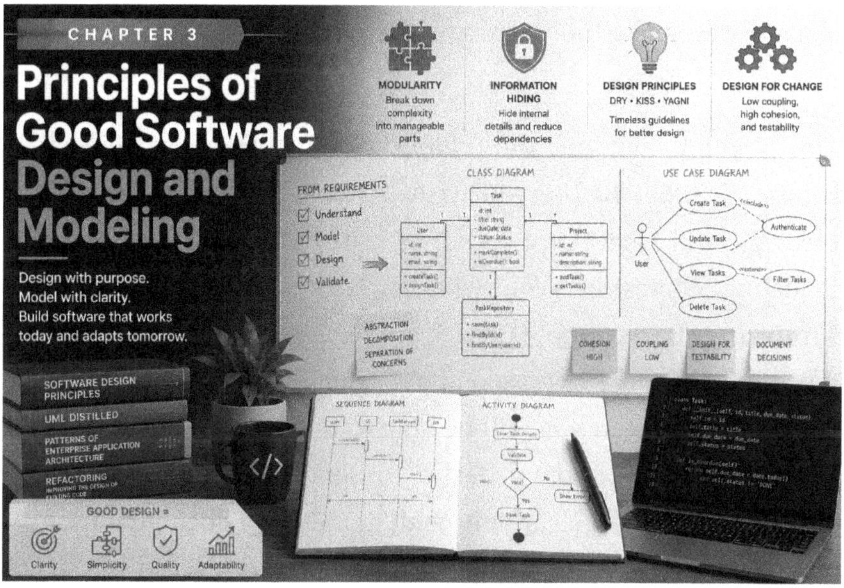

In the previous chapter, you learned how to gather and document requirements — the statements that describe what a system must do and how well it must do it. Requirements tell you *what* to build. Design is where you decide *how* to build it. This chapter bridges that gap. It introduces the principles that separate software you can maintain and extend from software that collapses under its own weight after a few months of changes.

Good design is not decoration. It is the difference between a codebase that welcomes new features and one that fights you at every turn. Poorly designed software still runs, at least for a while, but it becomes progressively harder and more expensive to change. In this chapter you will learn the core principles professional engineers use to structure their systems: abstraction, decomposition, modularity, information hiding, and a handful of memorable heuristics like DRY, KISS, and YAGNI. You will also learn to recognize the warning signs of bad design before it takes root.

The second half of the chapter shifts from principles to communication. Before you write code, you often need to think through and share your design with others. That is where modeling comes in. You will be introduced to the **Unified Modeling Language (UML)** and the most common diagram types engineers use to reason about structure and behavior. By the end of this chapter, you will be able to take a set of requirements, shape them into a sound design, evaluate that design critically, and communicate it clearly through models and documentation.

3.1 From Requirements to Design

Requirements describe a problem. Design describes a solution. The transition between the two is one of the most important – and most misunderstood – steps in software engineering. Requirements say "users must be able to reset their password." Design decides which classes, functions, and data stores make that possible. This section shows you how to make that leap deliberately rather than by accident, and it introduces two mental tools you will use constantly: abstraction and decomposition.

Understanding this transition matters because a common mistake among newer developers is to jump straight from a requirement to writing code. That works for tiny scripts, but it fails for anything larger. Design gives you a chance to think about structure before you commit to it in code, when changes are still cheap.

Moving from Requirements to Design

A **design** is a plan for how software will be organized to satisfy its requirements. When you move from requirements to design, you shift from describing observable behavior to describing internal structure. A requirement might state that "the system shall calculate shipping costs based on weight and destination." The design decides whether that logic lives in a `ShippingCalculator` class, which methods it exposes, what data it needs, and how it connects to the rest of the system.

This transition is rarely a single step. You typically move from broad, sweeping decisions down to fine, specific ones. That progression is captured by two levels of design.

High-Level and Low-Level Design

High-level design describes the overall shape of the system: its major components, how they are organized, and how they communicate. It answers questions like "Do we have a web front end talking to a backend API?" or "Where does the database sit?" High-level design is sometimes called architecture, and it establishes boundaries that are expensive to change later.

Low-level design fills in the details inside those boundaries. It defines specific classes, their methods, the algorithms they use, and the exact data structures involved. If high-level design decides that a `ShippingCalculator` component exists, low-level design decides that it has a `calculate(weight, destination)` method that returns a `Decimal` .

```
# High-level design decision: a dedicated component for shipping.
# Low-level design decision: its exact interface and data.

from decimal import Decimal

class ShippingCalculator:
    def __init__(self, rate_table):
        self._rate_table = rate_table

    def calculate(self, weight_kg: float, destination: str) -> Decimal:
        base_rate = self._rate_table.get(destination, Decimal("20.00"))
        return base_rate + Decimal(str(weight_kg)) * Decimal("1.50")
```

This example shows both levels at work. The *decision to have a separate calculator at all* is high-level: it isolates shipping logic in one place. The *specific method signature and formula* are low-level: they define exactly how that component behaves. Notice how the class hides its rate table behind a simple `calculate` method — callers do not need to know how the number is produced. That idea, hiding the "how" behind a clear interface, is the heart of the next two tools.

Abstraction

Abstraction is the practice of focusing on the essential characteristics of something while ignoring its irrelevant details. When you drive a car, you use a steering wheel and pedals without thinking about the combustion happening inside the engine. The controls are an abstraction over a very complex machine.

In software, abstraction lets you work with a concept at the level that matters for your current task. When you call `list.sort()` in Python, you do not care whether it uses Timsort internally – you care that the list ends up sorted. A well-designed abstraction exposes *what* something does and hides *how* it does it. This is powerful because it lets you change the "how" later without breaking any code that relies on the "what."

```
class PaymentGateway:
    """An abstraction over payment processing.
    Callers know they can charge a card; they do not know how."""

    def charge(self, card_token: str, amount: Decimal) -> bool:
        # Details of talking to Stripe, retries, currency conversion,
        # and error handling all live behind this simple method.
        raise NotImplementedError
```

Here, `PaymentGateway.charge` is an abstraction. Any code that processes an order can call `charge` and receive a simple success-or-failure answer. All the messy reality of network calls and third-party APIs stays hidden behind that method. If you later switch payment providers, code that depends only on this abstraction does not need to change.

Decomposition

Where abstraction hides detail, **decomposition** breaks a large problem into smaller, more manageable parts. A checkout system is too big to reason about all at once. Decompose it, and you get separate concerns: validating the cart, calculating totals, processing payment, and confirming the order. Each part is small enough to understand, build, and test on its own.

Abstraction and decomposition are complementary. Decomposition determines *what the parts are*, and abstraction determines *how each part presents itself* to the others. Together, they let you build large systems out of small, comprehensible pieces.

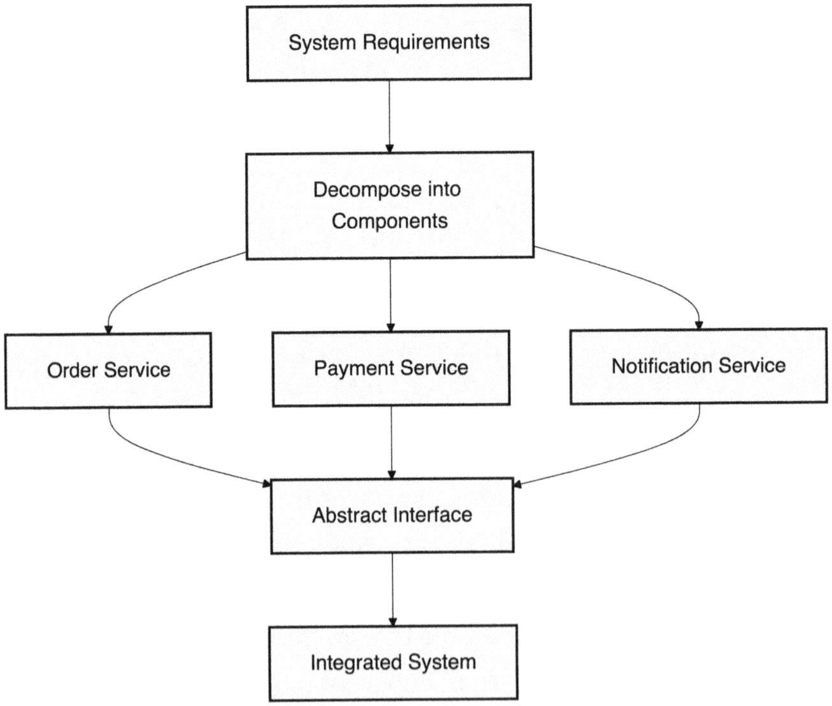

```
class CheckoutService:
    def __init__(self, cart_validator, pricing, payments):
        self._cart_validator = cart_validator
        self._pricing = pricing
        self._payments = payments

    def checkout(self, cart, card_token):
        self._cart_validator.validate(cart)
        total = self._pricing.total_for(cart)
        return self._payments.charge(card_token, total)
```

This `CheckoutService` demonstrates decomposition in action. The checkout process has been split into three collaborators, each responsible for one job. The service itself just coordinates them. Because each part is an abstraction, `CheckoutService` reads almost like a plain-English description of checkout, and any one part can be developed or replaced independently.

Summary

- Design translates requirements (*what* the system does) into structure (*how* it does it).
- **High-level design** defines major components and their relationships; **low-level design** defines classes, methods, and algorithms.
- **Abstraction** exposes essential behavior while hiding implementation details, letting the "how" change without breaking callers.
- **Decomposition** breaks large problems into small, understandable parts.
- Abstraction and decomposition work together: decomposition finds the parts, abstraction defines their interfaces.

3.2 Modularity and Information Hiding

Once you have decomposed a system into parts, you need principles for how those parts should be built and how they should relate to one another. This section covers four closely related ideas — modularity, encapsulation, information hiding, and separation of concerns — that together form the foundation of maintainable software. They are so intertwined that it is easy to blur them, so we will define each precisely and show how they reinforce each other.

These principles matter because they control how change propagates through a system. In poorly organized code, a small change in one place forces changes everywhere else. In well-organized code, changes stay local. Learning to build that kind of locality is one of the most valuable skills you can develop as an engineer.

Modularity

Modularity is the degree to which a system is composed of separate, self-contained parts called modules. A **module** is a unit of software — a class, a file, or a package — that groups related functionality behind a defined boundary. Think of modules like the components of a home theater system. The speaker, the receiver, and the TV are separate units connected by standard cables. You can replace the speakers without touching the TV.

A modular system is easier to understand because you can study one module at a time. It is easier to test because modules can be tested in isolation. And it is easier to change because well-defined boundaries limit how far a modification spreads.

```python
# email_notifier.py  — a self-contained module

class EmailNotifier:
    def __init__(self, smtp_client):
        self._smtp = smtp_client

    def send_welcome(self, email_address: str) -> None:
        self._smtp.send(
            to=email_address,
            subject="Welcome!",
            body="Thanks for signing up.",
        )
```

This module has one job: sending notification emails. It groups everything related to that job in one place and exposes a clear method. The rest of the application can send a welcome email without knowing anything about SMTP. If you later switch to a different email provider, only this module changes.

Encapsulation

Encapsulation is the bundling of data together with the operations that act on that data, while restricting direct access to the data from the outside. In Python, encapsulation is expressed partly through convention: a leading underscore signals that an attribute is internal and should not be touched directly.

Encapsulation protects the integrity of your data. If the only way to modify an object's state is through its methods, those methods can enforce rules. A bank account can guarantee its balance is never set to a negative number, because nothing outside the class can change the balance directly.

```python
class BankAccount:
    def __init__(self, opening_balance: Decimal):
        self._balance = opening_balance  # internal state

    def withdraw(self, amount: Decimal) -> None:
        if amount > self._balance:
            raise ValueError("Insufficient funds")
        self._balance -= amount

    @property
    def balance(self) -> Decimal:
        return self._balance
```

The `_balance` attribute is encapsulated. Outside code cannot reduce the balance without going through `withdraw`, which enforces the overdraft rule. The `balance` property exposes the value for reading but not for arbitrary writing. This bundling of data and rules together is exactly what encapsulation provides.

Information Hiding

Information hiding is the principle of concealing the internal details of a module so that other parts of the system cannot depend on them. It is closely related to encapsulation, but the emphasis is different. Encapsulation is the *mechanism* (bundling and access control); information hiding is the *goal* (hiding decisions that are likely to change).

The key insight, first articulated by David Parnas, is that you should hide the design decisions most likely to change. If clients cannot see a decision, they cannot depend on it, and you are free to change it later. In the `BankAccount` example, the fact that the balance is stored as a `Decimal` is hidden. You could switch to storing cents as an integer internally, and no calling code would break.

Separation of Concerns

Separation of concerns is the principle that each part of a system should address a single, distinct concern. A **concern** is any coherent area of responsibility — persistence, presentation, business logic, and so on. When concerns are mixed, a change to one drags in changes to others.

```
# Separated concerns: each class has one responsibility.

class OrderRepository:       # concern: persistence
    def save(self, order): ...

class OrderValidator:        # concern: business rules
    def validate(self, order): ...

class OrderView:             # concern: presentation
    def render(self, order): ...
```

Each class here handles exactly one concern. If the database changes, you touch `OrderRepository`. If a validation rule changes, you touch `OrderValidator`. If the display format changes, you touch `OrderView`. Because the concerns are separated, no single change ripples across all three. This is separation of concerns applied at the class level; the same principle applies to files, packages, and entire services.

Summary

- **Modularity** organizes a system into self-contained parts with defined boundaries, so changes stay local.
- **Encapsulation** bundles data with the operations on it and restricts direct outside access, protecting data integrity.
- **Information hiding** conceals design decisions likely to change so nothing can depend on them.
- **Separation of concerns** gives each part a single, distinct responsibility, preventing changes from rippling across the system.
- Together these principles make software easier to understand, test, and modify.

3.3 Core Design Principles

The principles in the previous sections give you a structural foundation. This section gives you three memorable heuristics that guide day-to-day design decisions. They are short, punchy, and easy to remember on purpose — engineers repeat them constantly because they work. You will learn what each one means, when it applies, and, just as importantly, when taking it too far causes problems.

These heuristics matter because most bad design does not come from a single catastrophic decision. It comes from a thousand small ones: a copy-pasted block here, an over-engineered abstraction there, a feature built for a customer who never arrives. DRY, KISS, and YAGNI are the antidotes to those small mistakes.

Don't Repeat Yourself (DRY)

DRY stands for "Don't Repeat Yourself." It states that every piece of knowledge in a system should have a single, authoritative representation. When the same logic appears in multiple places, a change to that logic must be made everywhere it appears — and sooner or later, someone forgets one.

```
# Violates DRY — tax logic duplicated
def invoice_total(subtotal):
    return subtotal + subtotal * 0.08

def receipt_total(subtotal):
    return subtotal + subtotal * 0.08

# Honors DRY — one source of truth
TAX_RATE = 0.08

def with_tax(subtotal):
    return subtotal + subtotal * TAX_RATE
```

In the first version, the tax rate lives in two functions. If the rate changes, you must update both, and a missed update produces inconsistent results. In the DRY version, the rate and the calculation live in exactly one place. Change `TAX_RATE` once and every caller is correct. Be careful, though: DRY is about knowledge, not about text that merely looks similar. Two functions that happen to share a line of code but represent different concepts should stay separate.

Keep It Simple (KISS)

KISS stands for "Keep It Simple, Stupid." It urges you to favor the simplest solution that satisfies the requirement. Complexity is the enemy of maintainability. Clever code that impresses in a code review often becomes the code nobody dares to touch six months later.

```
# Overly clever
def is_even(n):
    return not bool(n & 1) ^ False

# Simple and obvious
def is_even(n):
    return n % 2 == 0
```

Both functions produce the same result, but the second one is instantly understandable. Simplicity is not about writing less code for its own sake; it is about writing code whose intent is obvious. When you find yourself proud of how clever a solution is, pause and ask whether a simpler version would serve your future self better.

You Aren't Gonna Need It (YAGNI)

YAGNI stands for "You Aren't Gonna Need It." It warns against building functionality based on speculation about future needs. Developers love to add flexibility "just in case," but most of that speculative flexibility is never used. It adds complexity now to solve a problem that may never exist.

```
# YAGNI violation: speculative flexibility no one asked for
class Report:
    def export(self, fmt="pdf", encrypt=False, watermark=None,
               compression="none", cloud_provider=None):
        ...

# YAGNI honored: build only what today's requirement needs
class Report:
    def export_pdf(self, path):
        ...
```

The first version tries to anticipate every possible export scenario. Most of those parameters will never be used, yet every one of them must be maintained, tested, and understood. The second version does exactly what the current requirement asks. When a real need for another format arrives, you can extend the design then – with the benefit of knowing the actual requirements.

These three principles reinforce one another. DRY eliminates redundancy, KISS controls complexity, and YAGNI controls scope. Applied together, they keep a design lean and focused.

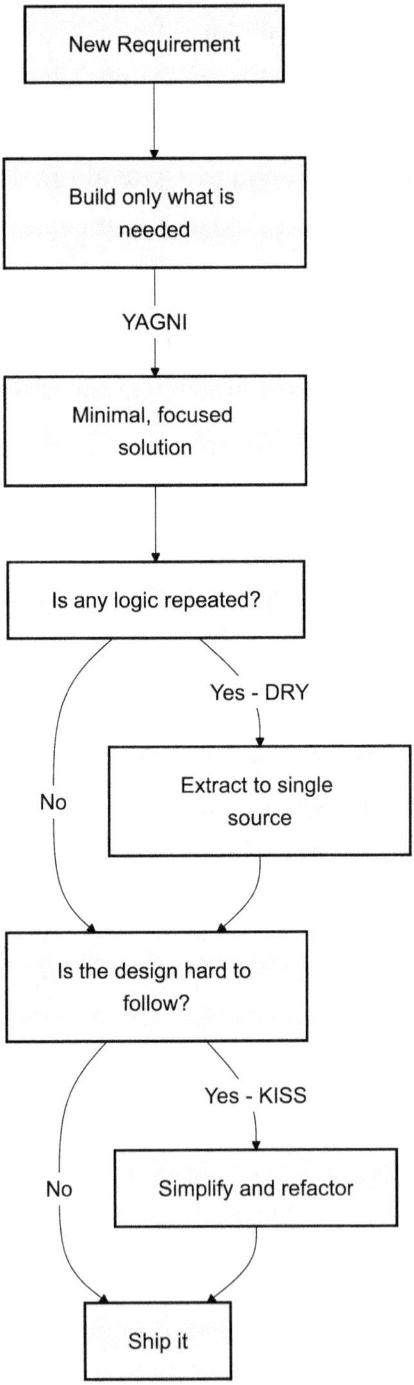
New Requirement
Build only what is needed
YAGNI
Minimal, focused solution
Is any logic repeated?
Yes - DRY
Extract to single source
No
Is the design hard to follow?
Yes - KISS
Simplify and refactor
No
Ship it

Summary

- **DRY** keeps each piece of knowledge in a single authoritative place, so changes only happen once.
- **KISS** favors the simplest solution that meets the requirement, prioritizing clarity over cleverness.
- **YAGNI** avoids building speculative features you do not yet need.
- These principles are heuristics, not absolute laws — apply DRY to knowledge, not coincidental similarity.
- Together, DRY, KISS, and YAGNI control redundancy, complexity, and scope.

3.4 Designing for Change and Recognizing Poor Design

Software that never changes is rare. Requirements evolve, dependencies get replaced, and features accumulate. The measure of a good design is not how it looks on day one but how gracefully it absorbs change over months and years. This section teaches you the two properties that most affect changeability — cohesion and coupling — and shows you concrete techniques for designing systems that welcome change and are easy to test. It closes by teaching you to recognize the smells of poor design so you can catch problems early.

This is where the abstract principles from earlier sections become practical judgment. You will learn to look at a design and ask: if this requirement changes, how much will break?

Cohesion and Coupling

Cohesion measures how closely related the responsibilities within a single module are. High cohesion is good: a module with high cohesion does one thing and does it well. A `PasswordHasher` that only hashes and verifies passwords is highly cohesive. A `Utils` class that hashes passwords, formats dates, and sends emails has low cohesion — it is a grab bag of unrelated functions.

Coupling measures how strongly one module depends on another. Loose coupling is good: modules interact through small, stable interfaces and know little about each other's internals. Tight coupling is dangerous because a change in one module forces changes in the modules bound to it.

The golden rule is **high cohesion, loose coupling**. Aim for modules that are internally focused and externally independent. These two properties are related: when responsibilities are well separated (high cohesion), modules tend to depend on each other less (loose coupling).

Designing for Change

To design for change, you first identify what is *likely* to change and isolate it behind a stable interface. The parts of your system most likely to change — external services, file formats, third-party APIs — are called **volatile dependencies**. The trick is to keep your core logic talking only to a stable abstraction, with the volatile detail hidden behind an interchangeable implementation.

A common way to do this is the **Adapter pattern**. Your business logic depends on an interface you control. Each external service gets a small adapter that translates between that interface and the service's real API. Swapping providers becomes a matter of writing a new adapter.

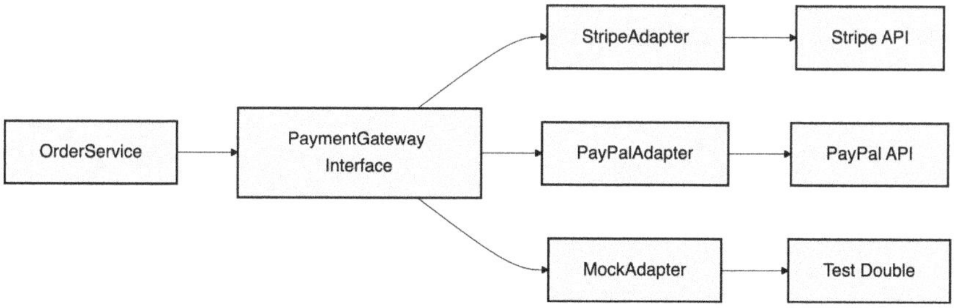

```python
from abc import ABC, abstractmethod

class PaymentProcessor(ABC):        # stable interface your code depends on
    @abstractmethod
    def charge(self, amount: Decimal) -> bool: ...

class StripeAdapter(PaymentProcessor):
    def charge(self, amount: Decimal) -> bool:
        # translate to Stripe's real API here
        return True

class PayPalAdapter(PaymentProcessor):
    def charge(self, amount: Decimal) -> bool:
        # translate to PayPal's real API here
        return True
```

Your checkout logic accepts a `PaymentProcessor` and never mentions Stripe or PayPal directly. To switch providers, you pass in a different adapter. The volatile dependency — the specific payment API — is fully isolated. Nothing in your core logic changes when the provider does.

Designing for Testability

Designs that are easy to change are usually easy to test, because both rely on loose coupling. When a class depends on abstractions rather than concrete implementations, you can substitute a fake or mock version in tests. This is called **dependency injection**: instead of a class creating its own dependencies, they are passed in from outside.

```python
class Checkout:
    def __init__(self, payments: PaymentProcessor):
        self._payments = payments      # injected, not created internally

    def pay(self, amount: Decimal) -> bool:
        return self._payments.charge(amount)

# In a test, inject a fake that never touches a real payment API:
class FakeProcessor(PaymentProcessor):
    def charge(self, amount): return True

assert Checkout(FakeProcessor()).pay(Decimal("10.00")) is True
```

Because `Checkout` receives its `PaymentProcessor` rather than constructing one, the test can supply a `FakeProcessor`. The test runs instantly and never contacts a real payment service. A design that resists testing — one where you cannot substitute dependencies — is usually a design that also resists change.

Recognizing Poor Software Design

Experienced engineers learn to spot **code smells**, which are surface signs that hint at deeper design problems. Common smells include:

- **Rigidity:** a small change forces a cascade of changes elsewhere.
- **Fragility:** changing one part breaks unrelated parts.
- **Tight coupling:** modules know too much about each other's internals.
- **Low cohesion:** a class does many unrelated things (a "God class").
- **Duplication:** the same logic appears in several places (a DRY violation).

- **Long methods and long parameter lists:** signs that too much is happening in one place.

None of these smells is automatically fatal, but each is a signal worth investigating. The earlier you notice them, the cheaper they are to fix.

Summary

- **Cohesion** measures how focused a module is; **coupling** measures how dependent modules are on each other. Aim for high cohesion and loose coupling.
- Design for change by isolating **volatile dependencies** behind stable interfaces, often using the Adapter pattern.
- **Dependency injection** makes designs testable by allowing fakes to replace real dependencies.
- Designs that are easy to test are usually easy to change, and vice versa.
- **Code smells** like rigidity, fragility, duplication, and God classes are early warning signs of poor design.

3.5 Introduction to Modeling and UML

So far this chapter has focused on how to structure software. Now we turn to how you *think about* and *communicate* that structure before and during construction. Software is invisible. Unlike a bridge or a building, you cannot walk around it and see its shape. Modeling gives software a visible form so that teams can reason about it together. This section introduces modeling in general and UML in particular, then covers the two most common diagram types: use-case and class diagrams.

Modeling matters because most software is built by teams, and teams need a shared language. A diagram sketched in ten minutes can prevent a week of building the wrong thing. You do not need to model everything — but knowing how to model the right things is a core professional skill.

Why Software Engineers Model Systems

A **model** is a simplified representation of a system that emphasizes certain aspects while omitting others. Engineers model systems for the same reason architects build scale models: to explore and communicate design decisions cheaply, before committing expensive resources.

Models serve several purposes. They help you *reason* about a design before you build it, exposing gaps and contradictions early. They help you *communicate* with teammates, stakeholders, and your future self. And they serve as *documentation* that outlives any single conversation. A good model captures the essence of a design without drowning in detail — that selective simplification is the whole point.

Introduction to UML

The **Unified Modeling Language (UML)** is a standardized set of notations for modeling software systems. Before UML, every team invented its own diagramming conventions, and diagrams from one project were meaningless on another. UML unified these into a common visual vocabulary that engineers everywhere can read.

UML diagrams fall into two broad families. **Structural diagrams** describe the static structure of a system — what parts exist and how they are arranged. **Behavioral diagrams** describe how the system behaves over time — how parts interact and how processes unfold. You do not need to memorize all of UML. In practice, a handful of diagram types cover the vast majority of real-world needs, and those are the ones this chapter teaches.

Use-Case Diagrams

A **use-case diagram** captures who uses a system and what they need it to do. It shows **actors** — the users or external systems that interact with your software — on the outside, and **use cases** — the goals those actors want to accomplish — as ovals inside a boundary. It deliberately avoids internal detail; its job is to frame the system's scope from the user's point of view.

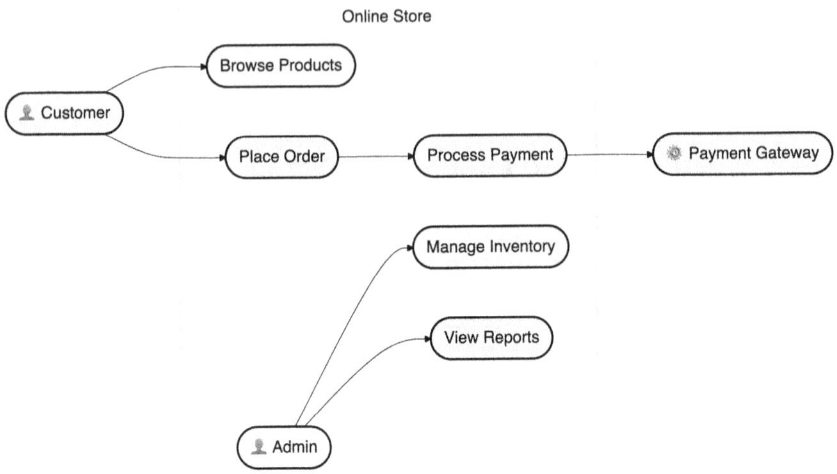

Use-case diagrams are most valuable early in a project, when you are still clarifying scope. They answer two questions at a glance: who are the users, and what does each of them need? Because they contain no technical detail, they are ideal for conversations with non-technical stakeholders. If someone points at your diagram and says "you forgot that managers can approve refunds," the diagram has done its job — it surfaced a missing requirement before any code was written.

Class Diagrams

A **class diagram** shows the static structure of a system: the classes that exist, their attributes (data), their methods (operations), and the relationships between them. It is the most widely used UML diagram because it maps so directly onto object-oriented code.

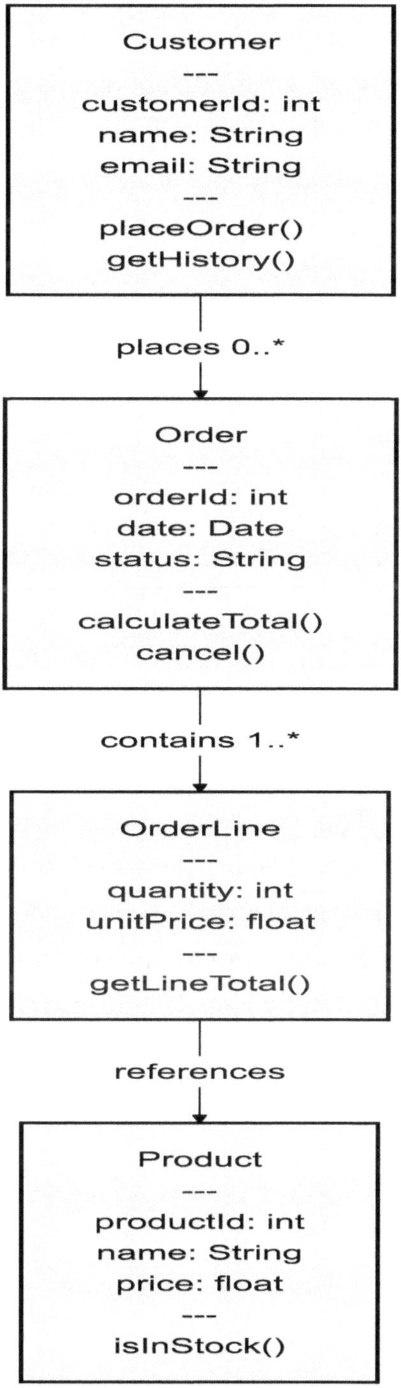
Customer
---
customerId: int
name: String
email: String
---
placeOrder()
getHistory()
places 0..*
Order
---
orderId: int
date: Date
status: String
---
calculateTotal()
cancel()
contains 1..*
OrderLine
---
quantity: int
unitPrice: float
---
getLineTotal()
references
Product
---
productId: int
name: String
price: float
---
isInStock()

A class in a class diagram is drawn as a box with three compartments: the class name at top, its attributes in the middle, and its methods at the bottom. Relationships between classes are drawn as lines, with different notations for different relationships — for example, an arrow for association or a line ending in a diamond for aggregation. The following code shows how a class diagram translates into Python.

```
class Author:
    def __init__(self, name: str):
        self.name = name

class Book:
    def __init__(self, title: str, author: Author):
        self.title = title
        self.author = author        # association: a Book has an Author

    def summary(self) -> str:
        return f"{self.title} by {self.author.name}"
```

Here `Author` and `Book` would each be a box in a class diagram. Their attributes (`name` , `title`) appear in the middle compartment and their methods (`summary`) in the bottom. The line connecting them represents the association captured in code by `Book` holding a reference to an `Author` . A class diagram and object-oriented code are two views of the same underlying structure — which is exactly why this diagram type is so useful for design.

Summary

- A **model** is a simplified representation that emphasizes some aspects of a system and omits others.
- Engineers model to reason about designs, communicate with others, and document decisions cheaply.
- **UML** provides a standardized visual vocabulary, split into structural and behavioral diagram families.
- **Use-case diagrams** frame scope by showing actors and the goals they need the system to fulfill.
- **Class diagrams** show the static structure — classes, attributes, methods, and relationships — and map directly onto object-oriented code.

3.6 Behavioral and Structural Diagrams

The previous section introduced two foundational UML diagrams. This section broadens your toolkit with four more that engineers reach for regularly. Two of them — sequence and activity diagrams — are behavioral: they describe how a system acts over time. The other two — component and deployment diagrams — are structural: they describe how the system is organized and where it runs. Learning when to reach for each is more valuable than memorizing their notation.

These diagrams matter because different questions demand different views. "In what order do these objects talk to each other?" is a different question from "Where does this code actually run in production?" Each diagram type answers a specific kind of question well.

Sequence Diagrams

A **sequence diagram** shows how objects or components interact over time by exchanging messages. Participants are drawn across the top, each with a vertical **lifeline** descending below it. Messages are horizontal arrows between lifelines, read from top to bottom in chronological order. Sequence diagrams excel at showing the step-by-step flow of a single scenario, such as a user logging in.

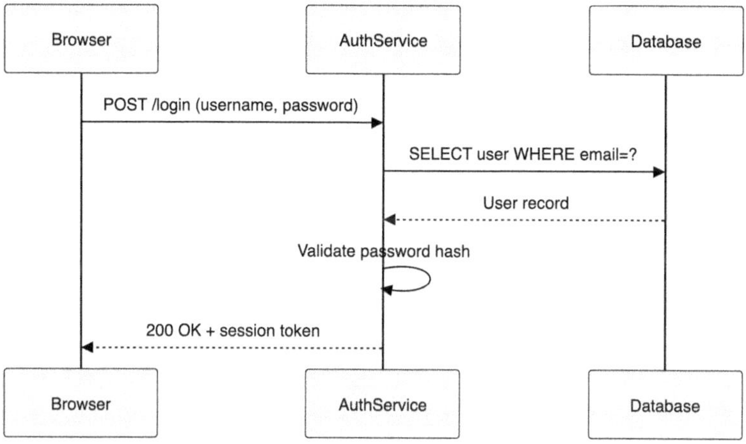

Reading a sequence diagram top to bottom tells you the exact order of interactions: who calls whom, and what comes back. This makes them invaluable for understanding or documenting a specific workflow, especially one that crosses several components. They are also excellent for spotting problems — if you see one object making a dozen calls to another, you may have found a coupling issue worth addressing.

Activity Diagrams

An **activity diagram** models the flow of a process or workflow, much like a flowchart. It uses actions connected by arrows, with **decision nodes** for branching and **fork/join** bars for parallel activities. Activity diagrams are ideal for modeling business processes and complex logic where the order of steps and the conditions between them matter.

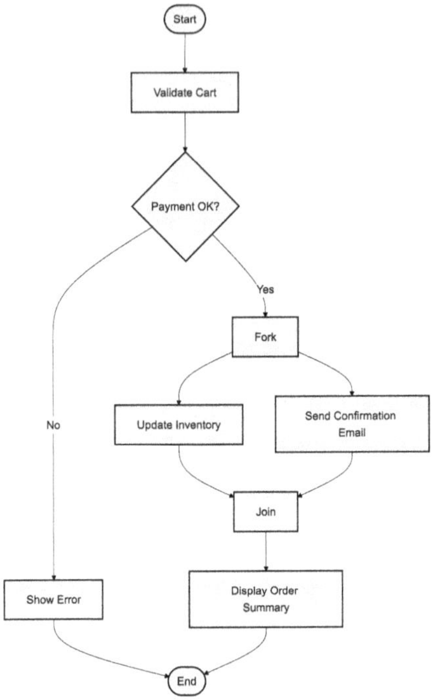

The strength of an activity diagram is its ability to show branching and parallelism clearly. A decision node captures an either/or choice, while parallel branches show work that can happen simultaneously — such as reserving inventory and charging a card at the same time. When a requirement involves conditional logic and concurrent steps, an activity diagram communicates it far more clearly than prose.

Component Diagrams

A **component diagram** shows the high-level building blocks of a system and their dependencies. A **component** is a self-contained, replaceable unit of software — often a service, library, or subsystem — that exposes its functionality through well-defined interfaces. These diagrams operate at the architectural level, above individual classes.

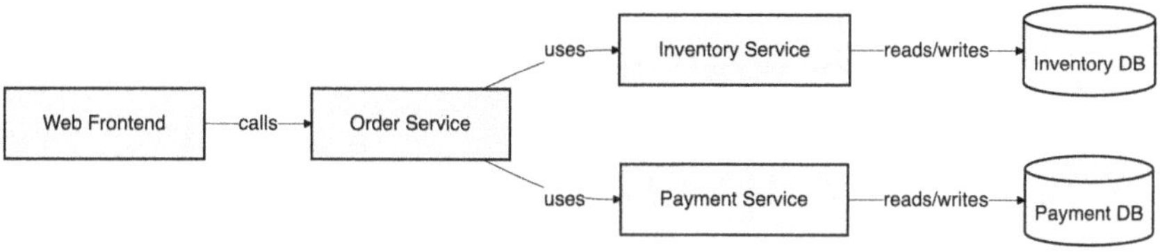

Component diagrams are most useful for reasoning about system architecture and dependencies. When one component depends on another, that dependency is drawn explicitly, which makes it easy to spot problematic coupling between services. If your order service depends on five other services, the diagram shows that dependency load at a glance, prompting the question of whether the design can be simplified.

Deployment Diagrams

A **deployment diagram** shows the physical arrangement of software on hardware. It depicts **nodes** — physical or virtual machines, containers, or devices — and shows which software artifacts run on each, along with the communication paths between them.

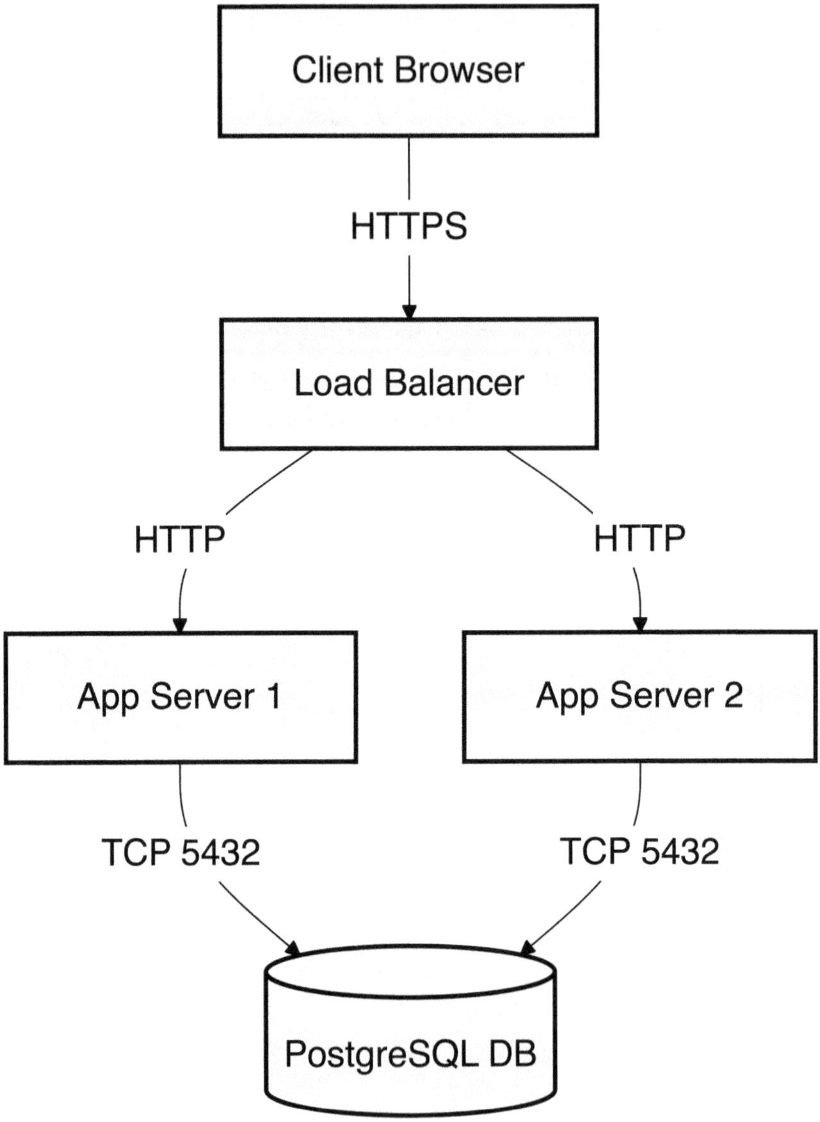

Where a component diagram answers "how is the software organized?", a deployment diagram answers "where does it run?" This is essential for planning infrastructure, reasoning about performance and security, and communicating with operations teams. A classic three-tier layout — browser, application server, and database — becomes immediately clear in a deployment diagram, along with the network boundaries between each tier.

Summary

- **Sequence diagrams** show the time-ordered exchange of messages between participants in a single scenario.
- **Activity diagrams** model workflows with branching decisions and parallel paths, like an enhanced flowchart.
- **Component diagrams** show architectural building blocks and their dependencies, helping you spot excessive coupling.
- **Deployment diagrams** show where software runs by mapping artifacts onto physical or virtual nodes.
- Choose a diagram based on the question you need to answer — behavior over time, or structure and placement.

3.7 Data Models and Effective Documentation

Most software exists to manage data, so modeling that data well is as important as modeling behavior. This final section covers data modeling with entity-relationship diagrams and data-flow modeling, then steps back to address a crucial practical question: how do you keep models and documentation genuinely useful rather than letting them rot into misleading clutter? You will also learn when informal diagrams beat formal UML, and how to document the design decisions that matter most.

This section matters because a model or document that is out of date is worse than none at all — it actively misleads. The goal is not to produce impressive artifacts but to produce useful ones that a real team will trust and maintain.

Entity-Relationship Models

An **entity-relationship model**, or **ER model**, describes the data a system manages in terms of entities, their attributes, and the relationships between them. An **entity** is a thing the system stores information about, such as a customer or an order. A **relationship** connects entities, and its **cardinality** describes how many of one entity relate to how many of another — one-to-one, one-to-many, or many-to-many.

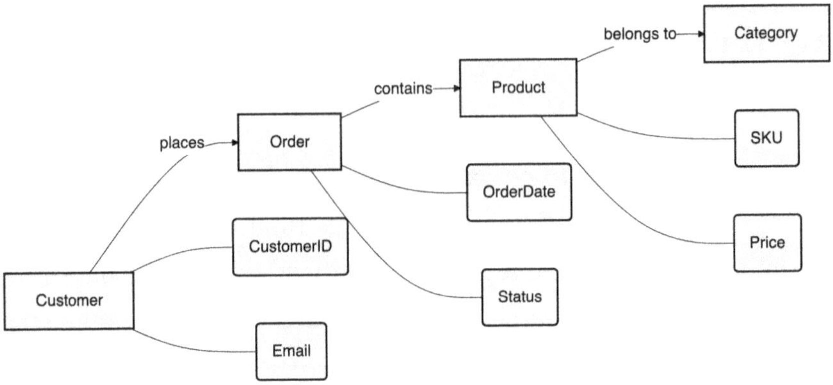

ER models are the standard tool for designing relational databases. Each entity typically becomes a table, each attribute a column, and each relationship a foreign key or join table. Getting the ER model right early prevents painful data migrations later. Cardinality is especially important: recognizing that a customer can place *many* orders, but each order belongs to *one* customer, directly shapes how your tables are structured.

Modeling Data Flow

Where an ER model shows how data is *stored*, a **data-flow model** shows how data *moves* through a system. A **data-flow diagram (DFD)** depicts processes that transform data, data stores that hold it, external entities that produce or consume it, and the flows of data between them. It ignores control logic and timing, focusing purely on where data comes from and where it goes.

Data-flow modeling is useful for understanding systems where the movement and transformation of information is the central concern — reporting pipelines, ETL processes, and integrations between systems. By tracing a piece of data from its source to its final destination, you can identify redundant transformations, missing validation steps, or unnecessary copies of data.

Keeping Models Useful

A model is only valuable while it reflects reality. The single biggest failure of modeling in practice is letting diagrams drift out of sync with the code. A stale diagram that shows an architecture the system no longer has will mislead every new engineer who trusts it.

To keep models useful, follow a few guidelines:

- **Model selectively.** Diagram only the parts that are complex, important, or frequently misunderstood. Do not diagram trivial code.
- **Match detail to purpose.** A diagram for a stakeholder conversation needs less detail than one guiding implementation.
- **Keep models close to the code.** Store diagrams in the repository so they travel with the software and are more likely to be updated.
- **Discard models that have served their purpose.** A whiteboard sketch used to settle a design debate can be photographed and thrown away.

UML vs. Informal Architecture Diagrams

Formal UML is precise and standardized, but that precision is not always worth the effort. **Informal architecture diagrams** – boxes and arrows drawn without strict notation – are often more effective for quick communication, especially with mixed audiences. A napkin sketch that everyone understands beats a perfect UML diagram that only specialists can read.

Use formal UML when precision matters: when the diagram must be unambiguous, when it will guide implementation, or when it serves as long-lived reference documentation. Use informal diagrams when you are exploring ideas, communicating broad structure, or talking with non-technical stakeholders. The goal is always communication, and you should choose whichever style communicates best for the situation.

Documenting Design Decisions

The most valuable documentation is often not a diagram at all but a record of *why* a decision was made. Six months later, no one remembers why you chose one database over another, and someone will be tempted to "fix" the decision without understanding its reasons. A lightweight record prevents that.

Many teams use **Architecture Decision Records (ADRs)** – short documents that capture a single decision, the context that prompted it, the options considered, and the consequences. A good ADR fits on one page and answers the question a future engineer will inevitably ask: "Why is it done this way?"

```
# ADR-007: Use the Adapter Pattern for Payment Providers

Status: Accepted
Context: We currently use Stripe but may switch providers within a year.
Decision: Core checkout logic depends on a PaymentProcessor interface;
          each provider gets its own adapter.
Consequences: Core logic is insulated from provider changes. Adding a
          provider means writing one new adapter, with no changes to checkout.
```

This ADR captures the reasoning behind a design decision in a form anyone can read in under a minute. It records not just *what* was decided but *why*, and what the trade-offs are. When a new engineer later wonders why the payment code is structured around an interface, this document answers them without a meeting. Documenting decisions this way is a small habit that pays enormous dividends in maintainability.

Summary

- **Entity-relationship models** describe stored data as entities, attributes, and relationships with cardinality — the foundation of database design.
- **Data-flow diagrams** show how data moves and transforms through a system, ignoring control logic and timing.
- Models stay useful only when they are selective, matched to their purpose, kept close to the code, and discarded when done.
- **Informal diagrams** often communicate better than formal UML for exploration and mixed audiences; use formal UML when precision matters.
- **Architecture Decision Records** capture *why* a decision was made, preventing costly misunderstandings later.

Chapter Summary

This chapter took you from requirements to a well-structured, well-communicated design. You began by learning how to translate *what* a system must do into *how* it will be built, using abstraction to hide detail and decomposition to break big problems into small ones. Those two tools underpin everything that followed. Modularity, encapsulation, information hiding, and separation of concerns are all specific applications of the same core idea: put related things together, hide what is likely to change, and keep the pieces loosely connected so that change stays local.

The design heuristics – DRY, KISS, and YAGNI – gave you practical guardrails for everyday decisions, while cohesion, coupling, and the techniques for designing for change and testability gave you a way to evaluate whether a design will age well. You can now look at a piece of software and reason critically about it: Is this class doing one thing? Are these modules too tightly bound? Is this flexibility something we actually need? Recognizing code smells turns that reasoning into a practical skill you can apply immediately.

Finally, you learned that design is not only something you *do* but something you *communicate*. UML and data models give software a visible shape, letting teams reason together before writing code, and each diagram type answers a specific question about structure or behavior. Just as importantly, you learned to keep models honest and to document the reasoning behind your decisions. Together, these skills move you from someone who writes code that works today to someone who designs systems that keep working, and keep changing gracefully, for years to come.

Chapter Lab: Analyzing Poor Design and Modeling the Course Project

In the first lab, you will examine a poorly designed piece of software, identify the code smells and principle violations it contains — such as tight coupling, low cohesion, and DRY violations — and refactor it into a cleaner design that applies the principles from this chapter. In the second lab, you will produce a set of UML diagrams for your ongoing course project, including a use-case diagram, a class diagram, and at least one behavioral diagram, choosing the diagram types that best communicate your system's structure and behavior. Together these labs let you apply both halves of the chapter: evaluating and improving design, and modeling a design so others can understand it.

Chapter 4: Object-Oriented Design and SOLID Principles

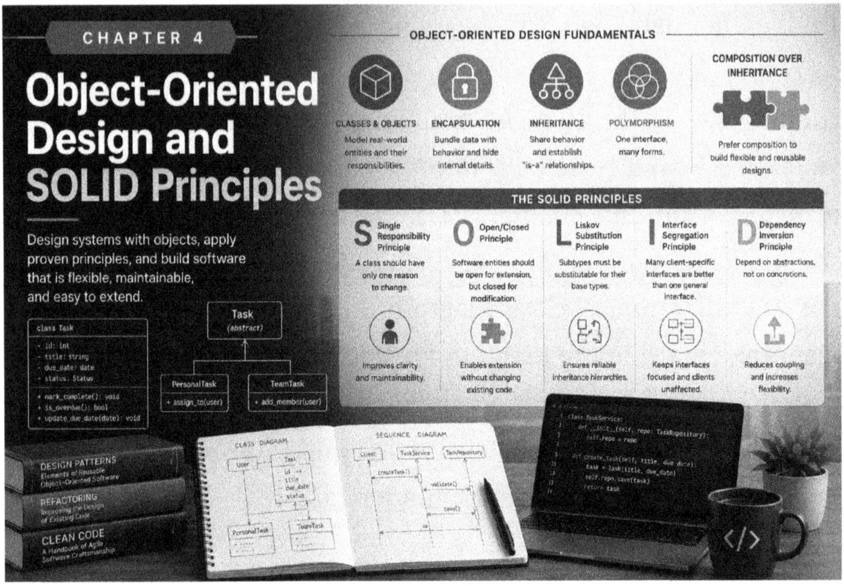

Every program you write is a collection of decisions about how to organize code. In the earlier chapters you learned how to structure logic, manage data, and write functions that do one job well. Those skills carry you a long way, but as programs grow, the way you arrange your code becomes just as important as the code itself. A poorly organized program of ten thousand lines is far harder to change than a well-organized one of fifty thousand. This chapter is about the discipline of organizing code so that it stays flexible, understandable, and easy to extend.

You will begin with the fundamentals of **object-oriented design**, learning how to model real-world concepts as classes with clear responsibilities. From there you will explore the tools that let objects work together — inheritance, polymorphism, and composition — and learn when to reach for each one. Then you will meet the SOLID principles, a set of five guidelines that professional engineers use to keep object-oriented systems maintainable over years of change. Finally, you will put it all together by learning dependency injection and by refactoring existing code to follow these principles.

By the end of this chapter you will be able to design classes that carry a single, well-defined responsibility, choose between inheritance and composition with confidence, program against interfaces rather than concrete implementations, and recognize and fix common design problems in real Python code. These are the skills that separate code that merely runs from code that other engineers can trust and build upon.

4.1 Object-Oriented Design Fundamentals

Object-oriented programming gives you a way to bundle data and the behavior that operates on that data into a single unit. But knowing the syntax of classes is not the same as knowing how to design good ones. **Object-oriented design** is the practice of deciding what objects your program needs, what each object should know, and what each object should be able to do. Get these decisions right and your program almost writes itself. Get them wrong and every change becomes a struggle.

In this section you will learn how to think in objects. You will see how to assign clear responsibilities to classes, how to hide internal details through encapsulation, and how to expose simple ideas through abstraction. These four concepts form the foundation that everything else in this chapter builds upon.

Object-Oriented Design

Good object-oriented design starts with a simple question: what are the "things" in my problem, and what does each thing do? Consider a program that manages a library. The things in that domain include books, members, and loans. Each of these becomes a candidate for a class. **A class is a blueprint that describes the data an object holds and the operations it can perform.**

The goal of design is to make each class model a single, coherent concept. When a class represents one clear idea, its purpose is obvious, its code is easy to find, and changes stay contained. When a class tries to represent several ideas at once, it becomes a tangle that no one wants to touch.

```
class Book:
    def __init__(self, title, author, isbn):
        self.title = title
        self.author = author
        self.isbn = isbn
        self.is_available = True

    def check_out(self):
        if not self.is_available:
            raise ValueError(f"'{self.title}' is already checked out.")
        self.is_available = False

    def return_book(self):
        self.is_available = True
```

This `Book` class models exactly one concept: a book in the library. It holds the data that describes a book and the operations that make sense for a book — checking it out and returning it. Notice that the class does not know anything about members, fines, or the library building. Keeping that knowledge out of `Book` is a deliberate design choice, and it is what makes the class easy to understand and reuse.

Classes and Responsibilities

Every class you write carries one or more **responsibilities** — the things it is accountable for doing or knowing. A helpful way to reason about design is to describe each class in a single sentence. If you cannot describe a class without using the word "and," it may be doing too much.

The `Book` class above has a clear responsibility: it manages the state of a single book. It does not decide how books are stored in a database, and it does not format book information for display on a web page. Those are separate responsibilities that belong to separate classes. This idea — that a class should have one reason to change — will return in force when you study the Single Responsibility Principle later in this chapter.

Assigning responsibilities well is the heart of design. When responsibilities are scattered across many classes, no one class understands the whole picture and bugs slip through the cracks. When too many responsibilities pile into one class, that class becomes a bottleneck that every developer must edit and no developer fully understands.

Encapsulation

Encapsulation is the practice of bundling data together with the methods that operate on it, while restricting direct access to that data from the outside. The goal is to protect an object's internal state so that it can only be changed in valid ways. Think of a vending machine: you press buttons and insert coins, but you cannot reach inside and rearrange the products directly. The machine controls its own state.

```python
class BankAccount:
    def __init__(self, balance=0):
        self._balance = balance

    def deposit(self, amount):
        if amount <= 0:
            raise ValueError("Deposit must be positive.")
        self._balance += amount

    def withdraw(self, amount):
        if amount > self._balance:
            raise ValueError("Insufficient funds.")
        self._balance -= amount

    @property
    def balance(self):
        return self._balance
```

Here the balance is stored in `self._balance`. The leading underscore is a Python convention signaling that the attribute is internal and should not be touched directly from outside the class. Every change to the balance flows through `deposit` or `withdraw`, and each of those methods enforces rules that keep the balance valid. The `balance` property lets callers read the value without being able to overwrite it. Encapsulation gives you a single, trusted place to guard the integrity of your data.

Abstraction

Abstraction is the practice of exposing only the essential features of something while hiding the complicated details. When you drive a car you use a steering wheel and pedals — a simple interface — without needing to understand the combustion happening inside the engine. Abstraction lets you work with ideas at the level you care about.

In the `BankAccount` example, the caller thinks in terms of depositing and withdrawing money. They never see the arithmetic, the validation, or the underscore-prefixed variable. Those details are abstracted away. Encapsulation and abstraction work together: encapsulation hides the data, and abstraction presents a clean set of operations in its place. A well-designed class is one you can use correctly without reading its source code, because its public methods tell you everything you need to know.

Summary

- **Object-oriented design** is the practice of deciding what objects a program needs and what each one is responsible for.
- A well-designed **class** models a single, coherent concept and can be described in one sentence without the word "and."
- **Encapsulation** bundles data with its methods and restricts direct access, giving you one trusted place to protect an object's state.
- **Abstraction** exposes only the essential operations of an object while hiding its complex internal details.
- Encapsulation and abstraction together let you use a class correctly without needing to understand how it works internally.

4.2 Inheritance, Polymorphism, and Composition

Once you can design individual classes, the next question is how to make them work together and share behavior. Object-oriented languages give you several tools for this. **Inheritance** lets one class build on another. **Polymorphism** lets different objects respond to the same request in their own way. **Composition** lets you assemble objects out of other objects. Each tool solves a different problem, and knowing which to reach for is a key design skill.

In this section you will learn how these mechanisms work in Python and, just as importantly, when to use each. You will finish by comparing composition and inheritance directly, because choosing between them is one of the most common design decisions you will face.

Inheritance

Inheritance is a mechanism that lets a new class, called the subclass, take on the attributes and methods of an existing class, called the superclass. It expresses an "is-a" relationship: a savings account *is a* kind of bank account. The subclass inherits everything the superclass offers and can add to it or change it.

```
class SavingsAccount(BankAccount):
    def __init__(self, balance=0, interest_rate=0.02):
        super().__init__(balance)
        self.interest_rate = interest_rate

    def add_interest(self):
        interest = self.balance * self.interest_rate
        self.deposit(interest)
```

The `SavingsAccount` class extends `BankAccount`. The call to `super().__init__(balance)` runs the parent class's constructor so the balance is set up correctly. `SavingsAccount` gains `deposit`, `withdraw`, and `balance` for free, and it adds a new method, `add_interest`, that reuses the inherited `deposit`. Inheritance lets you avoid duplicating the shared logic that all bank accounts need. Use it only when the "is-a" relationship truly holds — a subclass should be a genuine, specialized kind of its parent.

Polymorphism

Polymorphism means that objects of different classes can be treated through a common interface, each responding to the same method call in its own way. The word literally means "many forms." In practice, it lets you write code that works with a family of related objects without caring exactly which one it has.

```
class CheckingAccount(BankAccount):
    def add_interest(self):
        pass  # Checking accounts earn no interest.

accounts = [SavingsAccount(1000), CheckingAccount(500), SavingsAccount(2000)]

for account in accounts:
    account.add_interest()
    print(f"Balance: {account.balance}")
```

The loop calls `add_interest` on every account without checking its type. Each object decides for itself what that call means: a `SavingsAccount` adds interest, while a `CheckingAccount` does nothing. This is the power of polymorphism — you can add new account types later, and as long as they provide an `add_interest` method, this loop keeps working unchanged. Polymorphism is what makes object-oriented code extensible.

Composition

Composition is a design technique where a class is built by containing instances of other classes rather than inheriting from them. It expresses a "has-a" relationship: a car *has an* engine. Instead of saying an object *is a* kind of something, you say it is *made up of* other objects that do specialized work.

```
class Engine:
    def start(self):
        return "Engine started."

class Car:
    def __init__(self):
        self.engine = Engine()

    def start(self):
        return self.engine.start()
```

The `Car` class does not inherit from `Engine`. Instead it holds an `Engine` object and delegates the work of starting to it. This keeps each class focused: the `Engine` knows how to run, and the `Car` knows how to coordinate its parts. If you later need an `ElectricEngine`, you can give the car a different engine object without changing the `Car` class much at all. Composition builds complex behavior by combining simple, independent pieces.

Composition vs. Inheritance

Both inheritance and composition let you reuse code, but they do so in different ways with different consequences. Inheritance creates a tight bond between subclass and superclass — a change in the parent ripples down to every child. Composition creates a looser connection, because the containing class only depends on the public methods of the parts it holds.

A widely respected guideline is to **favor composition over inheritance**. The reason is flexibility. Inheritance locks in a relationship at the moment you write the class, while composition lets you swap parts at runtime. Deep inheritance hierarchies also tend to become fragile: a small change high up can break subclasses in surprising ways.

That said, inheritance is not wrong — it is simply narrower. Reach for inheritance when there is a genuine "is-a" relationship and the subclass truly is a specialized version of its parent. Reach for composition when the relationship is "has-a," when you need to assemble behavior from interchangeable parts, or when you are unsure. As a rule of thumb, ask whether the new class *is* the old thing or merely *uses* the old thing.

Summary

- **Inheritance** expresses an "is-a" relationship and lets a subclass reuse and extend the behavior of a superclass.
- **Polymorphism** lets objects of different classes respond to the same method call in their own way, making code extensible.
- **Composition** expresses a "has-a" relationship by building a class from instances of other classes it delegates to.
- Composition creates looser coupling than inheritance and allows parts to be swapped at runtime.
- Favor composition over inheritance; use inheritance only when a genuine "is-a" relationship exists.

4.3 Interfaces and an Introduction to SOLID

As your programs grow, the connections between classes matter more than the classes themselves. The single most valuable habit you can develop is programming against **interfaces** — agreements about what an object can do — rather than against specific implementations. This habit lets you change parts of your system without those changes rippling everywhere.

In this section you will learn what an interface is, how Python expresses interfaces, and why depending on them makes code flexible. Then you will get your first look at SOLID, the set of five principles that will occupy the rest of the chapter. This section is the bridge between the fundamentals you have learned and the disciplined design principles ahead.

Interfaces and Contracts

An **interface** is a set of methods that a class promises to provide, without specifying how those methods work. It defines a **contract**: any class that fulfills the interface can be used wherever that interface is expected. Interfaces let you focus on *what* an object does rather than *how* it does it or *what class* it happens to be.

Python does not require formal interface declarations the way some languages do, but it offers **abstract base classes** to make contracts explicit. An abstract base class defines methods that subclasses must implement.

```python
from abc import ABC, abstractmethod

class PaymentMethod(ABC):
    @abstractmethod
    def pay(self, amount):
        ...

class CreditCard(PaymentMethod):
    def pay(self, amount):
        return f"Paid {amount} by credit card."

class PayPal(PaymentMethod):
    def pay(self, amount):
        return f"Paid {amount} via PayPal."

def checkout(method: PaymentMethod, amount):
    return method.pay(amount)
```

The `PaymentMethod` abstract base class defines the contract: every payment method must have a `pay` method. Both `CreditCard` and `PayPal` fulfill that contract in their own way. The `checkout` function accepts any `PaymentMethod` and calls `pay` without knowing or caring which concrete class it received. This is programming to an interface. You can add a `Cryptocurrency` payment method tomorrow, and `checkout` will handle it without a single change.

Introduction to SOLID

SOLID is an acronym for five design principles that guide you toward code that is easy to maintain and extend. The principles were popularized by Robert C. Martin, and each one addresses a common source of pain in growing software systems. The letters stand for:

- **S** – Single Responsibility Principle
- **O** – Open/Closed Principle

- **L** — Liskov Substitution Principle
- **I** — Interface Segregation Principle
- **D** — Dependency Inversion Principle

These principles are not rigid laws; they are guidelines that experienced engineers apply with judgment. What they share is a common goal: managing dependencies so that change in one part of a system does not force change everywhere else. Notice that the interface work you just saw is already a preview of SOLID — depending on the `PaymentMethod` contract instead of a concrete class is the essence of the Dependency Inversion Principle. In the next section you will study all five principles in depth.

Summary

- An **interface** is a contract describing what methods a class must provide, without specifying how they work.
- Python expresses interfaces informally through duck typing and formally through **abstract base classes**.
- Programming to an interface lets you swap implementations freely, because callers depend only on the contract.
- **SOLID** is a set of five principles — Single Responsibility, Open/Closed, Liskov Substitution, Interface Segregation, and Dependency Inversion — for maintainable design.
- The shared goal of SOLID is to manage dependencies so that changes stay contained rather than rippling across a system.

4.4 The Five SOLID Principles

Now that you have met SOLID at a high level, it is time to study each principle in detail. Each one targets a specific way that code becomes rigid, fragile, or hard to reuse. Learning to recognize the smell each principle addresses is as valuable as learning the principle itself.

In this section you will work through all five principles with concrete Python examples. For each, you will see what problem it solves, how to apply it, and what your code looks like before and after. Together they form a coherent toolkit for building software that welcomes change instead of resisting it.

Single Responsibility Principle

The **Single Responsibility Principle (SRP)** states that a class should have only one reason to change. In other words, a class should have a single, well-defined responsibility. When a class does several unrelated things, a change to any one of them risks breaking the others.

```
# Violates SRP: this class formats, saves, and emails a report.
class Report:
    def generate(self, data):
        return f"Report: {data}"

    def save_to_file(self, content, path):
        with open(path, "w") as f:
            f.write(content)

    def email(self, content, address):
        print(f"Emailing report to {address}")
```

This `Report` class has three reasons to change: the report format, the file storage mechanism, and the emailing logic. If your email provider changes, you must edit a class that also handles files. The fix is to split each responsibility into its own class — a `ReportGenerator`, a `FileSaver`, and an `EmailSender` — so each has a single reason to change. Smaller, focused classes are easier to test, reuse, and reason about.

Open/Closed Principle

The **Open/Closed Principle (OCP)** states that software entities should be open for extension but closed for modification. You should be able to add new behavior without editing existing, tested code. The tool that makes this possible is usually polymorphism.

```
class Discount(ABC):
    @abstractmethod
    def apply(self, price):
        ...

class NoDiscount(Discount):
    def apply(self, price):
        return price

class PercentageDiscount(Discount):
    def __init__(self, percent):
        self.percent = percent

    def apply(self, price):
        return price * (1 - self.percent / 100)

def final_price(price, discount: Discount):
    return discount.apply(price)
```

To add a new kind of discount — say, a fixed-amount discount — you write a new subclass of `Discount`. You do not touch `final_price` or any existing discount class. The existing code is closed for modification but the system is open for extension.

Compare this to an approach using a long chain of `if/elif` statements checking a discount type: every new discount would force you to edit that chain, risking bugs in code that already works.

Liskov Substitution Principle

The **Liskov Substitution Principle (LSP)** states that objects of a subclass should be usable anywhere objects of the superclass are expected, without breaking the program. A subclass must honor the contract of its parent. If it does not, inheritance becomes a trap.

```
class Bird:
    def move(self):
        return "Moving around."

class Sparrow(Bird):
    def move(self):
        return "Flying."

class Penguin(Bird):
    def move(self):
        return "Waddling."
```

Here every `Bird` subclass can stand in for a `Bird` because they all honor the same `move` contract. The classic violation is a `fly` method: if `Bird` promised `fly` and `Penguin` overrode it to throw an error, then substituting a penguin for a bird would crash code that expected any bird to fly. LSP pushes you to design base classes around behavior that every subclass can genuinely support. When a subclass cannot honor the parent's contract, that is a sign inheritance is the wrong tool.

Interface Segregation Principle

The **Interface Segregation Principle (ISP)** states that no class should be forced to depend on methods it does not use. Instead of one large, general-purpose interface, prefer several small, focused ones. Fat interfaces force implementers to provide methods that make no sense for them.

```python
class Printer(ABC):
    @abstractmethod
    def print_document(self, doc): ...

class Scanner(ABC):
    @abstractmethod
    def scan(self, doc): ...

class SimplePrinter(Printer):
    def print_document(self, doc):
        return f"Printing {doc}"
```

Imagine instead a single `MultiFunctionDevice` interface requiring `print_document` , `scan` , and `fax` . A simple printer that only prints would be forced to implement `scan` and `fax` , probably by raising errors. By splitting the interface into `Printer` and `Scanner` , each device implements only the contracts it truly supports. A machine that does both simply implements both interfaces. Small interfaces keep classes honest and clients decoupled.

Dependency Inversion Principle

The **Dependency Inversion Principle (DIP)** states that high-level modules should not depend on low-level modules; both should depend on abstractions. It also says abstractions should not depend on details — rather, details should depend on abstractions. In practice this means your business logic should depend on interfaces, not on concrete classes like a specific database.

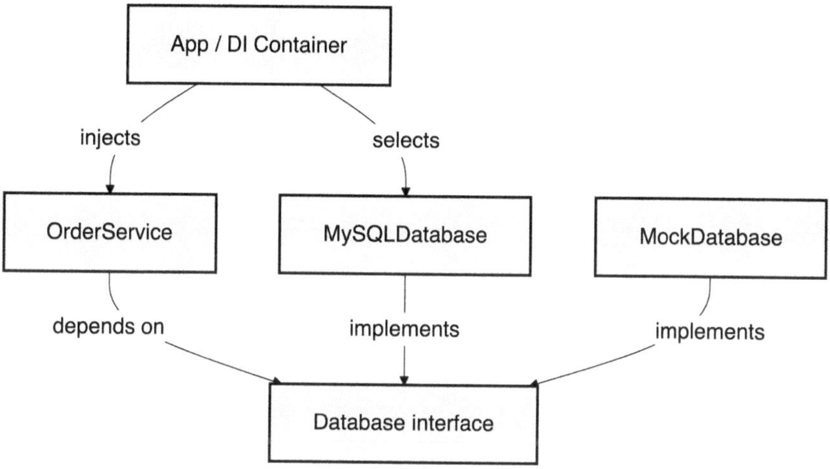


```
class Database(ABC):
    @abstractmethod
    def save(self, record): ...

class MySQLDatabase(Database):
    def save(self, record):
        print(f"Saving {record} to MySQL.")

class OrderService:
    def __init__(self, database: Database):
        self.database = database

    def place_order(self, order):
        self.database.save(order)
```

The `OrderService` is a high-level module holding your business logic. It depends on the abstract `Database`, not on `MySQLDatabase`. The concrete `MySQLDatabase` also depends on the `Database` abstraction by implementing it. Because of this, you can hand `OrderService` a `PostgresDatabase` or even a fake in-memory database for testing, and it will not notice the difference. The direction of the dependency has been inverted: both the policy and the detail now point at a shared abstraction.

Summary

- The **Single Responsibility Principle** says a class should have only one reason to change.
- The **Open/Closed Principle** says code should be open for extension but closed for modification, usually achieved through polymorphism.
- The **Liskov Substitution Principle** says subclasses must be usable in place of their base class without breaking the program.
- The **Interface Segregation Principle** says classes should not be forced to depend on methods they do not use.
- The **Dependency Inversion Principle** says high-level and low-level modules should both depend on abstractions rather than on each other.

4.5 Applying SOLID in Practice

Principles are only useful when you can apply them to real code. In this final section you will learn **dependency injection**, the practical technique that makes the Dependency Inversion Principle work, and you will walk through refactoring a messy legacy class into a clean, SOLID design. This is where theory becomes craft.

You will see that applying SOLID is rarely about following a checklist. It is about recognizing where a class is doing too much or depending on too much, then untangling those concerns one at a time. The skills here directly prepare you for the chapter lab.

Dependency Injection

Dependency injection is the practice of giving an object its dependencies from the outside rather than having it create them itself. Instead of a class building the objects it needs internally, those objects are passed in — usually through the constructor. This small change is what makes the Dependency Inversion Principle practical.

```python
class EmailNotifier:
    def send(self, message):
        print(f"Email: {message}")

class OrderProcessor:
    def __init__(self, notifier):
        self.notifier = notifier  # injected from outside

    def process(self, order):
        # ... business logic ...
        self.notifier.send(f"Order {order} processed.")

# Wiring happens at the edge of the application.
processor = OrderProcessor(EmailNotifier())
processor.process("A-1001")
```

Notice that `OrderProcessor` never creates its own notifier. The notifier is *injected* through the constructor, so the caller decides what kind of notifier to use. To send SMS messages instead, you pass in a different notifier — no change to `OrderProcessor` is needed. This also makes testing simple: in a test you can inject a fake notifier that records messages instead of sending them. Dependency injection is the mechanism that turns loosely coupled design from a nice idea into working code.

Applying SOLID to Existing Code

Most of the time you will apply SOLID not to blank files but to existing code that has grown tangled. A common example is the **God class** – a single class that has accumulated data access, business logic, and notification duties all at once. Such a class violates SRP, is hard to test, and forces unrelated changes into the same file.

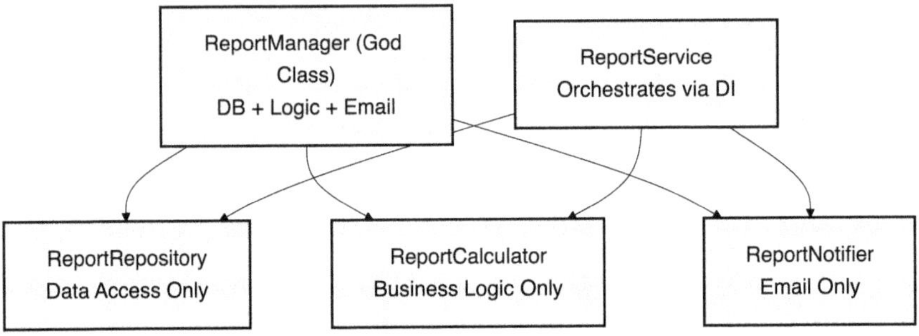

Refactoring a God class follows a repeatable rhythm. First you identify the distinct responsibilities buried inside it. Then you extract each responsibility into its own focused class. Finally you use dependency injection to wire the pieces back together, so the coordinating class depends on abstractions rather than doing everything itself.

```python
# Before: a God class doing everything.
class UserManager:
    def register(self, email):
        # validate, save to DB, and send email all in one place
        print(f"Saving {email} to database")
        print(f"Sending welcome email to {email}")

# After: responsibilities separated and injected.
class UserRepository:
    def save(self, email):
        print(f"Saving {email} to database")

class WelcomeMailer:
    def send(self, email):
        print(f"Sending welcome email to {email}")

class RegistrationService:
    def __init__(self, repository, mailer):
        self.repository = repository
        self.mailer = mailer

    def register(self, email):
        self.repository.save(email)
        self.mailer.send(email)
```

In the refactored version, storage lives in `UserRepository`, emailing lives in `WelcomeMailer`, and `RegistrationService` simply coordinates them. Each class now has a single reason to change, and the service receives its collaborators through injection. You can test the registration flow with fake objects, swap the mailer for an SMS sender, or change the database without touching the coordination logic. Refactoring this way, one responsibility at a time, keeps the code working at every step while steadily improving its design.

Summary

- **Dependency injection** supplies an object's dependencies from the outside, usually through its constructor.
- Injection makes the Dependency Inversion Principle practical and makes classes far easier to test with fake collaborators.
- A **God class** mixes many responsibilities and is a common target for SOLID refactoring.
- Refactoring proceeds by identifying responsibilities, extracting each into a focused class, and wiring them together with injection.
- Applying SOLID is an incremental craft of untangling concerns, not a checklist to follow blindly.

Chapter Summary

This chapter took you from the basics of object-oriented design to the disciplined principles that professional engineers rely on. You began by learning to model concepts as focused classes and to protect their behavior through encapsulation and abstraction. Those fundamentals matter because every principle that followed depends on them — you cannot manage responsibilities in a class that has no clear responsibility to begin with. You then explored inheritance, polymorphism, and composition, learning that while all three enable reuse, composition's flexibility usually makes it the safer default.

The heart of the chapter was the shift from thinking about individual classes to thinking about the dependencies between them. Programming to interfaces set the stage, and the five SOLID principles gave you a shared vocabulary for the design decisions engineers make every day. Each principle attacks a specific weakness: SRP fights tangled responsibilities, OCP fights fragile modification, LSP fights broken inheritance, ISP fights bloated contracts, and DIP fights rigid coupling to concrete details. Dependency injection tied these ideas into a technique you can apply in real code.

You can now do something you could not do at the start of this chapter: look at a piece of software and reason about whether it will be easy or painful to change. You can spot a class that does too much, an interface that demands too much, or a dependency pointing the wrong way — and you can fix each one. These are the design instincts that underpin every large, long-lived software system, and they will serve you in every language and framework you work with from here forward.

Chapter Lab: Refactoring a Python Application Using SOLID Principles

In this lab you will take a small but poorly structured Python application built around a God class and refactor it into a clean, maintainable design. You will apply the Single Responsibility Principle to separate its concerns, program to interfaces to decouple its components, and use dependency injection to wire everything back together. By the end you will have transformed rigid, hard-to-test code into a flexible system that welcomes change, applying every major concept from this chapter in a single connected exercise.

Chapter 5: Software Design Patterns

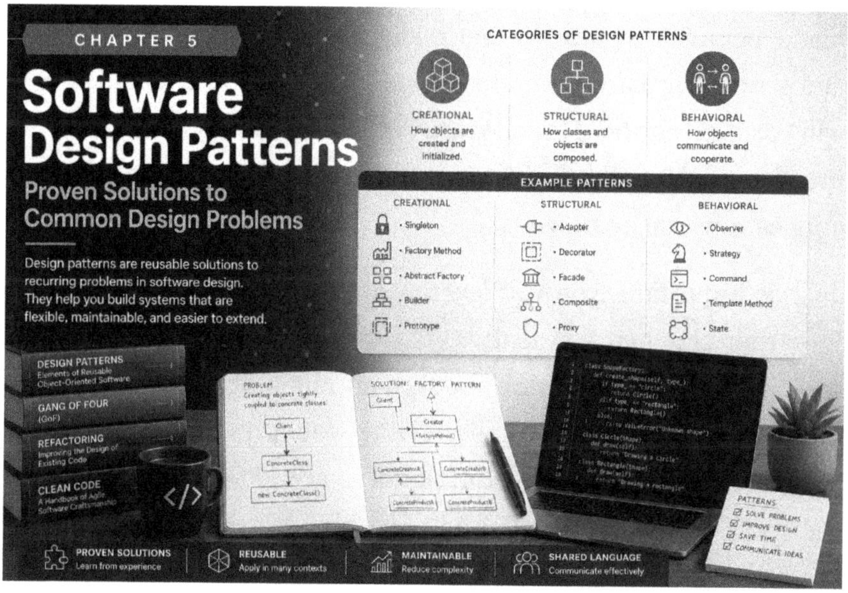

Every experienced developer eventually notices something curious: the same problems keep showing up. You need to create objects without hardcoding their exact types. You need one part of your system to react when another part changes. You need to swap out one algorithm for another without rewriting everything around it. These problems appear across languages, industries, and decades. Over time, the software community discovered that certain solutions worked so reliably that they were worth naming, documenting, and reusing. Those solutions are called design patterns.

In this chapter, you will learn what design patterns are, why they became a shared vocabulary among professional developers, and how to apply the most important ones in your own Python code. You will study creational patterns that manage how objects are made, behavioral patterns that manage how objects communicate, and structural patterns that manage how objects fit together. You will also meet the Model-View-Controller architecture and the practice of dependency injection, both of which shape how real applications are organized.

Just as important, you will learn when *not* to reach for a pattern. In earlier chapters you learned to write clean functions, organize code into classes, and think about maintainability. Design patterns build directly on those skills, giving you proven templates for structuring larger systems. But patterns are tools, not trophies. By the end of this chapter, you will be able to recognize patterns in the frameworks you already use, implement several of them from scratch, and make thoughtful decisions about when a pattern helps and when it just adds noise.

5.1 What Design Patterns Are and Why They Matter

Before you can use design patterns well, you need a clear mental model of what they actually are. Many beginners assume a pattern is a chunk of code they can copy and paste. It is not. A pattern is closer to a recipe or a blueprint — a description of a solution that you adapt to your specific situation. In this section, you will learn the true definition of a design pattern, understand why patterns matter to working developers, and see how the major patterns are grouped into three families.

Understanding this foundation matters because patterns are, above all, a form of communication. When a colleague says "let's use a factory here," an enormous amount of meaning is packed into those few words. Learning that shared language is one of the fastest ways to grow from a hobbyist into a professional engineer.

What Is a Design Pattern?

A **design pattern** is a general, reusable solution to a commonly occurring problem in software design. Notice the word *general.* A pattern does not solve one specific bug in one specific program. Instead, it describes the shape of a solution that you can apply to many different programs, each time filling in the details that fit your case.

Think of a design pattern like an architectural blueprint for a staircase. The blueprint tells you the essential elements — steps, a railing, a slope that people can climb safely. It does not tell you the exact wood, the exact color, or the exact number of steps. You adapt those details to the building you are constructing. In the same way, a design pattern tells you the essential elements of a solution while leaving the concrete details to you.

Patterns were popularized by a 1994 book, *Design Patterns: Elements of Reusable Object-Oriented Software*, written by four authors often called the "Gang of Four." They catalogued twenty-three patterns they had observed appearing again and again in well-designed systems. They did not invent these solutions. They discovered and documented them, much like a naturalist naming species that already existed in the wild.

A useful way to describe any pattern is with three parts: the **problem** it addresses, the **solution** it proposes, and the **consequences** — the trade-offs you accept when you use it. Every pattern has consequences. There is no such thing as a free improvement in software design, and part of being a professional is understanding what a pattern costs as well as what it gives.

Why Design Patterns Matter

The most immediate benefit of design patterns is a shared vocabulary. Software is built by teams, and teams need to communicate design decisions quickly and precisely. Consider the difference between these two sentences a developer might say in a code review:

- "We should create a separate class whose only job is to decide which type of report object to build, so the calling code doesn't have to know about all the concrete report classes."
- "We should use a factory here."

Both sentences describe the same idea. The second one takes two seconds and every experienced developer understands it instantly. That is the power of a named pattern.

Beyond communication, patterns encode hard-won wisdom. Each pattern represents a solution that many developers tried, refined, and validated over years. When you apply a well-known pattern, you inherit that collective experience. You are less likely to stumble into a design that seems clever at first but becomes painful to maintain later.

Patterns also make code easier to understand and change. When a new developer joins your team and recognizes a familiar pattern in your codebase, they can predict how the code behaves without reading every line. This predictability reduces the time it takes to onboard people and lowers the risk of introducing bugs during changes.

Finally, patterns support one of the central goals of good software design: managing change. Most patterns work by isolating the parts of a system that are likely to vary. When requirements shift — and they always do — a well-placed pattern lets you make the change in one small area rather than rewriting large portions of the program.

Creational, Structural, and Behavioral Patterns

The Gang of Four organized their patterns into three families, and this classification remains a helpful way to think about them today. Each family addresses a different kind of concern.

Creational patterns deal with object creation. They give you flexible, controlled ways to produce objects rather than scattering `new`-style construction calls throughout your code. Examples include the Factory pattern and the Singleton pattern. The core question a creational pattern answers is: *how do we make objects without tightly binding our code to their exact types?*

Structural patterns deal with how objects and classes are composed to form larger structures. They help you assemble pieces so that the overall system stays flexible and comprehensible. Examples include the Adapter and Facade patterns. The core question here is: *how do we combine objects into bigger units while keeping the connections clean?*

Behavioral patterns deal with how objects communicate and how responsibilities are distributed. They focus on the flow of control and data between objects at runtime. Examples include the Strategy and Observer patterns. The core question is: *how do* *objects interact and share work without becoming hopelessly entangled?*

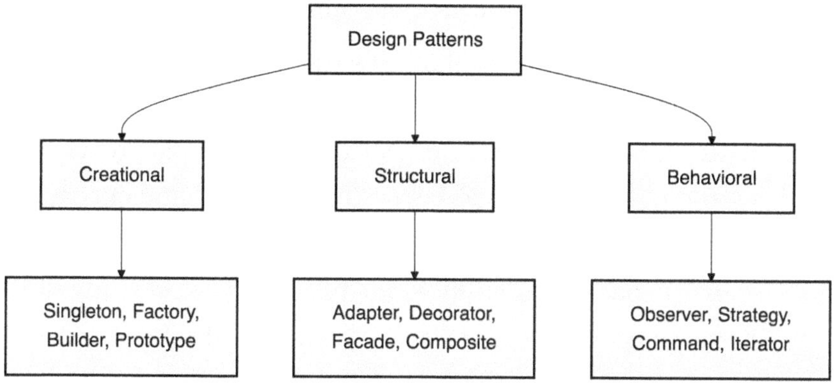

Keeping these three families in mind gives you a quick way to reason about any pattern you encounter. When you meet an unfamiliar pattern, ask which family it belongs to. If it is about making objects, it is creational. If it is about arranging objects, it is structural. If it is about objects talking to each other, it is behavioral. That single question orients you immediately.

Summary

- A **design pattern** is a general, reusable solution to a common design problem — a blueprint you adapt, not code you copy.
- Patterns give teams a shared vocabulary, encode proven wisdom, and make code easier to understand and change.
- Every pattern involves trade-offs; a professional weighs the consequences as carefully as the benefits.
- Patterns fall into three families: **creational** (object creation), **structural** (object composition), and **behavioral** (object communication).
- When you meet a new pattern, identifying its family quickly tells you what kind of problem it solves.

5.2 Creational and Behavioral Patterns

Now that you understand what patterns are and how they are grouped, it is time to build some. In this section you will implement three of the most widely used patterns in everyday development: the Factory pattern from the creational family, and the Strategy and Observer patterns from the behavioral family. These three appear constantly in real codebases, so learning them well pays off immediately.

Each pattern here solves a problem you have probably already felt, even if you did not have a name for it. You will see how the Factory removes hardcoded type decisions, how the Strategy lets you swap algorithms cleanly, and how the Observer lets objects react to changes without tight coupling.

Factory Pattern

The **Factory pattern** provides a single place responsible for creating objects, so that the rest of your code does not need to know the exact classes being instantiated. The problem it solves is a common one: as a program grows, you often need to create one of several related objects based on some input, and those decisions get scattered across many files. When a new type is added, you have to hunt down every place that makes decisions and update it.

Imagine an application that exports reports in different formats. Without a factory, every part of the program that needs a report has to know about every format class. A factory centralizes that knowledge.

```python
class PdfReport:
    def render(self):
        return "Rendering a PDF report"

class CsvReport:
    def render(self):
        return "Rendering a CSV report"

class HtmlReport:
    def render(self):
        return "Rendering an HTML report"

class ReportFactory:
    @staticmethod
    def create_report(format_type):
        reports = {
            "pdf": PdfReport,
            "csv": CsvReport,
            "html": HtmlReport,
        }
        report_class = reports.get(format_type)
        if report_class is None:
            raise ValueError(f"Unknown format: {format_type}")
        return report_class()

report = ReportFactory.create_report("pdf")
print(report.render())
```

The output of this code is `Rendering a PDF report`. The key detail is that the calling code only knows the string `"pdf"` and the fact that whatever it receives has a `render` method. It knows nothing about the `PdfReport` class specifically. When you later add an `XmlReport`, you change only the `ReportFactory` — one location — and every caller automatically gains the new capability. This is the essence of the pattern: it isolates the decision about *which* class to create so that change stays contained.

Strategy Pattern

The **Strategy pattern** lets you define a family of interchangeable algorithms, put each one in its own class, and choose between them at runtime. The problem it solves is the tangle of `if` / `elif` branches that appears when a single operation can be done in several ways. Those branches make code hard to read and even harder to extend.

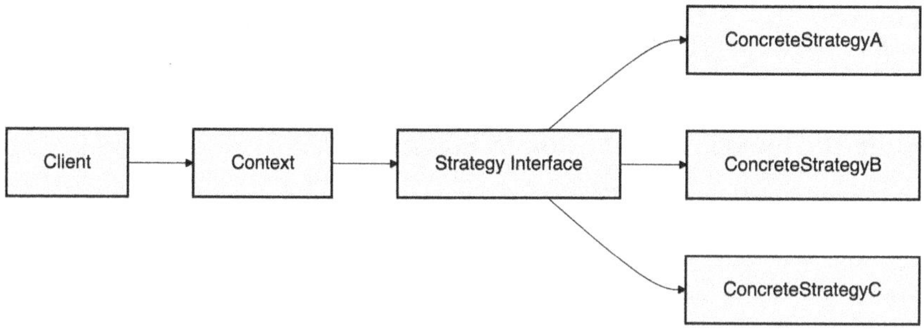

Consider an online store that calculates shipping costs differently depending on the shipping method. Instead of one giant function full of conditionals, you can express each calculation as a separate strategy.

```
class StandardShipping:
    def calculate(self, weight):
        return weight * 1.5

class ExpressShipping:
    def calculate(self, weight):
        return weight * 3.0 + 5.0

class Order:
    def __init__(self, weight, shipping_strategy):
        self.weight = weight
        self.shipping_strategy = shipping_strategy

    def shipping_cost(self):
        return self.shipping_strategy.calculate(self.weight)

order = Order(weight=4, shipping_strategy=ExpressShipping())
print(f"Shipping cost: ${order.shipping_cost():.2f}")
```

This prints `Shipping cost: $17.00`. The `Order` class is the **context** – it holds a reference to a strategy but does not care how the calculation works. Each strategy class implements the same `calculate` method, so they are interchangeable. To add a new shipping method, you write a new class and pass it in; you never touch `Order`. Notice also that you can switch the strategy at runtime simply by assigning a different object, which is impossible when the logic is baked into `if` statements.

Observer Pattern

The **Observer pattern** defines a one-to-many relationship between objects so that when one object changes state, all of its dependents are notified automatically. The problem it solves is coupling: you want several objects to react to an event without the source of the event knowing exactly who is listening.

You have almost certainly used this pattern as an end user. When you subscribe to a newsletter, you become an observer of the publisher. When the publisher releases a new issue, everyone subscribed receives it — the publisher does not need a hardcoded list of names in its own logic.

```
class NewsPublisher:
    def __init__(self):
        self._subscribers = []

    def subscribe(self, subscriber):
        self._subscribers.append(subscriber)

    def unsubscribe(self, subscriber):
        self._subscribers.remove(subscriber)

    def publish(self, headline):
        for subscriber in self._subscribers:
            subscriber.update(headline)

class EmailSubscriber:
    def __init__(self, name):
        self.name = name

    def update(self, headline):
        print(f"Emailing {self.name}: {headline}")

publisher = NewsPublisher()
publisher.subscribe(EmailSubscriber("Ada"))
publisher.subscribe(EmailSubscriber("Grace"))
publisher.publish("New Python release!")
```

Running this notifies both subscribers, printing a message for Ada and one for Grace. The `NewsPublisher` maintains a list of observers and loops over them when something happens, but it knows nothing about what each observer *does* with the news. One might send email, another might log to a file, another might update a dashboard. You can add and remove observers at any time. This decoupling is what makes the Observer pattern so powerful in event-driven systems and user interfaces.

Summary

- The **Factory pattern** centralizes object creation so the rest of your code depends on an interface rather than concrete classes.
- The **Strategy pattern** turns interchangeable algorithms into separate classes that can be swapped at runtime, replacing long conditional chains.
- The **Observer pattern** lets many objects react to a change in one object without the source knowing who is listening.
- All three patterns work by isolating what varies, keeping change contained to small, predictable areas.
- Behavioral patterns like Strategy and Observer focus on how objects communicate and divide responsibilities at runtime.

5.3 Structural Patterns and MVC

With creational and behavioral patterns behind you, this section turns to structural patterns — the ones concerned with how objects are assembled into larger wholes. You will learn the Adapter and Facade patterns, meet the Repository pattern that dominates data-access code, and then step up to a higher level with the Model-View-Controller architecture that organizes entire applications.

Structural patterns matter because real systems are made of many parts that must fit together. A pattern that keeps those connections clean is the difference between a codebase you can grow and one that collapses under its own complexity.

Adapter Pattern

The **Adapter pattern** lets two incompatible interfaces work together by wrapping one of them in a translating layer. The name is literal: it works exactly like a travel power adapter that lets a plug from one country fit a socket in another. The problem it solves comes up whenever you must integrate code you cannot change — a third-party library, a legacy module, or an external service — whose interface does not match what your application expects.

```python
class ModernLogger:
    def log(self, message):
        print(f"[LOG] {message}")

class LegacyPrinter:
    def write_line(self, text):
        print(f"OLD SYSTEM: {text}")

class PrinterAdapter:
    def __init__(self, legacy_printer):
        self.legacy_printer = legacy_printer

    def log(self, message):
        self.legacy_printer.write_line(message)

def run_report(logger):
    logger.log("Report generated")

run_report(ModernLogger())
run_report(PrinterAdapter(LegacyPrinter()))
```

Here, `run_report` expects any object with a `log` method. The `ModernLogger` already has one. The `LegacyPrinter` does not — it has `write_line` instead. Rather than rewriting the legacy class, you wrap it in a `PrinterAdapter` that exposes a `log` method and quietly forwards the call to `write_line`. The adapter translates between the two interfaces so the client code stays uniform. This is invaluable when you cannot or should not modify the original class.

Facade Pattern

The **Facade pattern** provides a simple, unified interface to a complex subsystem. The problem it solves is complexity leaking into client code. When using a system requires calling many objects in a precise order, every caller must understand those details, and mistakes become easy. A facade hides that complexity behind one clean entry point.

```python
class Inventory:
    def reserve(self, item):
        print(f"Reserved {item}")

class Payment:
    def charge(self, amount):
        print(f"Charged ${amount}")

class Shipping:
    def dispatch(self, item):
        print(f"Dispatched {item}")

class OrderFacade:
    def __init__(self):
        self.inventory = Inventory()
        self.payment = Payment()
        self.shipping = Shipping()

    def place_order(self, item, amount):
        self.inventory.reserve(item)
        self.payment.charge(amount)
        self.shipping.dispatch(item)

facade = OrderFacade()
facade.place_order("Laptop", 1200)
```

The client calls a single method, `place_order`, and the facade orchestrates the three subsystems in the correct order. The caller does not need to know that reserving inventory must happen before charging payment, or that shipping comes last. The facade encapsulates that workflow. If the process changes later — say you add a fraud check — you update the facade, and every caller benefits without any change on their side.

Repository Pattern

The **Repository pattern** provides a collection-like interface for accessing data, hiding the details of how and where that data is stored. The problem it solves is the entanglement of business logic with database code. When SQL queries or file operations are sprinkled throughout your application, changing your storage technology becomes a nightmare, and testing becomes difficult because your logic cannot run without a real database.

```
class User:
    def __init__(self, user_id, name):
        self.user_id = user_id
        self.name = name

class UserRepository:
    def __init__(self):
        self._users = {}

    def add(self, user):
        self._users[user.user_id] = user

    def get(self, user_id):
        return self._users.get(user_id)

    def all(self):
        return list(self._users.values())

repo = UserRepository()
repo.add(User(1, "Ada"))
repo.add(User(2, "Grace"))
print(repo.get(1).name)
```

This repository stores users in a dictionary, but the rest of your application does not know that. It only knows the methods `add`, `get`, and `all`. Later you could rewrite `UserRepository` to talk to a PostgreSQL database or a REST API, and as long as those three methods keep the same behavior, no other code changes. The in-memory version shown here is also perfect for testing, since your tests can run fast without any database at all.

Model-View-Controller

Model-View-Controller, usually abbreviated **MVC**, is an architectural pattern that divides an application into three layers with distinct responsibilities. The **Model** holds the data and business logic. The **View** presents information to the user. The **Controller** receives user input, tells the model what to do, and selects which view to display.

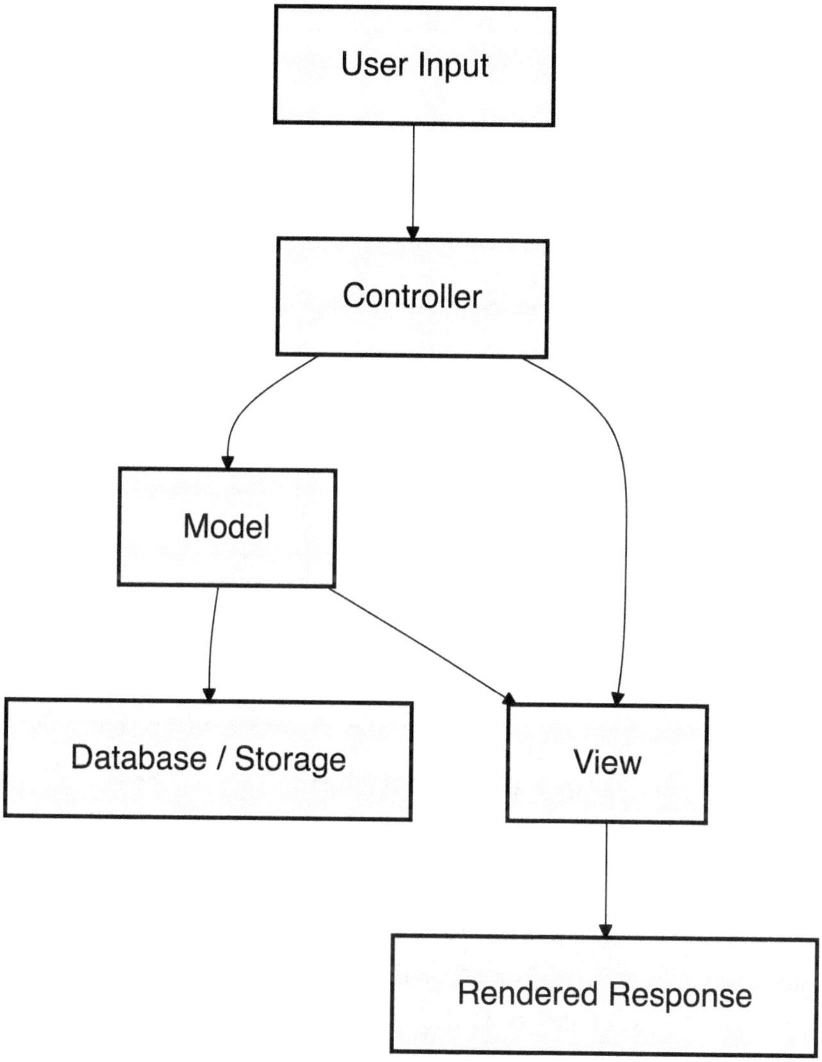

The reason MVC has endured for decades is that it enforces a clean separation of concerns. Each layer has one job, which means you can change how something looks without touching how it works, and change your business rules without touching your display code.

```python
class TaskModel:
    def __init__(self):
        self.tasks = []

    def add_task(self, description):
        self.tasks.append(description)

class TaskView:
    def show(self, tasks):
        for i, task in enumerate(tasks, start=1):
            print(f"{i}. {task}")

class TaskController:
    def __init__(self, model, view):
        self.model = model
        self.view = view

    def add_task(self, description):
        self.model.add_task(description)

    def display_tasks(self):
        self.view.show(self.model.tasks)

controller = TaskController(TaskModel(), TaskView())
controller.add_task("Write chapter")
controller.add_task("Review lab")
controller.display_tasks()
```

The `TaskModel` knows only about storing tasks. The `TaskView` knows only how to print them. The `TaskController` connects the two, responding to requests and coordinating the other layers. Notice that the model never imports the view and the view never imports the model — they are fully independent. This is why web frameworks like Django and Flask lean heavily on MVC-style separation: it keeps large applications organized and testable.

Summary

- The **Adapter pattern** wraps an incompatible interface so it works with code that expects a different one.
- The **Facade pattern** hides a complex subsystem behind a single, simple entry point.
- The **Repository pattern** separates business logic from data storage, making code easier to change and test.
- **Model-View-Controller** divides an application into data, presentation, and coordination layers that stay independent.
- Structural patterns and MVC all share one goal: keeping the connections between parts clean so systems can grow without collapsing.

5.4 Using Patterns Wisely

Learning patterns is exciting, and that excitement can be dangerous. Once you know several patterns, everything starts to look like a place to use one. This final section teaches you the discipline that separates good engineers from merely enthusiastic ones. You will learn dependency injection, how to spot patterns already present in the frameworks you use, and — most importantly — when to leave patterns out entirely.

The goal of this section is judgment. Patterns are means to an end, and that end is code that is easy to understand, change, and maintain. Any time a pattern works against those goals, the pattern is wrong for that situation.

Dependency Injection

Dependency injection, often shortened to **DI**, is the practice of giving an object the things it needs from the outside rather than letting it create them itself. The problem it solves is tight coupling. When a class constructs its own dependencies, it is permanently wedded to those exact implementations, which makes the class rigid and hard to test.

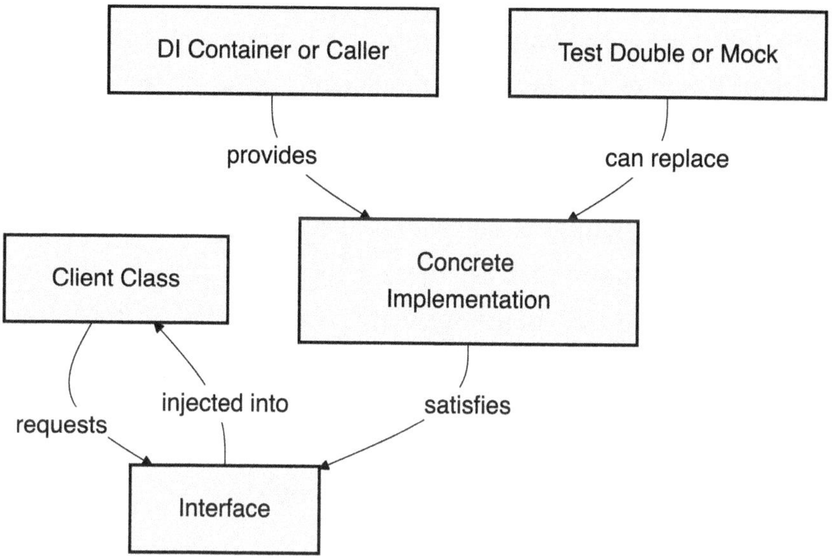

Look at the difference between a tightly coupled class and one that uses injection.

```
# Tightly coupled: creates its own dependency
class ReportServiceTight:
    def __init__(self):
        self.logger = ModernLogger()  # locked to one logger

    def generate(self):
        self.logger.log("Report generated")

# Injected: receives its dependency from outside
class ReportService:
    def __init__(self, logger):
        self.logger = logger

    def generate(self):
        self.logger.log("Report generated")

service = ReportService(ModernLogger())
service.generate()
```

The first class builds its own `ModernLogger`, so it can never use any other logger and cannot be tested without producing real log output. The second class accepts a logger as a parameter. This small change has large consequences. In production you pass a real logger; in a test you pass a fake one that records messages so you can verify them. The class no longer controls *which* logger it uses — it only knows that whatever it receives has a `log` method. Dependency injection is the mechanism that makes patterns like Strategy and Repository practical, because it is how you supply the interchangeable pieces.

Recognizing Patterns in Frameworks

You do not need to build patterns from scratch to benefit from them. The frameworks you already use are full of them, and learning to recognize the patterns helps you understand those tools far more deeply.

- When a web framework calls your view function every time a request arrives, that is dependency injection and the Observer idea at work.
- When an ORM like Django's gives you a `Model` class with `objects.get()` and `objects.all()`, you are using the Repository pattern.
- When Python's `sorted` function accepts a `key` argument that changes how comparison works, that is the Strategy pattern — you inject the algorithm.
- When a library gives you one simple client object that hides dozens of internal classes, that is a Facade.

Once you start looking, you will see patterns everywhere. This recognition is a practical skill. It lets you read documentation faster, because you already understand the shape of the design. It also gives you confidence that these patterns are not academic curiosities — they are the load-bearing structure of the software you rely on every day.

When Not to Use Design Patterns

A pattern is only valuable when it solves a problem you actually have. The most common mistake beginners make is applying a pattern preemptively, in case they might need its flexibility later. This is almost always a bad trade. You pay the cost of the pattern's extra complexity immediately, while the benefit is only hypothetical.

Consider the Factory pattern. It shines when you have several related classes and the choice between them varies. But if you only ever create one type of object, a factory adds a layer of indirection for no reason. A plain constructor call is clearer. The same logic applies to Strategy: if there is only one algorithm and no realistic prospect of another, wrapping it in a strategy class just hides a simple function behind ceremony.

A good rule of thumb is to wait until you feel the pain the pattern relieves. If you find yourself editing the same `if` / `elif` chain repeatedly to add new cases, *that* is the signal to introduce a Strategy or Factory. If you find business logic hopelessly tangled with database calls, *that* is the moment for a Repository. Patterns applied in response to real, observed problems almost always earn their keep. Patterns applied out of anxiety about the future usually do not.

Avoiding Overengineering

Overengineering is building more structure and flexibility than a problem requires. It is the natural failure mode of a developer who has just learned patterns and wants to use them. The result is code that is technically impressive but genuinely harder to read, harder to change, and slower to write than a simpler solution would have been.

The antidote is a principle you may have heard before: keep it simple. Prefer the most straightforward solution that solves the problem in front of you. Add complexity only when the simple solution starts to strain. Remember that every layer of abstraction you introduce is a layer that the next developer — possibly your future self — must understand before they can make a change.

Patterns are a vocabulary for managing complexity, but they are not free. Each one adds classes, indirection, and concepts a reader must hold in their head. The mark of a skilled engineer is not how many patterns they use but how well their code matches the actual difficulty of the problem. Sometimes the most professional decision you can make is to write three plain functions and move on.

Summary

- **Dependency injection** supplies a class's dependencies from outside, reducing coupling and making code easy to test.
- The frameworks you already use are built on patterns; recognizing them helps you learn and trust those tools.
- Apply a pattern only when you feel the specific pain it relieves, not preemptively "just in case."
- **Overengineering** adds flexibility a problem does not need, making code harder to read and change.
- The best engineers match the complexity of their solution to the real difficulty of the problem, and often choose simplicity.

Chapter Summary

This chapter moved you from understanding what design patterns are to using them with judgment. You began by learning that a pattern is a general, reusable blueprint rather than copyable code, and that patterns fall into three families — creational, structural, and behavioral — each addressing a different layer of concern. That classification gives you a mental map for any pattern you encounter, whether you meet it here or years from now in an unfamiliar codebase.

You then built real patterns. The Factory centralized object creation, Strategy made algorithms interchangeable, and Observer let objects react to change without tight coupling. On the structural side, Adapter and Facade tamed messy interfaces, Repository separated logic from storage, and Model-View-Controller organized an entire application into independent layers. Running through all of these is a single theme: good design isolates what varies so that change stays contained. Every pattern in this chapter is a different technique for achieving that one goal, and dependency injection is the mechanism that ties many of them together by letting you supply interchangeable pieces from the outside.

Most importantly, you learned restraint. Patterns are tools that carry real costs in complexity, and applying them out of enthusiasm rather than need leads to overengineered code that is harder to maintain than the problem justified. You can now recognize patterns in the frameworks you use every day, implement the essential ones yourself, and — the true mark of an engineer — decide when a simpler solution is the better one. These skills sit at the heart of professional software engineering and will shape how you architect systems for the rest of your career.

Chapter Lab: Implementing Design Patterns in Python

In this lab, you will implement several of the design patterns introduced in this chapter by building a small application that exercises them together. You will apply creational, behavioral, and structural patterns — including Factory, Strategy, Observer, and Repository — and use dependency injection to wire the pieces together cleanly. The lab also asks you to reflect on your choices, reinforcing the judgment you developed in Lesson 5.4 about when a pattern genuinely improves a design and when a simpler approach would serve better.

Chapter 6: Software Architecture

Every building you have ever walked into began as an architectural plan. Before a single brick was laid, someone decided where the load-bearing walls would go, how many floors the structure would have, and where the plumbing and electrical systems would run. Software works the same way. Before you write detailed functions and classes, you make high-level decisions about how the major pieces of your system fit together. Those decisions are what we call **software architecture**, and they shape everything that comes afterward.

In the previous chapters, you learned about writing clean code, managing requirements, and designing individual modules. Now we zoom out. Architecture is not about the details of any single function — it is about the shape of the whole system. It answers questions like: What are the major parts? How do they talk to each other? Where does each part run? What happens when the system needs to grow, or when something fails?

By the end of this chapter, you will be able to recognize and describe the most common architectural styles used in industry, from simple layered applications to sprawling microservice ecosystems. You will understand the tradeoffs behind each choice and learn how professionals document those choices. Most importantly, you will start thinking like an architect — someone who weighs competing concerns and makes deliberate decisions rather than letting a system's structure emerge by accident.

6.1 What Is Software Architecture?

Before we explore specific architectural styles, you need a solid definition of what architecture actually is — and, just as importantly, what it is not. Many developers use the word loosely, applying it to everything from database schemas to button placement. In this section you will learn to distinguish architecture from lower-level design, and you will meet the fundamental building blocks that every architecture is made of: components and services.

Getting this vocabulary right matters. When you can clearly separate architectural concerns from implementation details, you make better decisions and communicate more effectively with your team. Architecture decisions are expensive to reverse, so knowing which decisions belong at this level saves you from painful rework later.

What Is Software Architecture?

Software architecture is the set of high-level structures of a software system, comprising the major components, their externally visible properties, and the relationships among them. Put more simply, architecture is the collection of decisions that are hard to change later.

Think of a city plan. The plan decides where the highways run, where residential zones sit, and how water flows to each neighborhood. It does not decide the color of anyone's front door. Architecture is the highway system of your software. It defines the big pieces and how they connect, leaving the finer details to the design and implementation stages.

Architecture matters because it determines the qualities your system can achieve. A system built for a single user on one machine cannot suddenly serve millions of users just because you optimized a few functions. Those capabilities are baked in — or ruled out — at the architectural level. Getting the architecture right gives your team a stable foundation to build on. Getting it wrong creates friction that grows with every feature you add.

Architecture vs. Detailed Design

It helps to think of software decisions as living on a spectrum. At one end sits **architecture**: the broad, system-wide structure. At the other end sits **detailed design**: the specific implementation choices inside a single component, like which sorting algorithm to use or how to name a variable.

The line between them is not always sharp, but a useful test is the cost of change. If a decision would be expensive and disruptive to reverse — say, switching from a monolithic application to microservices — it is architectural. If a decision can be changed quietly within one module without affecting anything else, it is detailed design.

Consider a concrete example. Deciding that your application will separate its user interface, its business rules, and its data storage into distinct layers is an architectural decision. Deciding that a particular function inside the business layer uses a dictionary instead of a list is detailed design. The first decision shapes how the whole team works; the second affects only one small area.

```
# Detailed design: this choice lives inside one function
def find_customer(customers, customer_id):
    # Using a dictionary for O(1) lookup is a design decision
    lookup = {c["id"]: c for c in customers}
    return lookup.get(customer_id)
```

This code shows a detailed design decision in action. Whether `find_customer` uses a dictionary or a linear scan through a list changes the function's performance, but it does not change the structure of the system. You could rewrite this function tomorrow and no other part of the application would need to know. That local, contained quality is the hallmark of detailed design rather than architecture.

Components and Services

The vocabulary of architecture centers on two related ideas: components and services. A **component** is a modular part of a system that encapsulates a set of related functions and data behind a well-defined interface. A component hides its internal workings and exposes only what other parts of the system need to use it.

A **service** is a component that provides functionality over a network, typically to other components that may run on different machines. The key distinction is the boundary. Components inside the same program communicate through direct function calls, which are fast and simple. Services communicate across a network, which is slower and can fail, but which allows the pieces to be deployed, scaled, and maintained independently.

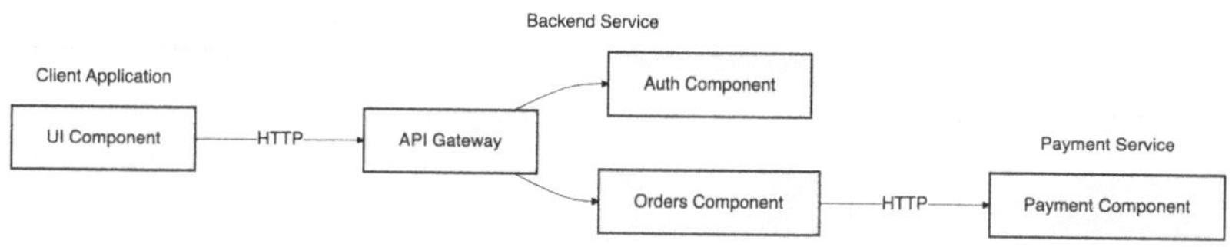

Understanding boundaries is central to thinking about architecture. When two components sit inside the same deployment boundary, calling one from the other is nearly free and always reliable. The moment you place a boundary between them — turning one into a service — every interaction now travels over a network. That change buys you flexibility but introduces latency, the possibility of failure, and the need to handle data serialization. Architects spend much of their time deciding where to draw these boundaries.

Summary

- Software architecture is the set of high-level structural decisions that are hard and expensive to change later.
- Architecture answers what the major pieces are and how they relate, while detailed design handles implementation choices inside a component.
- The cost of reversing a decision is a practical test for whether it is architectural or design-level.
- A component encapsulates related functions behind an interface; a service is a component accessed over a network.
- Boundaries determine whether communication is a fast local call or a slower, less reliable network call.

6.2 Classic Architectural Styles

Now that you understand what architecture is, let's look at the tried-and-true patterns that have shaped software for decades. An **architectural style** is a reusable, named way of organizing a system that solves a recurring set of problems. Just as a builder can choose between a bungalow, a townhouse, or a high-rise, you can choose between established architectural styles that others have refined over many years.

In this section you will learn four foundational styles: layered architecture, three-tier architecture, client-server, and Model-View-Controller. These appear constantly in real systems, often combined with one another. Recognizing them helps you understand existing codebases quickly and gives you a proven starting point for your own designs.

Layered Architecture

Layered architecture organizes a system into horizontal layers, where each layer has a specific responsibility and communicates only with the layers directly adjacent to it. A common arrangement uses three layers: a presentation layer that handles user interaction, a business logic layer that enforces the rules of the application, and a data access layer that talks to storage.

The guiding rule is that each layer offers a clean interface to the layer above and delegates work to the layer below. The presentation layer never reaches directly into the database. Instead it asks the business layer, which in turn asks the data layer. This strict flow keeps concerns separated and makes each layer easier to understand, test, and replace.

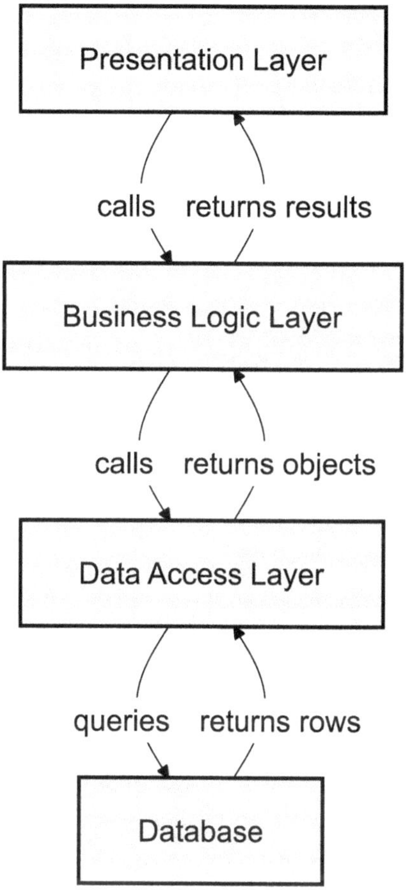

```python
# Data access layer
class UserRepository:
    def __init__(self, database):
        self.database = database

    def get_by_email(self, email):
        return self.database.query(
            "SELECT * FROM users WHERE email = ?", email
        )

# Business logic layer
class UserService:
    def __init__(self, repository):
        self.repository = repository

    def authenticate(self, email, password):
        user = self.repository.get_by_email(email)
        if user and user["password_hash"] == hash_password(password):
            return user
        return None

# Presentation layer
class LoginController:
    def __init__(self, user_service):
        self.user_service = user_service

    def handle_login(self, email, password):
        user = self.user_service.authenticate(email, password)
        if user:
            return f"Welcome back, {user['name']}!"
        return "Invalid credentials."
```

This example demonstrates the layered flow clearly. The `LoginController` in the presentation layer never touches the database directly. It calls `UserService`, which contains the authentication rules, and `UserService` in turn relies on `UserRepository` to fetch data. Each class depends only on the layer directly beneath it. If you later switched from a SQL database to a cloud storage service, only `UserRepository` would change — the business and presentation layers would remain untouched.

Three-Tier Architecture

Three-tier architecture is closely related to layered architecture but describes physical deployment rather than logical organization. Where layers are a conceptual stack, tiers are about where code actually runs. The three tiers are typically the presentation tier on the user's device, the application tier on a server, and the data tier on a database server.

The distinction matters because separating tiers physically lets you scale and secure them independently. You can put your database server behind a firewall, add more application servers when traffic spikes, and update the user interface without touching the backend. A single logical layer might be split across tiers, or several layers might run within one tier.

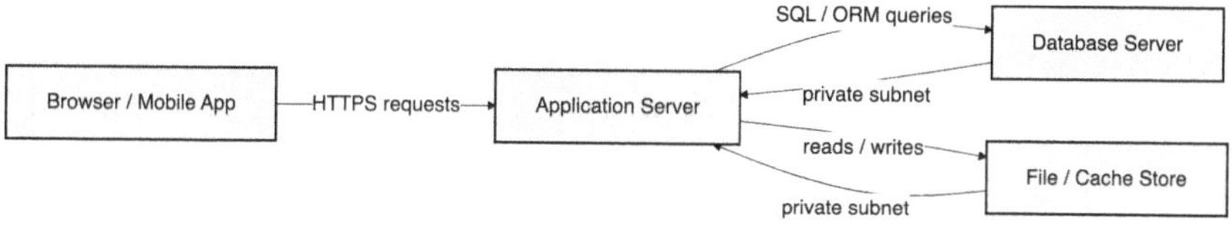

A web application illustrates this well. The browser on a user's laptop is the presentation tier. The API server running in a data center is the application tier. The database, often on its own dedicated machine, is the data tier. Each tier communicates with the next over a network, which is exactly why the boundaries you learned about in the previous section become so important here.

Client-Server Architecture

Client-server architecture divides a system into two roles: clients that request services and a server that provides them. The client initiates communication, sends a request, and waits for a response. The server listens for requests, does the work, and replies. This pattern underlies most of the internet.

The strength of client-server is centralization. The server holds the authoritative data and enforces the rules, while many clients — web browsers, mobile apps, other programs — connect to it. This makes it easy to update logic in one place and keep all clients consistent. The tradeoff is that the server can become a bottleneck or a single point of failure if it is not designed to handle load and stay available.

Model-View-Controller

Model-View-Controller, usually shortened to **MVC**, is a style for organizing applications that have a user interface. It divides responsibilities into three parts. The **Model** holds the data and business rules. The **View** displays information to the user. The **Controller** handles user input and coordinates between the Model and the View.

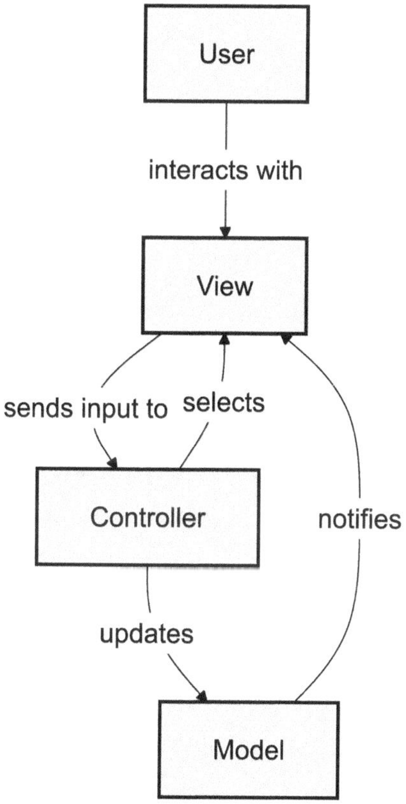

The value of MVC is separation of concerns within the user-facing part of an application. Designers can work on views while developers work on models, and each can change with minimal impact on the other. The pattern also makes testing easier, because the model contains the important logic and can be tested without any user interface at all.

```python
# Model: holds data and rules
class Counter:
    def __init__(self):
        self.value = 0

    def increment(self):
        self.value += 1

# View: displays the data
class CounterView:
    def render(self, value):
        print(f"Current count: {value}")

# Controller: coordinates input and updates
class CounterController:
    def __init__(self, model, view):
        self.model = model
        self.view = view

    def on_button_click(self):
        self.model.increment()
        self.view.render(self.model.value)
```

Notice how each class has a single, focused responsibility. The `Counter` model knows nothing about how it is displayed, so you could swap the `CounterView` for a graphical interface or a web page without changing the model at all. The `CounterController` is the glue: it responds to a button click, updates the model, and asks the view to refresh. This clean division is what makes MVC so durable and so widely adopted across web and desktop frameworks.

Summary

- An architectural style is a named, reusable way of organizing a system to solve recurring problems.
- Layered architecture separates concerns into horizontal layers that communicate only with adjacent layers.
- Three-tier architecture describes physical deployment across presentation, application, and data tiers.
- Client-server architecture centralizes logic and data on a server that many clients connect to.
- MVC separates a user-facing application into Model, View, and Controller to keep data, display, and coordination independent.

6.3 Monoliths, Services, and Microservices

The classic styles you just learned describe how to organize code within a system. This section tackles a different but related question: how many separately deployable pieces should your system be broken into? The answer ranges from a single unified application to dozens of tiny, independent services. Each point along that range carries real consequences for how your team builds, deploys, and scales the software.

You will learn about three approaches: the monolith, service-oriented architecture, and microservices. There is no universally correct choice among them. The right answer depends on your team size, your scaling needs, and how much operational complexity you can manage. Understanding all three lets you choose deliberately instead of following a trend.

Monolithic Architecture

A **monolithic architecture** packages all of an application's functionality into a single deployable unit. The user interface, business logic, and data access all live in one codebase and run as one process. When you deploy, you deploy the whole thing at once.

Monoliths get an unfair reputation as outdated, but they are often the right choice, especially early on. A monolith is simple to develop, test, and deploy. There is only one codebase to reason about, and communication between parts is fast because everything happens through direct function calls within the same process. Many successful, large-scale products run as monoliths for years.

The drawbacks appear as the system and team grow. A single large codebase becomes harder to understand. You cannot scale one part independently — if only the reporting feature is under heavy load, you still have to scale the entire application. And because everything ships together, one risky change can require redeploying the whole system.

Service-Oriented Architecture

Service-oriented architecture, or **SOA**, breaks an application into a set of services that each provide a distinct business capability and communicate over a network. SOA emerged in large enterprises that needed to integrate many systems built by different teams over many years.

A defining feature of traditional SOA is centralized communication. Services do not usually talk to each other directly. Instead they route messages through a shared piece of infrastructure called an **Enterprise Service Bus (ESB)**, which handles message routing, protocol translation, and orchestration between services.

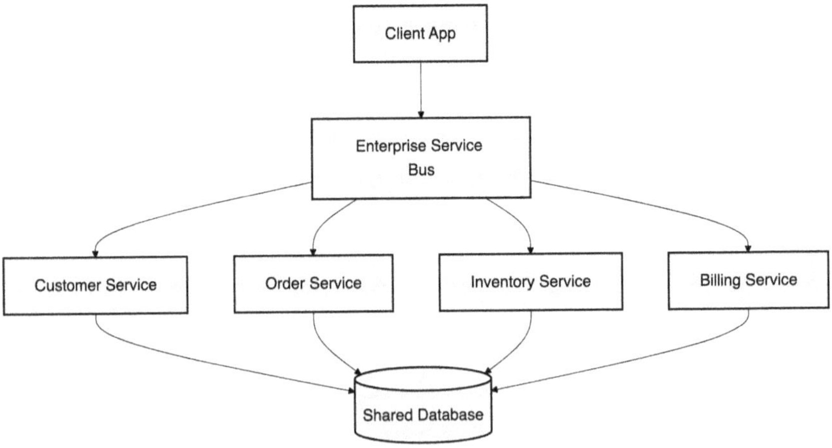

The ESB is both SOA's strength and its weakness. On one hand, it provides a single place to manage communication, apply security, and transform data between services that speak different formats. On the other hand, it concentrates a great deal of logic and traffic in one place, which can become a bottleneck and a source of tight coupling that SOA was meant to avoid.

Microservices

Microservices architecture takes the idea of splitting a system into services and pushes it further. The application becomes a collection of small, independent services, each owning a single business capability and its own data. Unlike traditional SOA, microservices usually communicate directly with one another over lightweight protocols, without a heavy central bus.

The appeal of microservices is independence. Each service can be developed, deployed, and scaled on its own by a small team. If one service needs more capacity, you scale only that service. If a bug appears in one service, you can fix and redeploy it without touching the rest. Teams can even use different programming languages for different services.

That independence comes at a steep operational cost. You now run many services instead of one, each needing monitoring, deployment pipelines, and network communication that can fail. Debugging a request that flows through a dozen services is far harder than tracing a function call within a monolith. Microservices reward mature teams with strong automation and punish those without it, which is why experienced architects often recommend starting with a monolith and extracting services only when a clear need arises.

Summary

- A monolith packages all functionality into a single deployable unit that is simple to build and deploy but hard to scale in parts.
- Service-oriented architecture splits a system into services that communicate through a central Enterprise Service Bus.
- The ESB centralizes routing and translation but can become a bottleneck and a source of coupling.
- Microservices break a system into small, independent services that each own their data and communicate directly.
- Microservices offer independent scaling and deployment at the cost of significant operational complexity.

6.4 Event-Driven and Distributed Systems

As systems grow beyond a single machine, new patterns become necessary for the pieces to cooperate. This section introduces the ideas that make large, modern systems possible: event-driven architecture, RESTful communication, and the broader concept of distributed systems. These approaches let independent parts of a system react to one another and coordinate across networks and continents.

By the end of this section you will understand how components can communicate without being tightly bound together, how the REST style organizes web APIs, and what challenges arise when your software runs across many machines at once. These ideas build directly on the service boundaries you learned about earlier in the chapter.

Event-Driven Architecture

Event-driven architecture is a style in which components communicate by producing and reacting to events rather than by calling each other directly. An **event** is a record that something happened — an order was placed, a payment was received, a user signed up. Components that generate events are called **producers**, and components that react to them are called **consumers**.

The connecting piece is usually a **message broker**, a central intermediary that receives events from producers and delivers them to interested consumers. Consumers **subscribe** to the kinds of events they care about, and the broker routes matching events to them. Crucially, a producer does not know or care who consumes its events.

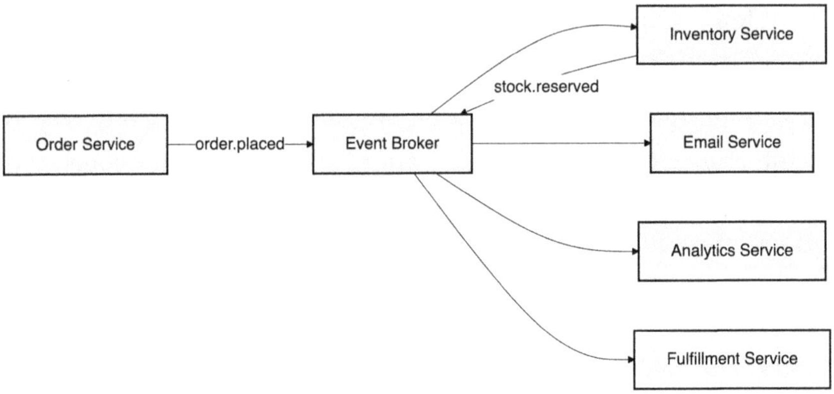

This decoupling is the great advantage of event-driven systems. Because producers and consumers only depend on the shape of the event, not on each other, you can add new consumers without changing any producer. When a user places an order, one consumer might send a confirmation email while another updates inventory and a third records analytics — all reacting independently to the same event. The tradeoff is that the flow of logic becomes harder to follow, since no single place describes the full sequence of what happens.

RESTful Systems

REST, which stands for Representational State Transfer, is an architectural style for designing networked systems, most commonly web APIs. A **RESTful** system exposes its functionality as **resources**, each identified by a URL, and manipulates those resources using standard HTTP methods like `GET`, `POST`, `PUT`, and `DELETE`.

The core idea is uniformity. Every resource is addressed the same way, and every interaction uses the same small set of verbs. `GET /users/42` retrieves the user with ID 42. `POST /users` creates a new user. This consistency makes REST APIs predictable and easy to learn, which is a major reason REST became the dominant style for communication between services.

```
# A simple RESTful endpoint using a Flask-style framework
@app.route("/users/<int:user_id>", methods=["GET"])
def get_user(user_id):
    user = user_service.find(user_id)
    if user is None:
        return {"error": "Not found"}, 404
    return {"id": user.id, "name": user.name}, 200

@app.route("/users", methods=["POST"])
def create_user():
    data = request.get_json()
    user = user_service.create(data["name"])
    return {"id": user.id, "name": user.name}, 201
```

This example shows two RESTful endpoints. The `get_user` function responds to a `GET` request on a specific user resource and returns the user's data along with the HTTP status code `200`, or `404` if the user does not exist. The `create_user` function responds to a `POST` request and returns status `201`, the conventional code meaning "created." Notice how the URL identifies the resource and the HTTP method describes the action. This alignment between verbs and resources is the essence of REST.

Distributed Systems

A **distributed system** is one whose components run on multiple networked computers and coordinate by passing messages. Almost every large modern application is a distributed system, whether it uses microservices, event-driven communication, or both.

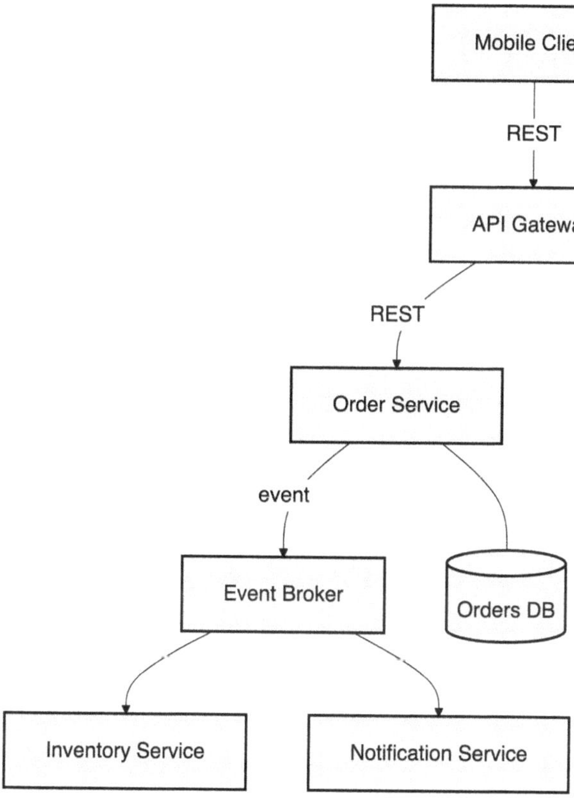

RESTful APIs and event brokers are the glue that holds distributed systems together. A single user action, like placing an order, can fan out across many independent services — one for orders, one for payments, one for shipping — each owning its own data and running on its own machines. This spreading of work is what lets systems handle enormous scale and stay running even when individual machines fail.

Distributed systems also introduce hard problems that simply do not exist in a single program. Networks are slow and unreliable, so messages can be delayed, duplicated, or lost. Keeping data consistent across many services is genuinely difficult, and a partial failure — where some services are up and others are down — must be handled gracefully. These challenges are why distributed systems demand careful design and why they are among the most respected skills in software engineering.

Summary

- Event-driven architecture decouples components by having producers emit events that consumers subscribe to through a broker.
- Decoupling lets you add new consumers without changing producers, at the cost of harder-to-follow logic.
- REST is a style that models functionality as resources addressed by URLs and manipulated with standard HTTP methods.
- A distributed system runs across multiple networked machines that coordinate by passing messages.
- Distributed systems enable massive scale and fault tolerance but must handle network failures, latency, and consistency.

6.5 Architectural Quality and Tradeoffs

Choosing an architecture is never about finding the single best option, because no such option exists. Every architectural decision improves some qualities while sacrificing others. This final section gives you the vocabulary to reason about those qualities and the discipline to record your decisions so future engineers understand why the system looks the way it does.

You will learn about the quality attributes that architects care about most — scalability, reliability, availability, and maintainability — and how they pull against one another. You will also learn about Architecture Decision Records, a simple and powerful tool for capturing the reasoning behind important choices.

Architectural Quality Attributes

Quality attributes, sometimes called non-functional requirements, are the measurable properties that describe how well a system performs its job rather than what it does. A system might correctly calculate an invoice, but quality attributes ask further questions: How fast? For how many users? How reliably? How easily can it be changed?

These attributes matter because they are shaped by architecture, not by individual features. You cannot bolt on scalability or security at the end of a project. They must be designed into the structure from the start. The most important quality attributes for most systems are scalability, reliability, availability, and maintainability, which we will examine in turn.

Scalability

Scalability is the ability of a system to handle increasing load by adding resources. As your user base grows, a scalable system can keep up by growing along with it, while a non-scalable system slows down or breaks.

There are two fundamental ways to scale. **Vertical scaling** means making a single machine more powerful by adding memory, processors, or faster storage. **Horizontal scaling** means adding more machines and spreading the load across them. Vertical scaling is simpler but has a hard ceiling — there is only so big one machine can get. Horizontal scaling has almost no ceiling but requires an architecture that can distribute work, which is exactly why distributed systems and microservices exist.

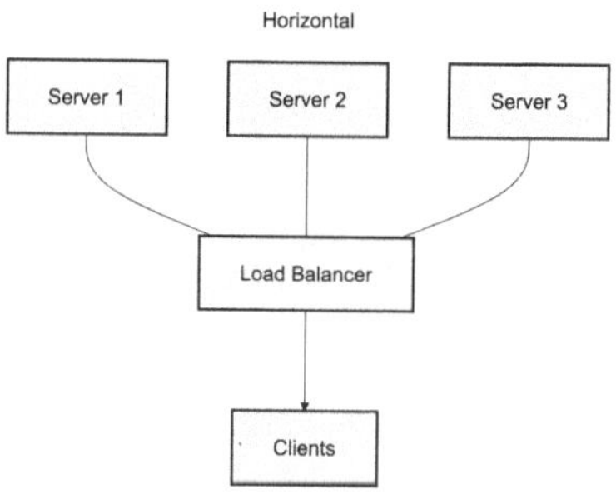

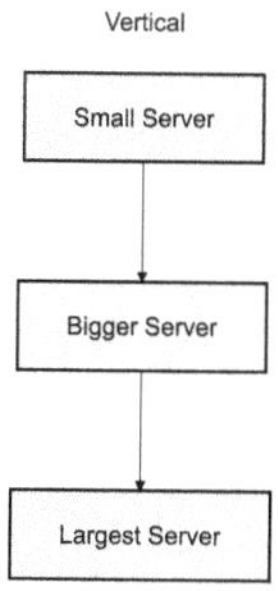

The architectural styles you have learned map directly onto scalability. A monolith is easy to scale vertically but harder to scale horizontally, because you must run copies of the entire application. Microservices scale horizontally with precision, letting you add capacity only to the service that needs it. This is one of the clearest examples of how architecture determines which qualities a system can achieve.

Reliability and Availability

Reliability is the probability that a system performs correctly over a period of time without failing. **Availability** is the proportion of time that a system is operational and ready to serve requests. The two are related but distinct: a system can be highly available yet occasionally return wrong answers, or highly reliable yet frequently offline for maintenance.

Distributed architectures improve availability through **redundancy** – running multiple copies of a component so that if one fails, another takes over. If you run three copies of a service across three machines, a single machine failure no longer takes the system down. This is a core reason large systems distribute themselves across many machines.

The catch is that redundancy adds complexity and cost. More copies mean more infrastructure to manage and more difficulty keeping data consistent across them. Architects constantly weigh the cost of higher availability against the business impact of downtime. For a hospital system, near-perfect availability is worth almost any cost; for an internal reporting tool, occasional downtime may be perfectly acceptable.

Maintainability

Maintainability is how easily a system can be understood, changed, and extended over time. It is one of the most valuable quality attributes because most of a software system's life is spent being maintained, not built. Code is read and modified far more often than it is written from scratch.

The architectural styles in this chapter directly affect maintainability. Clear layers and well-defined component boundaries make a system easier to reason about, because a change in one area is contained and its effects are predictable. This is the same benefit you saw with layered architecture and MVC: separating concerns means you can change one part without understanding or breaking everything else.

Maintainability also illustrates how quality attributes conflict. Splitting a monolith into microservices can improve maintainability for individual teams, since each owns a small, focused service. But it can hurt overall maintainability, because understanding how a request flows through many services is genuinely harder than reading a single codebase. There is no free lunch — improving one attribute often costs you another.

Architectural Tradeoffs and Architecture Decision Records

Because every choice involves tradeoffs, the mark of a good architect is not making perfect decisions but making informed, well-reasoned ones and recording why. Six months later, no one remembers why the team chose a message broker over direct REST calls, and without that reasoning, future engineers either blindly follow the decision or blindly reverse it. Both are dangerous.

An **Architecture Decision Record**, or **ADR**, is a short document that captures a single significant architectural decision, its context, and its consequences. ADRs are typically stored alongside the code in version control, so the reasoning lives with the system it describes. A good ADR is brief — often a single page — and follows a consistent structure.

A typical ADR includes these sections:

- **Title**: a short name for the decision, often numbered.
- **Status**: whether the decision is proposed, accepted, or superseded.
- **Context**: the situation and forces that led to the decision.
- **Decision**: what was decided.
- **Consequences**: the resulting tradeoffs, both positive and negative.

The real value of an ADR lies in the context and consequences sections. Anyone can state a decision, but recording the forces that shaped it and the tradeoffs you knowingly accepted turns a mysterious choice into a teachable one. When circumstances change and a decision needs revisiting, the ADR tells the next engineer exactly what assumptions were made, so they can judge whether those assumptions still hold. This simple habit transforms architecture from tribal knowledge into a durable, shared understanding.

Summary

- Quality attributes describe how well a system performs, and they are determined by architecture, not individual features.
- Scalability is the ability to handle growing load, achieved through vertical scaling (bigger machines) or horizontal scaling (more machines).
- Reliability measures correctness over time while availability measures uptime, and redundancy improves availability at the cost of complexity.
- Maintainability, how easily a system can be changed, is shaped by clear boundaries and often conflicts with other attributes.
- Architecture Decision Records capture the context, decision, and consequences of significant choices so future engineers understand the reasoning.

Chapter Summary

This chapter moved you from writing code to shaping systems. You began by learning what software architecture actually is — the set of high-level, hard-to-reverse decisions that define a system's major parts and how they relate. From there you saw that these parts are built from components and services, separated by boundaries that determine whether communication is a fast local call or a slower network exchange. That single idea of boundaries threads through everything that followed.

You then explored a progression of architectural choices. The classic styles — layered, three-tier, client-server, and MVC — showed you how to organize code within a system by separating concerns. The discussion of monoliths, SOA, and microservices raised the question of how many deployable pieces a system should have, and the section on event-driven and distributed systems showed how those pieces cooperate across networks. Each step built on the last: you cannot understand microservices without understanding service boundaries, and you cannot understand distributed systems without understanding how services communicate through REST and events.

Finally, you learned that architecture is fundamentally about tradeoffs. Scalability, reliability, availability, and maintainability all pull against one another, and no architecture maximizes them all. What separates a professional from a novice is not making flawless choices but making deliberate ones and documenting the reasoning with tools like Architecture Decision Records. You can now look at a system, name its architecture, explain the qualities that architecture enables, and reason about the tradeoffs it accepts — skills that sit at the heart of software engineering.

Chapter Lab: Converting a Simple Application into a Layered Architecture

In this lab you will take a small, tangled application in which user interface, business logic, and data access are all mixed together, and you will restructure it into a clean layered architecture. You will apply the separation-of-concerns principles from Lesson 6.1 and the layered architecture pattern from Lesson 6.2, drawing clear boundaries between components so that each layer depends only on the one beneath it. By the end you will have hands-on experience turning a hard-to-maintain program into one whose structure supports the quality attributes discussed in Lesson 6.5.

Chapter 7: Source Control and Collaborative Development

Every professional software project you will ever work on has one thing in common: it changes constantly. Code gets written, rewritten, broken, and fixed. Features are added, bugs are squashed, and sometimes decisions are reversed months after they were made. Without a reliable way to track those changes, software development quickly descends into chaos. This is where source control comes in, and it is one of the most important skills you can develop as a software engineer.

In this chapter, you will learn how to use **source control** to manage the history of your code, collaborate safely with other developers, and organize your work in a way that scales from a solo project to a team of hundreds. We will focus on Git, the tool that has become the industry standard, and explore the workflows that professional teams use every day. By the end, you will understand how to commit changes, work on branches, merge your work back together, and participate in the review processes that keep large codebases healthy.

These skills build directly on the engineering discipline you have developed in earlier chapters. Just as writing clean, testable code makes your programs easier to maintain, using source control well makes your collaboration easier to manage. Once you understand these principles, you will be ready to contribute to real-world projects with confidence.

7.1 Why Source Control Matters

Imagine writing a large essay without any way to undo your changes. Every edit is permanent, and if you delete a paragraph you later want back, it is gone forever. Now imagine three people editing that same essay at the same time, each saving over the others' work. This is what software development looks like without source control, and it is exactly the problem that these tools were invented to solve.

In this section, you will learn what source control is, why it has become essential to modern software engineering, and how the tool called Git approaches the problem. You will also learn about repositories, the containers that hold your project's history. Understanding these foundations will make everything else in this chapter click into place.

What Source Control Solves

Source control, also called **version control**, is a system that records changes to a set of files over time so that you can recall specific versions later. Think of it as an unlimited undo button that spans your entire project and remembers not just what changed, but who changed it, when, and why.

Source control solves several problems at once. It gives you a complete history of your project, so you can see how the code evolved and roll back to any earlier state. It lets multiple developers work on the same codebase without overwriting each other's changes. And it provides a safety net that encourages experimentation, because you always know you can return to a known-good version.

Before dedicated tools existed, developers often copied their entire project folder and named the copies things like `project_final`, `project_final_v2`, and `project_really_final`. This approach is fragile, error-prone, and impossible to scale. Source control replaces it with a disciplined, automated system.

Introduction to Git

Git is a **distributed version control system** created in 2005 to manage the development of the Linux kernel. Today it powers the vast majority of software projects in the world. The word "distributed" is important: unlike older systems that stored history on a single central server, Git gives every developer a complete copy of the project's entire history on their own machine.

This distributed design has real benefits. You can work offline, commit your changes locally, and view the full history without contacting a server. When you are ready, you synchronize your work with others by pushing and pulling changes. Because everyone has a full copy, there is no single point of failure that can wipe out your project's history.

Git tracks changes efficiently by storing **snapshots** of your files rather than a list of edits. Each time you record a change, Git captures the state of your project at that moment. If a file has not changed, Git simply links to the previous identical version, which keeps storage compact.

Repositories

A **repository**, often shortened to **repo**, is the container that holds your project along with its complete history. When you place a project under Git's control, a hidden folder named `.git` is created inside it. This folder is the repository; it stores every snapshot, every change record, and all the metadata Git needs to reconstruct any version of your work.

You create a repository by initializing Git inside a project folder. The following example shows how to start a new repository from the command line.

```
# These are shell commands, run in your terminal
# (shown here for reference, not Python code)

# Move into your project folder
cd my_project

# Initialize a new Git repository
git init

# Check the current status of the repository
git status
```

The `git init` command creates the `.git` folder and turns an ordinary directory into a Git repository. From that point on, Git begins tracking the folder. The `git status` command reports the current state of your repository, including which files have changed and which are ready to be recorded. You will run `git status` constantly as you work, because it tells you exactly where you stand.

There are two kinds of repositories you will encounter. A **local repository** lives on your own machine, while a **remote**

repository lives on a server such as GitHub or GitLab and acts as a shared point of coordination for a team. Most workflows involve both: you do your work locally, then synchronize with a remote so others can see it.

Summary

- **Source control** records the history of your files over time, giving you an unlimited undo and a complete record of who changed what and why.
- Copying project folders manually is fragile and does not scale; source control automates version tracking reliably.
- **Git** is a **distributed** version control system, meaning every developer holds a full copy of the project history and can work offline.
- A **repository** is the container for your project and its history, created with `git init` and stored in a hidden `.git` folder.
- Repositories can be **local** (on your machine) or **remote** (on a shared server), and most workflows use both together.

7.2 Commits, Branches, and Merging

Now that you understand what a repository is, it is time to learn how you actually record and organize changes inside one. The three concepts at the heart of everyday Git use are commits, branches, and merging. Together they let you save your progress in meaningful steps, explore different lines of work in isolation, and bring that work back together.

In this section, you will learn how to create commits that capture your changes, how to use branches to work on separate ideas without interfering with each other, and how to merge those branches back together. You will also learn how to handle merge conflicts, which are a normal and manageable part of collaborative development. These skills form the practical core of working with Git.

Commits

A **commit** is a saved snapshot of your project at a specific point in time. Each commit records the state of your tracked files, along with a message describing what changed and metadata about who made the change and when. Commits are the building blocks of your project's history, and a good series of commits reads like a clear story of how your code evolved.

Creating a commit is a two-step process in Git. First you **stage** the changes you want to include, then you record them as a commit. Staging lets you choose precisely which changes belong together, so you can group related edits into a single meaningful commit.

```
# Shell commands for creating a commit

# Stage a specific file
git add calculator.py

# Stage all changed files at once
git add .

# Record the staged changes as a commit with a message
git commit -m "Add division function with zero-check"
```

The `git add` command moves changes into the **staging area**, a holding zone where you assemble the exact set of changes for your next commit. The `git commit` command then records those staged changes permanently in the repository's history. The `-m` flag lets you provide a **commit message** directly on the command line. A good message explains *why* a change was made, not just *what* changed, because the code itself already shows the what.

Writing clear commit messages is a professional habit worth developing early. Months from now, you or a teammate may need to understand why a change was made. A message like "Fix bug" is nearly useless, while "Fix crash when user submits empty search field" tells the whole story at a glance.

Branches

A **branch** is an independent line of development within your repository. When you create a branch, you get a separate space to make commits without affecting the main line of work. This lets you develop a new feature or experiment with an idea while keeping the stable version of your code untouched.

Think of a branch like a parallel draft of a document. You can rewrite whole sections freely, knowing the original stays safe. If your draft works out, you merge it back in; if it does not, you simply discard it. Every Git repository starts with one default branch, usually named `main` .

```
# Shell commands for working with branches

# Create a new branch and switch to it in one step
git checkout -b add-user-login

# List all branches (the current one is marked with *)
git branch

# Switch back to the main branch
git checkout main
```

The `git checkout -b` command creates a new branch and immediately switches your working directory to it, so any commits you make now belong to that branch. The `git branch` command lists all branches and marks the one you are currently on. Switching branches with `git checkout` changes the files in your working directory to match that branch, which is why branches feel like separate workspaces even though they live in the same repository.

Branches are cheap and fast in Git, which encourages you to create them liberally. A common practice is to create a fresh branch for every distinct task, an idea we will return to when we discuss feature branches in the next section.

Merging

Merging is the process of combining the changes from one branch into another. When your work on a branch is finished, you merge it back into the main branch so that its changes become part of the shared history. Merging is how the parallel lines of development eventually come together.

```
# Shell commands for merging

# Switch to the branch you want to merge into
git checkout main

# Merge the feature branch into main
git merge add-user-login
```

Here you first switch to `main`, the branch that will receive the changes, and then run `git merge` with the name of the branch you want to bring in. Git compares the two branches and combines their changes automatically. When the branches have touched different files or different parts of the same file, Git can usually complete the merge without any input from you. This is called a **clean merge**.

Resolving Merge Conflicts

Sometimes two branches change the same lines of the same file in different ways. When this happens, Git cannot decide which version is correct, so it stops and asks you to resolve the situation. This is called a **merge conflict**, and while it can look intimidating at first, it is a normal part of collaboration and entirely manageable.

When a conflict occurs, Git edits the affected file to show you both versions, marked with special conflict markers.

```
def calculate_total(items):
<<<<<<< HEAD
    return sum(item.price for item in items)
=======
    return sum(item.price * item.quantity for item in items)
>>>>>>> add-quantity-support
```

The markers divide the file into sections. Everything between `<<<<<<< HEAD` and `=======` is the version from your current branch, while everything between `=======` and `>>>>>>>` is the version from the branch being merged. To resolve the conflict, you edit the file to contain the correct final version, delete all three marker lines, then stage and commit the result. In this example the second version is clearly more complete, so you would keep it and remove the rest.

Resolving conflicts is a judgment call that requires you to understand what each version intends. This is one reason clear commit messages and good communication with teammates matter so much. When you understand *why* each change was made, deciding how to reconcile them becomes far easier.

Summary

- A **commit** is a saved snapshot of your project, created by staging changes with `git add` and recording them with `git commit`.
- Clear **commit messages** explain why a change was made and make your project history readable and useful.
- A **branch** is an independent line of development that lets you work in isolation without disturbing the stable code.
- **Merging** combines the changes from one branch into another, often automatically as a clean merge.
- A **merge conflict** occurs when two branches change the same lines differently; you resolve it by editing the file to its correct final state and removing the conflict markers.

7.3 Collaborative Git Workflows

Knowing the mechanics of commits, branches, and merges is only half the story. The other half is knowing how to use those tools with other people in a way that keeps a shared codebase stable and understandable. This is the domain of collaborative workflows, the agreed-upon conventions that teams follow to coordinate their work.

In this section, you will learn about feature branches, pull requests, and code reviews, the three pillars of modern collaborative development. You will also survey a few common branching strategies that teams adopt to organize their work. These practices turn Git from a personal tool into the backbone of professional teamwork.

Feature Branches

A **feature branch** is a branch created to develop a single feature, fix, or task, and then discarded once that work is merged. Instead of committing directly to `main` , you create a dedicated branch, do your work there, and merge it back when it is complete and tested. This keeps `main` in a stable, working state at all times.

The **feature-branch workflow** is the foundation of most professional development. Because each branch is focused on one task, its history is easy to follow, its changes are easy to review, and its risk is contained. If a feature turns out to be a bad idea, you can abandon the branch without any impact on the rest of the project.

```
# Shell commands for a feature-branch workflow

# Start from an up-to-date main branch
git checkout main
git pull

# Create a focused feature branch
git checkout -b feature/password-reset

# ...make commits as you work...

# Push the branch to the remote so others can see it
git push -u origin feature/password-reset
```

This sequence shows the typical start of a feature. You first update your local `main` with `git pull` so you begin from the latest shared code, then create a well-named feature branch. The `git push -u origin` command uploads your branch to the remote repository and links your local branch to it, so future pushes and pulls need no extra arguments. Naming branches with a prefix like `feature/` is a common convention that makes their purpose obvious.

Pull Requests

A **pull request**, sometimes called a **merge request**, is a formal proposal to merge one branch into another. It is not a Git feature itself but a feature of hosting platforms like GitHub and GitLab. When you open a pull request, you are asking your team to review your changes and approve them before they become part of the shared codebase.

A pull request bundles together everything reviewers need: the list of commits, a summary of the changes, a description of what the feature does, and a place to discuss the work line by line. It creates a checkpoint between "the code is written" and "the code is merged," and that checkpoint is where quality control happens.

Pull requests also serve as documentation. Long after a feature ships, the pull request remains as a record of what changed, why it changed, and what the team discussed along the way. This history is invaluable when someone later needs to understand a decision.

Code Reviews

A **code review** is the process by which one or more developers examine another developer's changes before they are merged. Reviews usually happen inside a pull request, where reviewers can comment on specific lines, ask questions, request changes, or approve the work. Code review is one of the most effective practices in all of software engineering.

The benefits go well beyond catching bugs, though it does that too. Reviews spread knowledge across the team, so no single person is the only one who understands a piece of code. They enforce consistency in style and design. And they give less experienced developers a steady stream of feedback that accelerates their growth.

When you review someone's code, be specific, be kind, and focus on the code rather than the person. Instead of "this is wrong," write "this loop will fail if the list is empty; could we add a guard for that case?" When you receive a review, treat feedback as a gift rather than a criticism. This mindset makes reviews a collaborative act rather than an adversarial one.

Branching Strategies

A **branching strategy** is a team's agreed-upon set of rules for how branches are created, named, and merged. Choosing a strategy brings consistency and predictability to a project. There is no single correct choice; the right strategy depends on the size of your team and how often you release.

Several strategies are common in the industry:

- **GitHub Flow** is a simple strategy where `main` is always deployable, and all work happens on short-lived feature branches merged through pull requests. It suits teams that deploy frequently.
- **Git Flow** is a more structured strategy with long-lived branches for development and releases, plus dedicated branches for features, releases, and hotfixes. It suits projects with scheduled, versioned releases.
- **Trunk-Based Development** keeps branches extremely short-lived and merges into `main` (the "trunk") many times a day, relying heavily on automated testing. It suits teams practicing continuous delivery.

The key takeaway is that the strategy itself matters less than the discipline of following one consistently. A team that agrees on clear rules and sticks to them will collaborate smoothly regardless of which strategy they picked.

Summary

- A **feature branch** isolates a single task, keeping the `main` branch stable and making changes easy to review and, if necessary, abandon.
- A **pull request** is a formal proposal to merge a branch, providing a checkpoint for review and a lasting record of the change.
- **Code review** catches bugs, spreads knowledge, and enforces consistency; give feedback that is specific and kind, and receive it graciously.
- A **branching strategy** is a team's agreed set of rules for managing branches, with common options including GitHub Flow, Git Flow, and Trunk-Based Development.
- Consistency in following a chosen strategy matters more than which specific strategy a team selects.

7.4 Versioning and Release Management

The final piece of collaborative development is managing how your software is versioned and released to the world. As your project matures and other people or systems begin to depend on it, you need a disciplined way to communicate what has changed between versions. A well-chosen version number tells your users, at a glance, whether an update is safe to adopt.

In this section, you will learn about semantic versioning, a widely adopted convention for numbering releases in a meaningful way. You will then see how release management ties versioning together with your branching and review workflows to deliver software reliably. This brings together everything you have learned in the chapter into a complete picture of how professional teams ship code.

Semantic Versioning

Semantic versioning, often abbreviated **SemVer**, is a convention for assigning version numbers in the form `MAJOR.MINOR.PATCH`, such as `2.4.1`. Each of the three numbers carries a specific meaning, and incrementing the right one communicates precisely what kind of change a release contains. This shared vocabulary lets developers reason about updates without reading the full changelog.

The rules are straightforward. You increment the **MAJOR** version when you make a change that breaks backward compatibility, meaning existing code that used your software may no longer work. You increment the **MINOR** version when you add new functionality in a backward-compatible way. And you increment the **PATCH** version when you make backward-compatible bug fixes. When you increment a higher number, the lower numbers reset to zero.

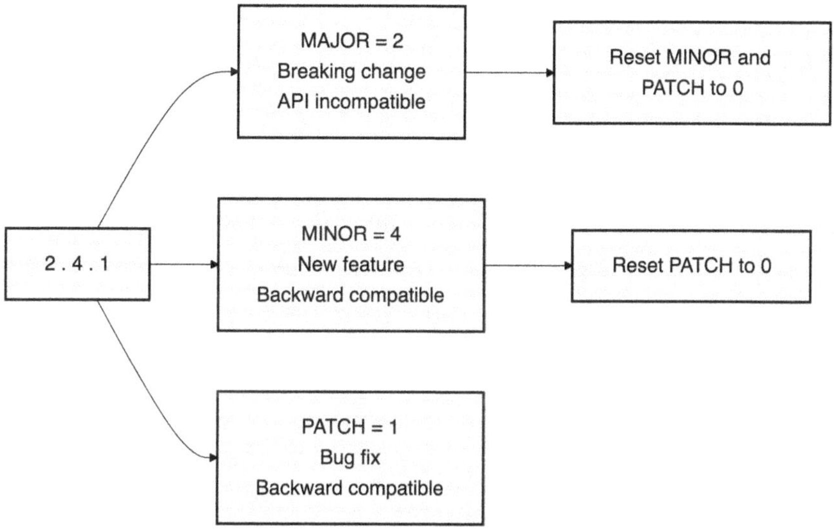

Consider a few examples. Moving from `1.4.2` to `1.4.3` signals a bug fix that is safe to adopt. Moving from `1.4.2` to `1.5.0` signals new features that will not break existing usage. Moving from `1.4.2` to `2.0.0` warns users that something incompatible has changed and they should read the release notes carefully before upgrading.

Semantic versioning is not just a courtesy; it enables automation. Package managers and dependency tools rely on these rules to decide which updates are safe to install automatically. Incrementing the wrong number misleads consumers and can silently break the systems that depend on your software.

Release Management

Release management is the practice of planning, building, testing, and shipping versions of your software in a controlled way. A **release** is a specific, versioned point in your project's history that you package and distribute to users. Good release management ensures that what you ship is stable, well-documented, and reproducible.

In Git, releases are commonly marked with **tags**. A tag is a permanent, named pointer to a specific commit, and unlike a branch it does not move. Tagging the exact commit that corresponds to a release lets you return to that precise state at any time.

```
# Shell commands for tagging a release

# Create an annotated tag for version 2.4.1
git tag -a v2.4.1 -m "Release version 2.4.1"

# Push the tag to the remote repository
git push origin v2.4.1
```

The `git tag -a` command creates an **annotated tag**, which stores the tagger's name, the date, and a message, making it ideal for marking official releases. The `-m` flag supplies that message. Because tags are not pushed to the remote by default, the explicit `git push origin v2.4.1` command is needed to share the tag with your team. Once tagged, that version becomes a stable reference point you can always rebuild or roll back to.

A key companion to any release is a **changelog**, a human-readable document that lists what changed in each version.

Combined with meaningful version numbers and tags, a changelog gives your users everything they need to decide whether and how to upgrade.

Collaborative Development Workflows

Everything in this chapter comes together in a complete collaborative development workflow. A typical cycle on a professional team weaves together the tools and practices you have learned into a repeatable process.

1. A developer pulls the latest `main` and creates a feature branch for their task.
2. They make focused commits with clear messages as they work.
3. They push the branch and open a pull request describing the change.
4. Teammates perform a code review, requesting changes or approving the work.
5. Once approved and passing automated tests, the branch is merged into `main`.
6. When enough changes accumulate, the team tags a release with an appropriate semantic version and updates the changelog.

This cycle repeats continuously, sometimes many times a day. Notice how each practice supports the others. Feature branches make pull requests focused, pull requests make code reviews possible, code reviews keep `main` stable, and a stable `main` makes reliable releases achievable. Semantic versioning then communicates the results of all that work to the outside world.

The power of this workflow is that it scales. The same fundamental steps that let two students collaborate on a school project also let thousands of developers build software like operating systems and web browsers. Once you internalize this cycle, you can join almost any professional team and be productive quickly.

Summary

- **Semantic versioning** uses `MAJOR.MINOR.PATCH` numbers to communicate whether a release contains breaking changes, new features, or bug fixes.
- Incrementing the correct number matters because tools and developers rely on SemVer rules to make safe update decisions.
- **Release management** controls how versions are planned, tested, and shipped, and Git **tags** mark exact release points permanently.
- A **changelog** documents what changed in each version, complementing version numbers and tags.
- A complete **collaborative workflow** ties feature branches, pull requests, code reviews, merges, and tagged releases into one repeatable cycle that scales to teams of any size.

Chapter Summary

This chapter moved you from the fundamentals of tracking a single file's history to the full lifecycle of professional, collaborative software development. You began by understanding why source control exists and what problems it solves, then learned how Git records your work through commits and organizes it through branches. Those two ideas, commits and branches, are the atoms of everything else in the chapter. Merging brought branches back together and taught you that conflicts are a normal, resolvable part of collaboration rather than a failure.

From there, the focus shifted from working alone to working with others. Feature branches, pull requests, and code reviews are not separate tools so much as layers of the same idea: isolate your work, propose it openly, and let your team improve it before it becomes permanent. Branching strategies gave those practices a consistent structure, and versioning and release management gave your finished work a clear voice to the outside world. Each concept reinforced the ones before it, culminating in a single repeatable workflow that a whole team can share.

You can now do something you could not do at the start of this chapter: participate confidently in a real software project alongside other engineers. You understand how to preserve a project's history, how to collaborate without stepping on your teammates' work, and how to ship versioned releases that others can depend on. These skills are not optional extras in modern software engineering; they are the daily reality of the profession, and mastering them is a major step toward becoming a professional developer.

Chapter Lab: Developing a Feature Using a Git Feature-Branch Workflow

In this lab, you will apply the complete feature-branch workflow to develop and deliver a new feature in a shared repository. You will create a dedicated feature branch, make a series of clear, well-scoped commits, and open a pull request that proposes your changes for review. Along the way you will practice the collaboration and merging skills from this chapter, including resolving a merge conflict and bringing your finished work safely back into the main branch.

Chapter 8: Writing Maintainable Software

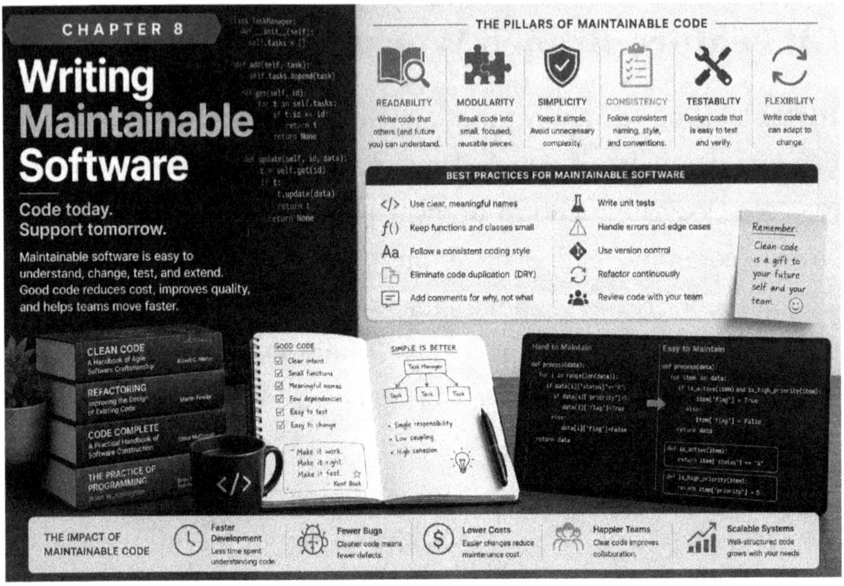

Most of the code you write in your career will be read far more often than it is written. Long after you have solved a problem and moved on, someone—often your future self—will return to that code to fix a bug, add a feature, or simply understand how it works. If that code is a tangled mess of cryptic names and duplicated logic, every change becomes slow, risky, and frustrating. Maintainable software is code written with those future readers in mind, and learning to produce it is one of the most valuable skills a software engineer can develop.

In this chapter, you will learn the practices that separate professional codebases from throwaway scripts. You will discover how to write clean, readable code, how to document your work effectively, and how to recognize the warning signs—called code smells—that indicate deeper problems. You will also learn how to refactor safely, manage dependencies and configuration, and measure the quality of what you produce. By the end, you will be able to look at a piece of software and judge not just whether it works, but whether it will keep working as it grows.

These ideas build directly on the design and testing principles from earlier chapters. Now that you understand how to structure programs and verify their behavior, you are ready to focus on the long-term health of a codebase. Maintainability is not a feature you add at the end—it is a discipline you apply with every line you write.

8.1 Writing Clean Code

Clean code is code that communicates its intent clearly to anyone who reads it. It is not about clever tricks or squeezing logic into the fewest possible lines. In fact, the cleverest-looking code is often the hardest to maintain. In this section, you will learn what makes code clean, how to name things well, how to write focused functions, and how to organize your code so that others can navigate it with ease.

The payoff for clean code is enormous. Teams that value readability spend less time deciphering old work and more time building new things. As you read through this section, keep one question in mind: *would a stranger understand this code without me explaining it?*

Clean Code

Clean code is code that is easy to read, easy to understand, and easy to change. It reveals its purpose without requiring the reader to run it in their head or trace through every branch. The most important property of clean code is clarity—each piece should do one thing, and it should be obvious what that thing is.

Consider two versions of the same logic. The first is technically correct but hard to follow:

```
def p(d):
    r = 0
    for i in d:
        if i[2] > 100 and i[3] == "A":
            r += i[2] * 0.9
    return r
```

Now compare it with a version that expresses the same computation clearly:

```
def calculate_discounted_total(orders):
    DISCOUNT_RATE = 0.10
    MINIMUM_FOR_DISCOUNT = 100

    total = 0
    for order in orders:
        if order.amount > MINIMUM_FOR_DISCOUNT and order.status == "ACTIVE":
            total += order.amount * (1 - DISCOUNT_RATE)
    return total
```

Both functions produce the same result, but the second one tells a story. The function name states its purpose, the constants explain the magic numbers, and the loop variable `order` makes the domain obvious. Notice that the second version is longer—clean code often uses more characters, because readability is worth more than brevity. This is the central trade-off: you are optimizing for the human reader, not the compiler.

Naming

Names are the single most powerful tool you have for making code readable. A good name eliminates the need for a comment. A bad name actively misleads the reader. When you name a variable, function, or class, you are documenting what it represents.

Follow these principles when choosing names:

- Use **intention-revealing names** that say what something is or does, such as `elapsed_days` rather than `d`.
- Avoid abbreviations unless they are universally understood, like `id` or `url`.
- Make names searchable—a variable named `max_retries` is easy to find; a bare `5` scattered through code is not.
- Use verbs for functions (`send_email`) and nouns for variables and classes (`email_message` , `EmailSender`).

```
# Unclear
def calc(n, r, t):
    return n * (1 + r) ** t

# Clear
def compound_interest(principal, annual_rate, years):
    return principal * (1 + annual_rate) ** years
```

The second version needs no documentation to explain its parameters. The moment you read `compound_interest(principal, annual_rate, years)` , you know exactly what the function computes and what to pass it. This is the goal of naming: to make the code self-explanatory. Time spent choosing a precise name is repaid every time someone reads that line.

Functions and Methods

A well-written **function** does one thing and does it well. When a function tries to do several things at once, it becomes harder to name, harder to test, and harder to reuse. A reliable rule of thumb is that if you struggle to name a function without using the word "and," it probably does too much.

Small functions also make code easier to read at different levels of detail. High-level functions read like a summary, while the details live in lower-level helpers.

```
def process_order(order):
    validate_order(order)
    charge_payment(order)
    send_confirmation(order)
    update_inventory(order)
```

This function is trivial to understand because each step is named and delegated to a focused helper. You can grasp the overall flow in seconds, and if you need detail about payment, you know exactly where to look. Each helper function can be tested independently, which connects directly to the testing practices you learned earlier. Keeping functions short and single-purpose is one of the most effective habits you can build.

Code Organization

Code organization is how you group related code together and separate unrelated code. Good organization means that when you look for something, you can guess where it lives. Related functions belong in the same module; related modules belong in the same package.

A common approach is to organize by feature or responsibility rather than by technical type. Keep the code that changes together, close together. Within a file, order your functions so that high-level entry points appear near the top and detailed helpers appear below—readers can then scan from general to specific.

```
# billing.py — all billing-related logic in one module

def generate_invoice(customer, items):
    subtotal = _calculate_subtotal(items)
    tax = _calculate_tax(subtotal, customer.region)
    return Invoice(customer, subtotal, tax)

def _calculate_subtotal(items):
    return sum(item.price * item.quantity for item in items)

def _calculate_tax(subtotal, region):
    return subtotal * TAX_RATES[region]
```

Here, everything about generating an invoice lives in one place. The public function `generate_invoice` appears first, and the private helpers—prefixed with an underscore by Python convention—follow below. This structure makes the module easy to navigate and signals clearly which functions are meant for outside use.

Summary

- Clean code prioritizes clarity and readability over cleverness or brevity.
- Intention-revealing names reduce the need for comments and make code self-explanatory.
- Functions should do one thing well; if a name needs "and," the function is doing too much.
- Organize code by responsibility, keeping related logic together and ordering functions from general to specific.

8.2 Documentation and Standards

Even the cleanest code sometimes needs explanation, and every team benefits from writing code in a consistent style. In this section, you will learn when and how to write comments and documentation, and how coding standards keep a codebase coherent as it grows and as new people join the team.

Documentation and standards work together to reduce the mental effort required to understand and contribute to a project. When code looks familiar and its trickier parts are explained, developers move faster and make fewer mistakes.

Comments and Documentation

The best comment is often the one you did not need to write, because the code was clear enough on its own. **Comments** should explain *why* something is done, not *what* is being done—the code already shows the what. A comment that merely restates the code adds noise and can become misleading when the code changes but the comment does not.

```
# Bad: restates the obvious
count = count + 1  # increment count

# Good: explains a non-obvious decision
# Retry up to 3 times because the payment gateway
# occasionally drops the first request after idle periods.
MAX_RETRIES = 3
```

The first comment tells you nothing the code does not already say. The second comment captures knowledge that is impossible to derive from the code alone—the reasoning behind a magic number. That kind of context is exactly what future maintainers need.

Documentation is more formal than comments and describes how to use a piece of code. In Python, the primary tool is the **docstring**, a string placed at the start of a module, class, or function.

```
def parse_duration(text):
    """Convert a duration string into total seconds.

    Args:
        text: A string like "1h30m" or "45s".

    Returns:
        The total number of seconds as an integer.

    Raises:
        ValueError: If the text cannot be parsed.
    """
    ...
```

This docstring tells a caller everything they need to use the function without reading its implementation: what it does, what to pass, what it returns, and how it can fail. Tools can extract docstrings to generate reference documentation automatically, so well-written docstrings serve double duty as both inline help and published documentation.

Coding Standards

Coding standards are the shared conventions a team agrees to follow, covering things like naming style, indentation, line length, and file organization. Standards matter not because one style is objectively better, but because consistency reduces friction. When all code looks the same, developers can read any file without adjusting to a new author's habits.

Python has an official style guide called **PEP 8**, which most projects adopt as a baseline. Rather than enforcing standards by hand, professional teams automate them with tools. A **linter** flags style and quality issues, and a **formatter** rewrites code into a consistent style automatically.

```
# Tools commonly used in Python projects:
#   black   - an automatic code formatter
#   flake8  - a linter that catches style and logic issues
#   isort   - sorts and groups import statements

# Example command line usage:
#   black .
#   flake8 src/
```

By running these tools, a team removes style debates from code review entirely—the formatter decides, and everyone moves on. The most effective approach enforces standards at multiple points, so problems are caught as early as possible rather than after code is shared.

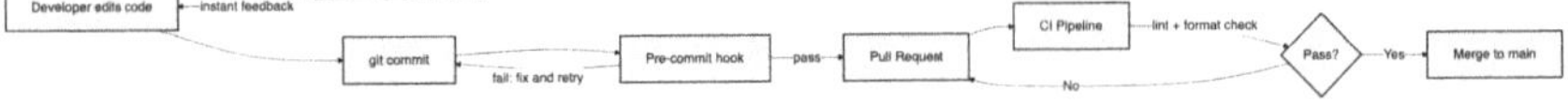

Enforcing standards at several layers means a developer gets instant feedback in their editor, a pre-commit hook catches anything missed before code is committed, and the continuous integration pipeline acts as a final safety net. Each layer catches what the previous one missed, and the earliest layers give the fastest feedback. This defense-in-depth approach keeps the codebase clean without relying on anyone's memory.

Summary

- Comments should explain *why*, not *what*; code that needs a "what" comment can usually be made clearer instead.
- Docstrings document how to use code and can be extracted into published reference documentation.
- Coding standards create consistency, which lets developers read any file without adjusting to a new style.
- Automated linters and formatters enforce standards at multiple layers, removing style debates and catching issues early.

8.3 Code Smells and Refactoring

Software rarely starts out messy—it gets that way gradually, one shortcut at a time. Learning to recognize the early warning signs of trouble lets you fix problems while they are still small. In this section, you will learn to identify **code smells**, apply **refactoring** to improve code safely, and eliminate one of the most common problems of all: duplication.

These skills change how you see code. Once you can name a smell, you can talk about it with your team and address it deliberately rather than living with a vague sense that "something is wrong here."

Code Smells

A **code smell** is a surface-level symptom that hints at a deeper problem in the code. A smell does not mean the code is broken—it means the code is likely to cause trouble as it evolves. Just as a smell in a kitchen suggests something needs attention, a code smell suggests a design that will resist change.

Common code smells include:

- **Long functions** that do too many things and are hard to follow.
- **Large classes** that have taken on too many responsibilities.
- **Duplicated code** that appears in multiple places.
- **Long parameter lists** that make functions hard to call correctly.

- **Magic numbers** and unexplained literal values scattered through the code.
- **Deeply nested conditionals** that are hard to reason about.

```
# Smell: deeply nested conditionals and unclear intent
def get_shipping_cost(order):
    if order:
        if order.items:
            if order.country == "US":
                if order.total > 50:
                    return 0
                else:
                    return 5
```

This function nests four levels deep and mixes several concerns. As soon as you add another country or discount tier, it will become unmanageable. The smell here is the nesting itself—it signals that the logic needs to be flattened and clarified.

Refactoring

Refactoring is the process of improving the internal structure of code without changing its external behavior. The key phrase is *without changing behavior*—refactoring is not the same as adding features or fixing bugs. You take working code and make it cleaner, relying on tests to prove that the behavior stayed the same.

Here is the nested function above, refactored to be flat and clear:

```
def get_shipping_cost(order):
    if not order or not order.items:
        raise ValueError("Order must contain items")

    if order.country != "US":
        return calculate_international_shipping(order)

    FREE_SHIPPING_THRESHOLD = 50
    STANDARD_SHIPPING = 5
    return 0 if order.total > FREE_SHIPPING_THRESHOLD else STANDARD_SHIPPING
```

This version handles invalid input up front, then returns early for the international case. By the time you reach the final line, only the simple domestic logic remains. The named constants replace the magic numbers, and the whole function reads top to bottom without deep nesting. Crucially, the function still returns exactly the same values it did before—only its structure has changed.

The safe way to refactor is in small steps, running your tests after each change. Because your tests describe the expected behavior, they will immediately catch any change you did not intend. This is why the testing skills from earlier chapters are the foundation of confident refactoring.

Eliminating Duplication

Duplicated code is one of the most damaging smells because it multiplies the cost of every change. When the same logic exists in three places, a fix must be applied three times, and it is easy to miss one. The principle of **DRY**—Don't Repeat Yourself—states that every piece of knowledge should have a single, authoritative representation in the code.

```
# Before: the same tax calculation duplicated
def price_with_tax_us(price):
    return price + price * 0.07

def price_with_tax_ca(price):
    return price + price * 0.13

# After: a single function parameterized by rate
TAX_RATES = {"US": 0.07, "CA": 0.13}

def price_with_tax(price, region):
    return price + price * TAX_RATES[region]
```

By extracting the shared logic into one function and moving the varying part—the rate—into data, you eliminate the duplication entirely. Adding a new region now means adding one entry to `TAX_RATES` rather than writing a new function. This makes the code shorter, but more importantly, it makes it correct by construction: there is only one place where the tax formula lives.

Summary

- Code smells are surface symptoms—like long functions, duplication, and deep nesting—that hint at deeper design problems.
- Refactoring improves internal structure without changing external behavior, and it relies on tests to stay safe.
- Small, test-backed steps make refactoring predictable rather than risky.
- The DRY principle eliminates duplication by giving every piece of knowledge a single authoritative home.

8.4 Managing Dependencies and Configuration

Real software rarely stands alone. It relies on external libraries, runs in different environments, needs to record what it is doing, and must survive unexpected inputs. In this section, you will learn how to manage dependencies and configuration, how to add useful logging, and how to write defensive code that fails gracefully.

These practices are what make software dependable in production. A program that works perfectly on your machine but breaks on the server, or that fails silently when something goes wrong, is not truly maintainable. The techniques here close that gap.

Managing Dependencies

A **dependency** is any external library your code relies on. Dependencies save enormous effort, but they also introduce risk: they can change, break, or conflict with one another. Managing them well means declaring exactly which versions your project needs so that it behaves the same way everywhere.

In Python, you typically declare dependencies in a file such as `requirements.txt` or `pyproject.toml`, and you install them into an isolated **virtual environment** so that different projects do not interfere with each other.

```
# requirements.txt - pin exact versions for reproducibility
requests==2.31.0
click==8.1.7
python-dateutil==2.8.2
```

Pinning exact versions ensures that everyone who installs the project—including the production server—gets the identical set of libraries you tested against. Without pinning, a library could quietly update to a new version that changes behavior, causing bugs that appear on some machines and not others. A virtual environment keeps these dependencies contained, so installing a library for one project never affects another.

Configuration Management

Configuration is the set of values that change how a program runs without changing its code—things like database addresses, API keys, and feature flags. A key principle is to separate configuration from code, so the same program can run in development, testing, and production simply by supplying different configuration.

A widely used approach is to read configuration from **environment variables**, which keeps secrets out of your source code entirely.

```
import os

DATABASE_URL = os.environ.get("DATABASE_URL", "sqlite:///local.db")
DEBUG = os.environ.get("DEBUG", "false").lower() == "true"
API_KEY = os.environ["API_KEY"]  # required — fail loudly if missing
```

Here, `DATABASE_URL` and `DEBUG` fall back to sensible defaults for local development, while `API_KEY` is required and will raise an error immediately if it is missing. Reading configuration this way means you never hardcode a production password into a file that might be committed to version control. It also makes deployment flexible, since operators can adjust behavior without touching the code.

Logging

Logging is the practice of recording what your program does as it runs, so you can understand its behavior later. Unlike `print` statements, a proper logging system lets you control how much detail is recorded and where it goes, and it timestamps and categorizes every message. When something goes wrong in production, logs are often your only window into what happened.

Python's built-in `logging` module organizes messages by severity, called **log levels**.

```
import logging

logging.basicConfig(level=logging.INFO)
logger = logging.getLogger(__name__)

def transfer_funds(account, amount):
    logger.debug("Transfer requested: %s for %.2f", account.id, amount)
    if amount > account.balance:
        logger.warning("Insufficient funds for account %s", account.id)
        return False
    account.balance -= amount
    logger.info("Transfer completed for account %s", account.id)
    return True
```

Each log call uses a level that matches the importance of the message. The `debug` call is detailed information useful during development, the `warning` flags a situation worth noticing, and the `info` records a normal milestone. By setting the level to `INFO` in `basicConfig`, the debug messages are suppressed in normal operation but can be turned on when you need to investigate a problem. Choosing the right level for each message is what makes logs useful rather than overwhelming.

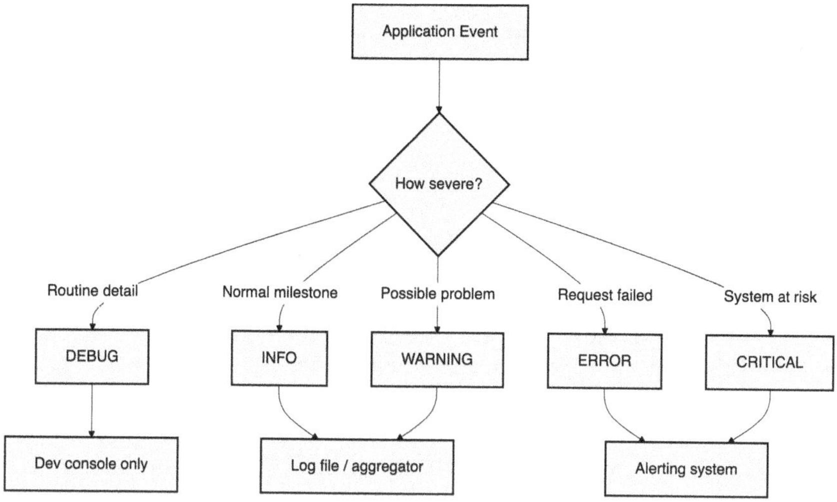

Understanding which audience each level serves helps you log deliberately. Debug messages support you during active development, info messages confirm the system is working normally, warnings flag conditions that may become problems, and errors record failures that need attention. Using levels consistently means you can filter the noise and focus on what matters in any given situation.

Defensive Programming

Defensive programming is the practice of writing code that anticipates and handles things going wrong. Inputs may be invalid, files may be missing, and network calls may fail. Defensive code checks its assumptions and responds to problems clearly instead of crashing in confusing ways or, worse, continuing with bad data.

```python
def load_user_config(path):
    if not path:
        raise ValueError("Config path must not be empty")

    try:
        with open(path) as file:
            return json.load(file)
    except FileNotFoundError:
        logger.warning("Config file %s not found; using defaults", path)
        return DEFAULT_CONFIG
    except json.JSONDecodeError as error:
        raise ValueError(f"Config file {path} is not valid JSON") from error
```

This function guards against several failure modes. It rejects an empty path up front, falls back to defaults if the file is missing, and turns an obscure JSON parsing error into a clear message that names the offending file. Notice the balance: a missing file is recoverable, so it logs a warning and continues, while corrupt data is a real problem, so it raises an error. Good defensive programming distinguishes between conditions you can recover from and those you cannot.

Summary

- Dependencies should be declared with pinned versions and installed in isolated virtual environments for reproducibility.
- Configuration should be separated from code, often through environment variables, to keep secrets safe and deployment flexible.
- Logging records program behavior using severity levels, each aimed at a different audience and use case.
- Defensive programming anticipates failures, recovering where possible and failing clearly where recovery is not.

8.5 Technical Debt and Code Quality

Every codebase accumulates compromises over time, and every team must decide how to measure and manage the quality of its work. In this section, you will learn what **technical debt** is and how to manage it, how **code reviews** catch problems and spread knowledge, and how teams **measure code quality** using a combination of signals.

These are the practices that keep a codebase healthy over years rather than weeks. They shift maintainability from an individual habit to a team responsibility, which is where it must live for any project of real size.

Technical Debt

Technical debt is the future cost of choosing a quick or easy solution now instead of a better one that would take longer. The metaphor is deliberate: like financial debt, technical debt lets you move fast in the short term, but it charges interest. Every shortcut makes future changes a little slower, and if you never pay it down, that interest can eventually overwhelm a project.

Not all technical debt is bad. Sometimes taking on debt deliberately—shipping a simpler version to meet a deadline—is a sound decision, as long as you track it and plan to repay it. The danger is *unintentional* debt that accumulates unnoticed. The healthiest teams make debt visible, often by recording it in the issue tracker with a note explaining what was compromised and why.

```
# TODO(debt): This linear search is fine for our current
# few-hundred records, but will be too slow past ~10k.
# Replace with an indexed lookup before onboarding large clients.
def find_customer(customers, email):
    for customer in customers:
        if customer.email == email:
            return customer
    return None
```

This comment turns an invisible compromise into a documented decision. Anyone reading it understands the trade-off, knows the conditions under which it must be addressed, and can find it later by searching for `TODO(debt)`. Acknowledging debt honestly is far better than pretending it does not exist.

Code Reviews

A **code review** is the practice of having another developer examine your changes before they are merged. Reviews catch bugs and design problems early, but their value goes further—they spread knowledge across the team and enforce shared standards. When two people understand every part of the codebase, no single person becomes a bottleneck.

Effective code reviews focus on things that matter: correctness, clarity, and design. They should not devolve into arguments about formatting, which is exactly why teams automate style with the tools you saw earlier. When you review, ask whether you could maintain this code six months from now, and when you receive a review, treat feedback as a gift rather than criticism.

Good review habits include:

- Keep changes small so reviewers can give thorough, focused feedback.
- Explain the *why* of a change in the description, not just the *what*.
- Comment on the code, never the person, and offer suggestions rather than commands.
- Automate style checks so reviews focus on substance.

Measuring Code Quality

You cannot manage what you cannot see, and **code quality** is notoriously hard to see. No single number captures it, but several complementary measures together paint a useful picture. Teams combine automated tools with human judgment to track whether quality is improving or degrading over time.

Common quality signals include **static analysis**, which inspects code without running it to find likely bugs and style issues; **test coverage**, which measures how much of the code your tests exercise; and **cyclomatic complexity**, which counts the number of independent paths through a function as a proxy for how hard it is to understand and test.

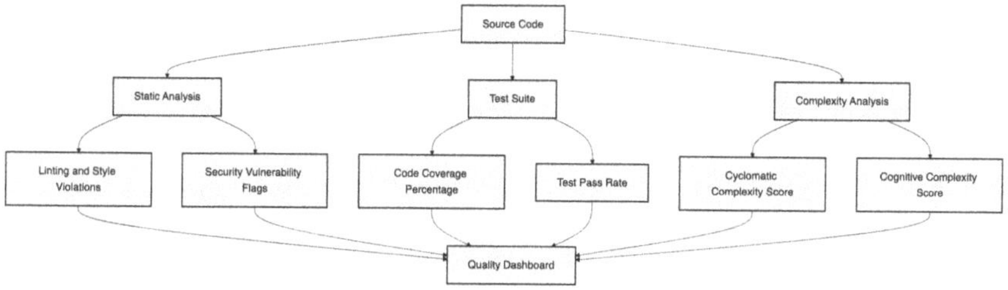

Each of these signals reveals something the others miss. Static analysis catches suspicious patterns, coverage shows untested gaps, and complexity flags functions that have grown too tangled. Relying on any one metric alone can mislead you—high coverage with no attention to complexity, for example, can still hide fragile code. The goal is not to chase a perfect score on any single measure but to use the combination as a conversation starter about where the codebase needs attention.

```
# Example tools that produce these signals:
#   pylint / mypy       - static analysis and type checking
#   coverage.py         - test coverage measurement
#   radon               - cyclomatic complexity analysis
#
#   coverage report --show-missing
#   radon cc src/ --min B
```

Running these tools regularly, ideally as part of your continuous integration pipeline, turns quality from a vague feeling into observable data. Over time you can watch trends—rising complexity or falling coverage—and act before small problems become large ones. Metrics guide attention; they never replace the judgment of a thoughtful engineer.

Summary

- Technical debt is the future cost of quick solutions; deliberate, tracked debt is manageable, while hidden debt is dangerous.
- Code reviews catch problems early and spread knowledge, and they work best when focused on substance rather than style.
- No single number measures code quality; teams combine static analysis, test coverage, and complexity to build a fuller picture.
- Quality tools run in continuous integration reveal trends over time, guiding attention without replacing engineering judgment.

Chapter Summary

This chapter has been about a single idea seen from many angles: software must be built to change. You began with clean code and naming, the foundation on which everything else rests, because code that cannot be read cannot be safely modified. From there you moved to documentation and standards, which extend that clarity across a whole team and keep a growing codebase coherent even as many hands contribute to it.

The middle of the chapter gave you tools for improving code that already exists. Recognizing code smells lets you spot trouble early, refactoring lets you fix it safely under the protection of tests, and the DRY principle helps you keep knowledge in one place. You then stepped outside individual functions to manage the wider concerns of real software—dependencies, configuration, logging, and defensive programming—all of which determine whether your code survives contact with the messy conditions of production.

Finally, you learned to think at the level of the whole project and team through technical debt, code reviews, and quality metrics. Together, these skills mean you can now do something you could not before: not just write code that works today, but shape code that will keep working, and keep being changeable, for years. That long-term view is what distinguishes a software engineer from someone who merely writes programs, and it is a lens you will carry into every project you touch.

Chapter Lab: Identifying Code Smells and Refactoring an Existing Application

In this lab, you will work with an existing application that functions correctly but suffers from a range of maintainability problems. You will apply the skills from this chapter to identify code smells, then refactor the code step by step to make it cleaner, better organized, and free of duplication while preserving its behavior. Along the way you will practice improving names, breaking up overgrown functions, and documenting the trade-offs you encounter.

Chapter 9: Software Testing and Quality Assurance

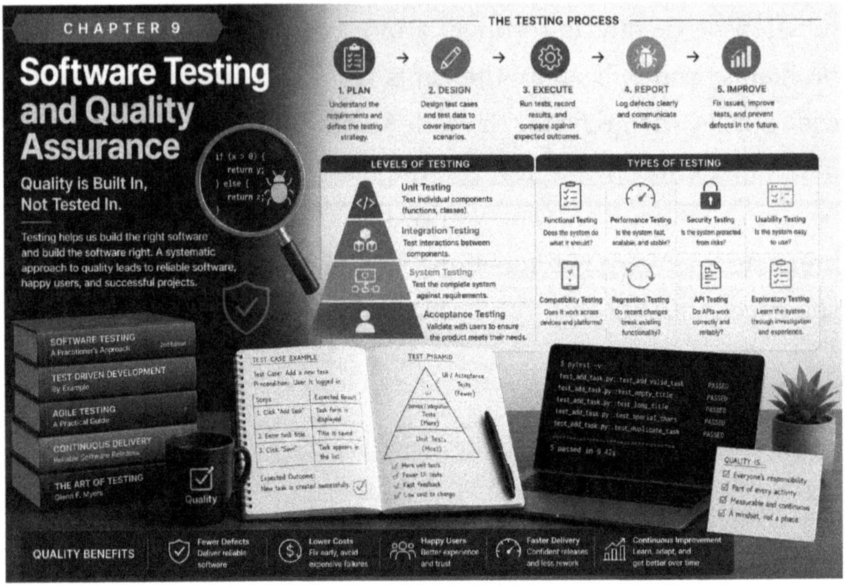

Every piece of software you write makes promises. A login form promises to reject bad passwords. A shopping cart promises to calculate the correct total. A payroll system promises to pay people the right amount. Software testing is how you check whether your code actually keeps those promises before your users find out that it doesn't. It is one of the most important disciplines in software engineering, and it separates code that works by accident from code that works on purpose.

In this chapter, you will learn why testing matters, how professional teams organize their tests into levels, and how to write tests that are clear, reliable, and useful. You will discover tools and techniques that let a computer run thousands of checks in seconds, and you will see how testing fits into the broader practice of quality assurance. By the end, you will be able to design a test suite for a real project, measure how much of your code it exercises, and understand how modern teams keep quality high while shipping software quickly.

This builds directly on the design and construction concepts from earlier chapters. Once you know how to structure functions, modules, and classes, the natural next question is: how do you prove they behave correctly? Testing answers that question, and it becomes the safety net that lets you change and grow a codebase with confidence.

9.1 Why Software Testing Matters

Software is complex, and humans make mistakes. Even a careful, experienced developer introduces defects — small logic errors, forgotten edge cases, and misunderstood requirements. Testing exists because the alternative, shipping untested code and hoping for the best, is far too risky. A defect caught during development might cost minutes to fix. That same defect discovered in production might cost hours of downtime, lost customers, or in critical systems, real physical harm.

In this section, you will learn the fundamental reasons testing pays off, the important distinction between verification and validation, and a model called the testing pyramid that helps teams decide what kinds of tests to write and how many of each. These ideas form the mental framework for everything else in the chapter.

Why Testing Pays Off

A **defect** is any flaw in software that causes it to behave differently from what is expected. The cost of a defect grows the longer it goes undetected. This is often called the cost-of-change curve, and the pattern is consistent across the industry: bugs are cheap to fix early and expensive to fix late.

Testing gives you several concrete benefits. It catches defects while they are still cheap. It documents how your code is supposed to behave, because a good test reads like a specification. It gives you the confidence to refactor, since a passing test suite tells you that your changes did not break existing behavior. And it protects against **regressions**, which are bugs that reappear in features that used to work.

```
def apply_discount(price, discount_percent):
    """Return the price after applying a percentage discount."""
    if discount_percent < 0 or discount_percent > 100:
        raise ValueError("Discount must be between 0 and 100")
    return price * (1 - discount_percent / 100)

# A quick manual check
print(apply_discount(100, 20))    # Expected: 80.0
print(apply_discount(50, 0))      # Expected: 50.0
```

This small function contains a promise: given a price and a valid discount percentage, it returns the discounted price. The manual checks below it confirm the promise for a couple of cases. Notice the `raise ValueError` line, which guards against invalid input. A defect might hide in that boundary logic — what happens at exactly `0` or exactly `100` ? Testing is how you systematically verify these boundaries instead of guessing.

Verification vs. Validation

Two words that sound similar but mean different things are verification and validation. **Verification** asks, "Are we building the product right?" It checks whether the software matches its specification — whether the code does what the design says it should do. **Validation** asks, "Are we building the right product?" It checks whether the software actually meets the user's real needs.

Consider an analogy. Imagine a builder constructing a house from a set of blueprints. Verification is confirming that the house matches the blueprints exactly — every wall is where the plan says it should be. Validation is confirming that the house is one the family actually wants to live in. You can verify a house perfectly and still fail validation if the blueprints described the wrong house.

Both matter. A program can pass every technical check yet still solve the wrong problem. In practice, unit and integration tests lean toward verification, while acceptance testing and user feedback lean toward validation. A mature team invests in both so that the software is not only correct but also genuinely useful.

The Testing Pyramid

The **testing pyramid** is a model that describes how to balance different kinds of tests. It suggests that you should have many small, fast tests at the base, fewer medium-sized tests in the middle, and only a handful of large, slow tests at the top.

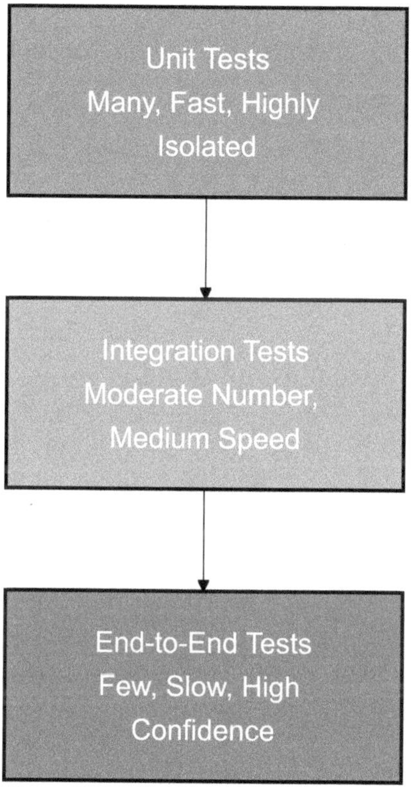

The base of the pyramid is made of **unit tests**, which check individual functions or classes in isolation. They are fast, cheap to write, and easy to debug because when one fails, you know exactly where the problem is. The middle layer holds **integration tests**, which verify that separate components work correctly together.

The top holds end-to-end or system tests, which exercise the whole application the way a user would.

The pyramid shape is deliberate. Tests at the top are slow, brittle, and expensive to maintain, so you want relatively few of them. Tests at the bottom are quick and precise, so you want many. Teams that invert this shape — writing mostly slow, high-level tests — often end up with test suites that take too long to run and break for confusing reasons. Following the pyramid keeps your feedback fast and your failures easy to diagnose.

Summary

- Testing exists because software is complex and defects are far cheaper to fix early than late.
- Testing catches bugs, documents expected behavior, enables safe refactoring, and prevents regressions.
- **Verification** checks that you built the product correctly; **validation** checks that you built the correct product.
- The **testing pyramid** recommends many fast unit tests, fewer integration tests, and few slow end-to-end tests.

9.2 Levels of Testing

Testing is not a single activity. Professional teams test their software at several distinct levels, each with a different scope and purpose. Understanding these levels helps you decide what to test, when, and how. It also helps you communicate with teammates, because terms like "unit test" and "acceptance test" carry precise meanings in the industry.

In this section, you will walk through the five most important levels of testing, from the smallest unit up to full acceptance testing, plus regression testing, which cuts across all of them. Each level answers a different question about the health of your software.

Unit Testing

A **unit test** verifies the smallest testable piece of your program — usually a single function or method — in isolation from the rest of the system. The goal is to confirm that one specific unit behaves correctly across a range of inputs, including normal cases, edge cases, and invalid inputs.

```python
import unittest

def apply_discount(price, discount_percent):
    if discount_percent < 0 or discount_percent > 100:
        raise ValueError("Discount must be between 0 and 100")
    return price * (1 - discount_percent / 100)

class TestApplyDiscount(unittest.TestCase):
    def test_normal_discount(self):
        self.assertEqual(apply_discount(100, 20), 80.0)

    def test_zero_discount(self):
        self.assertEqual(apply_discount(50, 0), 50.0)

    def test_invalid_discount_raises(self):
        with self.assertRaises(ValueError):
            apply_discount(100, 150)

if __name__ == "__main__":
    unittest.main()
```

This example uses Python's built-in `unittest` framework. Each method beginning with `test_` is a separate unit test. The `assertEqual` calls check that the function returns the expected value, and `assertRaises` confirms that invalid input triggers the expected exception. Because each test targets one behavior, a failure points you straight to the problem. This precision is exactly what makes unit tests the foundation of the pyramid.

Integration Testing

Integration testing checks that multiple units work correctly when combined. Individual functions might each pass their own unit tests but still fail when connected, because of mismatched assumptions, incorrect data formats, or unexpected interactions.

```python
def get_price_from_catalog(item_id, catalog):
    return catalog[item_id]

def checkout(item_id, discount, catalog):
    price = get_price_from_catalog(item_id, catalog)
    return apply_discount(price, discount)

# Integration test: two functions working together
def test_checkout_integration():
    catalog = {"book": 40.0, "pen": 5.0}
    result = checkout("book", 25, catalog)
    assert result == 30.0
    print("Integration test passed")

test_checkout_integration()
```

Here, `checkout` combines `get_price_from_catalog` and `apply_discount`. The integration test confirms that data flows correctly between them — that a lookup produces a price, and that the price flows into the discount calculation. A unit test would only check each function alone; the integration test verifies the seam where they meet.

System Testing

System testing evaluates the complete, integrated application as a whole to confirm it satisfies its overall requirements. Instead of testing a function or a pair of functions, you test the software the way it will actually run — with its database, its configuration, and its external services in place.

System tests are broader and slower than integration tests. They might launch the full application, submit a request through its public interface, and verify the end result. Because they cover so much at once, a failure can be harder to trace, which is why the pyramid tells you to keep their number small. Their value lies in catching problems that only appear when every part of the system is running together.

Acceptance Testing

Acceptance testing determines whether the software meets the needs and expectations of its users or customers. This is the level most closely tied to validation. While system testing asks whether the software works correctly, acceptance testing asks whether it does the right thing from the user's point of view.

Acceptance tests are often written in terms that a non-programmer can understand, expressed as scenarios such as "When a customer applies a valid coupon, their order total decreases." Sometimes the customer performs these tests directly. Sometimes they are automated with tools designed to express requirements in plain language. Either way, passing acceptance tests is often the signal that a feature is ready to ship.

Regression Testing

Regression testing is the practice of re-running existing tests to confirm that new changes have not broken previously working functionality. It is not a separate scope like the others; instead, it reuses your unit, integration, and system tests to guard against reintroduced bugs.

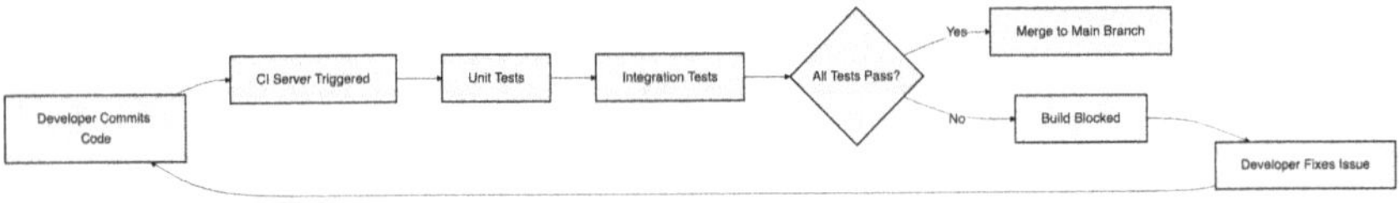

Regression testing is where automation truly earns its keep. Running your entire suite by hand after every change is impractical, but a computer can run thousands of tests in seconds. Modern teams wire their regression suite into an automated pipeline so that every code change is checked before it is allowed to merge. This turns regression testing from a chore into a constant, invisible safety net.

Summary

- **Unit tests** verify the smallest pieces of code in isolation and form the base of the pyramid.
- **Integration tests** confirm that separate components work correctly when combined.
- **System tests** evaluate the complete, integrated application against its overall requirements.
- **Acceptance tests** confirm the software meets user needs and are closely tied to validation.
- **Regression testing** re-runs existing tests to ensure new changes have not broken old behavior.

9.3 Writing Effective Tests

Knowing the levels of testing is only half the battle. To get real value, you need to write tests that are clear, reliable, and maintainable. Poorly written tests can be worse than no tests at all — they produce false alarms, break for the wrong reasons, and slow the team down. Good tests, by contrast, act as trustworthy documentation and a dependable safety net.

In this section, you will learn how to structure individual test cases, how to eliminate duplicated setup code with fixtures, and how to isolate the code under test from slow or unpredictable dependencies using mocking. These techniques apply at every level of the pyramid.

Test Cases

A **test case** is a single, self-contained check that exercises one behavior and verifies one expected outcome. The most reliable way to structure a test case is the **Arrange-Act-Assert** pattern: first arrange the inputs and setup, then act by calling the code under test, then assert that the result matches expectations.

```
import unittest

def word_count(text):
    if not text.strip():
        return 0
    return len(text.split())

class TestWordCount(unittest.TestCase):
    def test_counts_multiple_words(self):
        # Arrange
        text = "the quick brown fox"
        # Act
        result = word_count(text)
        # Assert
        self.assertEqual(result, 4)

    def test_empty_string_returns_zero(self):
        self.assertEqual(word_count("   "), 0)
```

Each test here checks exactly one thing and has a descriptive name that reads like a sentence. When `test_empty_string_returns_zero` fails, the name alone tells you what broke. The Arrange-Act-Assert comments in the first test make the structure explicit. Aim to keep each test focused; testing one behavior per case makes failures easy to diagnose and keeps your suite readable.

Test Fixtures

A **test fixture** is a fixed baseline environment that a test runs against — the setup steps needed before the test and the cleanup steps needed after. Without fixtures, you end up copying the same setup code into dozens of tests, which is tedious and error-prone. Worse, shared state left over from one test can silently corrupt another.

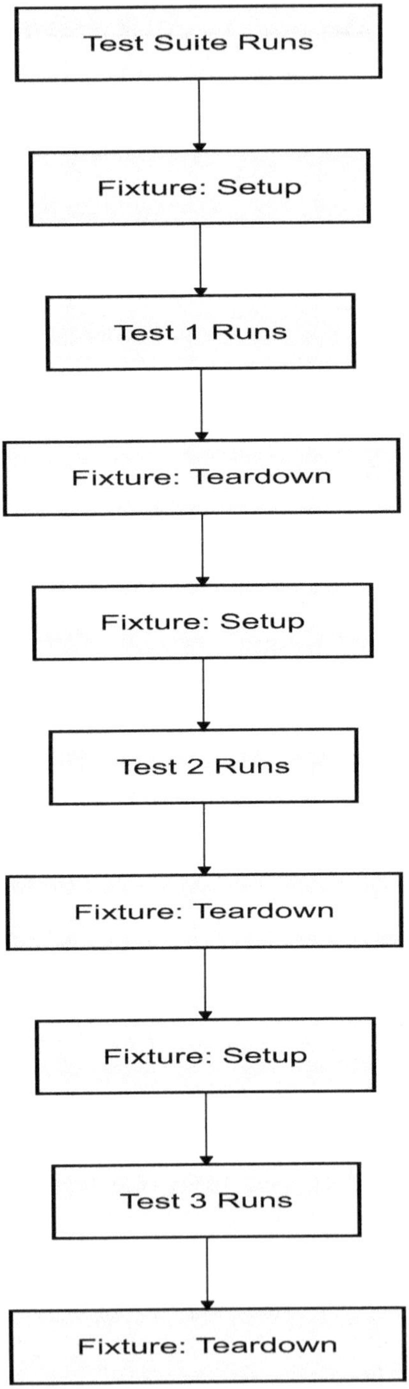
Test Suite Runs
Fixture: Setup
Test 1 Runs
Fixture: Teardown
Fixture: Setup
Test 2 Runs
Fixture: Teardown
Fixture: Setup
Test 3 Runs
Fixture: Teardown

```python
import unittest

class ShoppingCart:
    def __init__(self):
        self.items = []
    def add(self, item):
        self.items.append(item)
    def total(self):
        return sum(item["price"] for item in self.items)

class TestShoppingCart(unittest.TestCase):
    def setUp(self):
        # Runs before every test method
        self.cart = ShoppingCart()

    def test_empty_cart_total_is_zero(self):
        self.assertEqual(self.cart.total(), 0)

    def test_total_sums_items(self):
        self.cart.add({"name": "book", "price": 40})
        self.cart.add({"name": "pen", "price": 5})
        self.assertEqual(self.cart.total(), 45)
```

The `setUp` method is the fixture. It runs automatically before each test, giving every test a fresh, empty `ShoppingCart`. This guarantees that tests do not interfere with one another and eliminates duplicated setup code. Many frameworks also offer a `tearDown` method for cleanup, such as closing files or database connections after each test.

Mocking

Sometimes the code you want to test depends on something slow, unpredictable, or hard to control — a network call, a database, or the current time. **Mocking** is the technique of replacing such a dependency with a fake object that behaves in a controlled, predictable way. This keeps your test fast, isolated, and repeatable.

```
from unittest.mock import Mock

def get_weather_message(weather_service, city):
    temp = weather_service.get_temperature(city)
    if temp > 30:
        return f"It is hot in {city}"
    return f"It is mild in {city}"

def test_hot_weather_message():
    # Create a fake weather service
    fake_service = Mock()
    fake_service.get_temperature.return_value = 35

    result = get_weather_message(fake_service, "Austin")

    assert result == "It is hot in Austin"
    fake_service.get_temperature.assert_called_once_with("Austin")

test_hot_weather_message()
```

Here, `fake_service` is a `Mock` object standing in for a real weather service that would normally make a network request. The line `return_value = 35` tells the mock to always report a temperature of 35, so the test can reliably check the "hot" branch. The `assert_called_once_with` line even verifies that our code called the service correctly. With mocking, you test your own logic without depending on the internet or a live server.

Summary

- A **test case** should check one behavior and follow the Arrange-Act-Assert structure with a descriptive name.
- **Test fixtures**, such as `setUp` and `tearDown` , centralize setup and cleanup so each test starts from a clean slate.
- Fixtures prevent duplicated code and stop tests from corrupting each other through shared state.
- **Mocking** replaces slow or unpredictable dependencies with controlled fakes, keeping tests fast and reliable.

9.4 Automated Testing and Coverage

Running tests by hand does not scale. As a project grows to hundreds or thousands of tests, you need a computer to run them for you, quickly and consistently. Automated testing makes your safety net practical, and coverage tools help you understand how much of your code that net actually protects. Together, these tools transform testing from an occasional effort into a continuous discipline.

In this section, you will learn how to run tests automatically, how to measure test coverage and interpret it wisely, and how a workflow called test-driven development flips the usual order by writing tests first. These practices are the backbone of professional software development.

Automated Testing

Automated testing means using tools to run your tests without manual intervention. Python's `unittest` module and the popular third-party framework `pytest` both discover and execute your tests automatically. You write the tests once, then run the whole suite with a single command whenever you want confirmation that your code still works.

```python
# test_math_utils.py  - run with: pytest
def add(a, b):
    return a + b

def divide(a, b):
    if b == 0:
        raise ZeroDivisionError("Cannot divide by zero")
    return a / b

def test_add():
    assert add(2, 3) == 5

def test_divide():
    assert divide(10, 2) == 5

def test_divide_by_zero():
    import pytest
    with pytest.raises(ZeroDivisionError):
        divide(10, 0)
```

With `pytest`, any function whose name starts with `test_` is automatically discovered and run when you type `pytest` in the terminal. There is no boilerplate class to write — plain `assert` statements are enough. The framework reports which tests passed and which failed, along with helpful details for each failure. This automation is what makes it feasible to run your full regression suite after every change.

Test Coverage

Test coverage is a measurement of how much of your code is executed when your tests run, usually expressed as a percentage of lines or branches. A coverage tool watches your program while the tests run and reports which lines were exercised and which were never touched.

```python
# Run with: pytest --cov=my_module
def classify_number(n):
    if n > 0:
        return "positive"
    elif n < 0:
        return "negative"
    else:
        return "zero"

def test_positive():
    assert classify_number(5) == "positive"

# Note: no tests for negative or zero yet!
```

If you run coverage on this example, the tool will report that the `negative` and `zero` branches were never executed. That is exactly the kind of gap coverage helps you find. However, treat coverage as a guide, not a goal. High coverage does not guarantee good tests – you can execute a line without actually verifying its behavior. Aim to cover important logic and edge cases, and be suspicious of chasing 100 percent for its own sake.

Test-Driven Development

Test-driven development, or **TDD**, is a discipline in which you write a failing test *before* you write the code that makes it pass. It follows a short, repeating cycle often summarized as red, green, refactor: write a failing test (red), write the minimum code to pass it (green), then clean up the code while keeping the tests passing (refactor).

```
# Step 1 (RED): Write the test first, before is_palindrome exists.
def test_is_palindrome():
    assert is_palindrome("racecar") is True
    assert is_palindrome("hello") is False

# Step 2 (GREEN): Now write the simplest code that passes.
def is_palindrome(text):
    return text == text[::-1]
```

In TDD, you would run the test at Step 1 and watch it fail, because `is_palindrome` does not exist yet. That failure confirms the test actually checks something. Then you write the function in Step 2 and run the test again, this time watching it pass. Working this way keeps your design focused on real requirements, ensures every line of code is justified by a test, and produces a comprehensive test suite as a natural byproduct.

Summary

- **Automated testing** with tools like `unittest` and `pytest` runs your entire suite with a single command.
- Frameworks automatically discover test functions and report passes and failures with helpful detail.
- **Test coverage** measures how much of your code your tests exercise, revealing untested branches.
- Coverage is a useful guide but not a guarantee of quality; focus on meaningful behavior, not chasing 100 percent.
- **Test-driven development** writes a failing test first, then the minimal code to pass, following the red-green-refactor cycle.

9.5 Continuous Testing and Quality Assurance

Testing reaches its full potential when it becomes continuous – woven into the everyday flow of development rather than saved for the end. Modern teams run their tests automatically on every change, catching problems within minutes of when they are introduced. And testing itself is only part of a larger effort called quality assurance, which encompasses everything a team does to build good software.

In this final section, you will learn how continuous testing fits into an automated pipeline and how it keeps feedback fast. You will also see how quality assurance broadens the picture beyond testing alone, tying together the practices you have learned throughout this book.

Continuous Testing

Continuous testing is the practice of automatically running tests every time code changes, as part of a **continuous integration (CI)** pipeline. Instead of testing once before a big release, the pipeline tests constantly. Each commit triggers the suite, and developers get near-immediate feedback if they broke something.

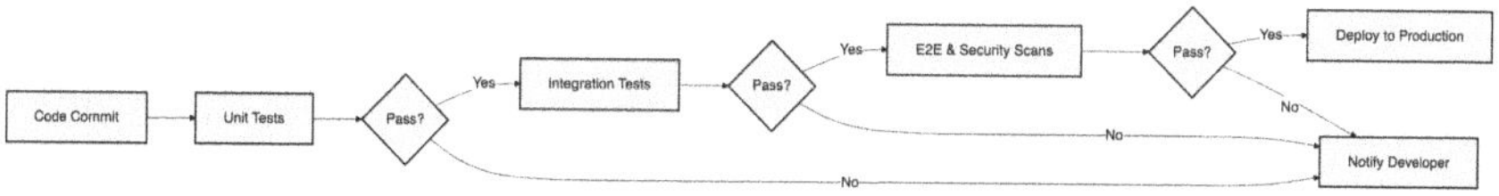

A typical pipeline is a series of gates. A change must pass each gate before moving to the next: run unit tests, then integration tests, then system tests, then perhaps a coverage check. If any gate fails, the pipeline stops and notifies the developer right away. This tight feedback loop is powerful. A bug introduced at 10:00 is discovered at 10:03, while the change is still fresh in the developer's mind, rather than weeks later when it has become tangled with other changes.

Continuous testing depends on the automation you learned in the previous section. Fast, reliable, automated tests are what make it possible to run the full suite on every commit without slowing the team down. This is also why the testing pyramid matters so much — a pipeline dominated by slow tests would take too long to give quick feedback.

Quality Assurance

Quality assurance (QA) is the broad set of activities and processes a team uses to ensure that software meets a required standard of quality. Testing is a central part of QA, but QA is bigger than testing. It includes code reviews, coding standards, static analysis tools, clear requirements, good design, and processes that prevent defects from being introduced in the first place.

It helps to distinguish two related ideas. **Quality control** focuses on finding defects in a finished product — testing is largely a quality control activity. **Quality assurance** focuses on improving the process so that fewer defects are created at all. A team practicing strong QA does not just catch bugs; it asks why bugs happen and changes how it works to prevent them.

Think of QA as the culture that surrounds testing. A team can have excellent tests and still ship poor software if its requirements are vague or its design is confused. Conversely, a team with strong QA practices — clear specifications, thoughtful reviews, automated pipelines, and a shared commitment to quality — produces software that is reliable, maintainable, and trustworthy. The techniques in this chapter are the tools; QA is the discipline that puts them to work.

Summary

- **Continuous testing** runs the full test suite automatically on every code change within a CI pipeline.
- Pipelines act as a series of gates that block flawed changes and notify developers immediately.
- Fast, automated tests and a healthy testing pyramid are what make continuous testing practical.
- **Quality assurance** is the broad discipline of ensuring software quality, encompassing testing, reviews, standards, and process.
- **Quality control** finds defects in the product, while **quality assurance** improves the process to prevent them.

Chapter Summary

This chapter took you from the fundamental question of *why* we test all the way to the disciplined practice of continuous testing and quality assurance. You began by understanding that testing exists because defects are cheap to fix early and costly to fix late, and you learned to distinguish verification from validation and to use the testing pyramid as a guide for balancing your efforts. Those ideas set the strategy; everything that followed filled in the tactics.

From there, you explored the levels of testing — unit, integration, system, acceptance, and regression — each answering a different question about your software's health. You then learned to write tests that are actually worth having: focused test cases, fixtures that keep each test clean and independent, and mocks that isolate your code from slow or unpredictable dependencies. Automation tied it all together, letting you run entire suites with a single command, measure coverage to find gaps, and even flip the process around with test-driven development. Finally, continuous testing showed how these tests become a constant safety net inside a pipeline, and quality assurance placed testing within the wider culture of building good software.

You can now do something you could not do reliably before: prove that your code keeps its promises and keep it correct as it grows and changes. This is a defining skill of professional engineers. Testing is not a chore bolted on at the end — it is the practice that gives you the confidence to design boldly, refactor freely, and ship software that people can trust.

Chapter Lab: Building an Automated Python Test Suite

In this lab, you will build a complete automated test suite for a small Python application, applying the skills developed throughout this chapter. You will write focused unit tests, use fixtures to manage setup, apply mocking to isolate an external dependency, and measure your test coverage to identify untested logic. By the end, you will have a runnable suite that demonstrates the levels and techniques of testing in a single, cohesive project.

Chapter 10: Secure Software Engineering

Every application you build lives in a hostile environment. The moment your software accepts input from a user, connects to a network, or stores someone's data, it becomes a target. Attackers probe for weaknesses automatically, at scale, around the clock. This reality means that security is not an optional feature you bolt on at the end of a project. It is a fundamental engineering responsibility that shapes how you design, write, test, and deploy code.

In this chapter, you will learn to think like both a builder and an attacker. You will discover how to treat security as a first-class concern throughout the software lifecycle rather than a last-minute scramble before release. You will study the core mechanisms that protect applications and their users: authentication, authorization, input validation, and data protection. You will also learn to manage the risks that come from the code you did not write yourself, including third-party dependencies and the broader software supply chain.

By the end of this chapter, you will be able to identify common vulnerabilities, apply secure-by-design principles, model threats against a system, and integrate security testing into an automated delivery pipeline. These skills build directly on the engineering practices from earlier chapters. Just as you learned to test and automate your builds, you will now learn to make security a continuous, automated part of that same process.

10.1 Security as an Engineering Responsibility

For a long time, many organizations treated security as someone else's problem. Developers wrote features, and a separate security team reviewed the finished product, often just before launch. This model fails badly. By the time a dedicated reviewer finds a design flaw, changing it is expensive and disruptive. Modern software engineering pushes security responsibility onto everyone who touches the code, starting from the earliest design decisions.

In this section, you will learn why security belongs to every engineer, how to design systems that resist attack by default, and how to systematically reason about the threats your software faces. These ideas form the foundation for everything else in the chapter.

Security as a Software Engineering Responsibility

Security is a property of the whole system, not a single component. A perfectly encrypted database means nothing if an attacker can log in with a stolen password. A flawless login page means nothing if the application leaks data through an unvalidated search field. Because vulnerabilities can appear anywhere, security cannot be delegated entirely to specialists who arrive at the end.

When you own the security of the code you write, several things change. You start asking "how could this be abused?" as you design a feature, not after you ship it. You treat a security bug with the same seriousness as a crash or data-corruption bug. You measure the cost of a defect not just in developer hours but in potential harm to users. This mindset is often called **shifting left**, meaning you move security concerns earlier in the development timeline where they are cheaper and easier to address.

Consider the economics. A design flaw caught during a whiteboard session costs almost nothing to fix. The same flaw caught in code review costs a few hours. Caught in production after a breach, it can cost millions in remediation, legal exposure, and lost trust. Security-conscious engineering is not just ethically right; it is dramatically cheaper.

Secure-by-Design Principles

Secure-by-design means building systems whose default behavior is safe, so that security does not depend on every developer remembering to do the right thing every time. Several time-tested principles guide this approach.

The **principle of least privilege** states that every component, user, and process should have only the permissions it needs to do its job, and no more. A service that reads reports does not need write access to the database. A background job that resizes images does not need permission to delete user accounts. When you minimize privileges, a compromised component can do far less damage.

Defense in depth means layering multiple independent controls so that no single failure exposes the whole system. If your login form validates input, your database uses parameterized queries, and your server runs with restricted permissions, an attacker must defeat all three layers rather than just one.

Two more principles round out the set. **Fail securely** means that when something goes wrong, the system defaults to a safe state. If an authorization check throws an error, deny access rather than granting it. **Minimize the attack surface** means reducing the number of ways an attacker can interact with your system. Every open port, exposed endpoint, and enabled feature is a potential entry point.

```
# Insecure: defaults to allowing access when a check fails
def can_access(user, resource):
    try:
        return check_permissions(user, resource)
    except Exception:
        return True  # dangerous fallback

# Secure: fails closed, denying access on any error
def can_access(user, resource):
    try:
        return check_permissions(user, resource)
    except Exception:
        log.warning("Permission check failed for %s", user.id)
        return False  # safe default
```

The two versions of `can_access` differ by a single return value, but the security implications are enormous. The first version treats an unexpected error as permission granted, which means a bug in `check_permissions` silently opens the door to everyone. The second version applies the fail-securely principle. When anything goes wrong, it logs the incident and denies access. The safe default protects your users even when your code has bugs, which it inevitably will.

Threat Modeling

Threat modeling is the practice of systematically identifying what could go wrong with a system before an attacker does it for you. Rather than reacting to breaches, you sit down early in the design and ask structured questions about who might attack, what they want, and where your defenses are weak.

A useful starting point is to draw how data moves through your system and mark the **trust boundaries**, the points where data passes from a less-trusted zone into a more-trusted one. The boundary between a user's browser and your web server is a trust boundary. So is the boundary between your application and its database. Any place where trust levels change deserves careful scrutiny.

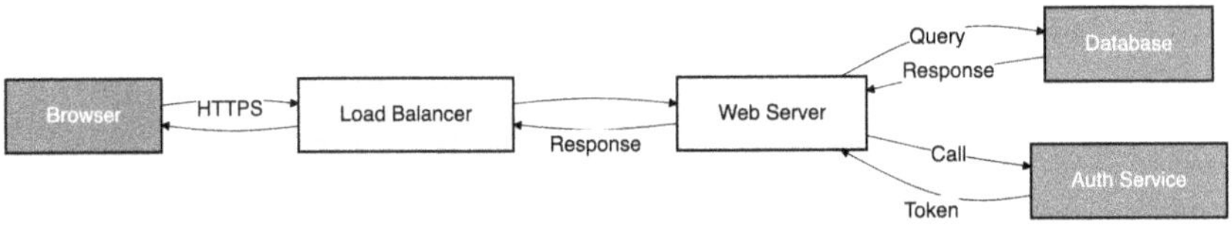

Once you can see the boundaries, you enumerate threats against each one. A popular framework for this is **STRIDE**, which prompts you to consider six categories of threat: Spoofing (pretending to be someone else), Tampering (altering data), Repudiation (denying an action), Information disclosure (leaking data), Denial of service (making the system unavailable), and Elevation of privilege (gaining unauthorized power). For each trust boundary, you walk through these categories and ask whether your design defends against them.

Threat modeling does not require expensive tools or a security PhD. A whiteboard, a diagram, and a team willing to think adversarially for an hour can surface the most dangerous flaws in a design. The goal is not to find every possible threat but to catch the serious, likely ones while they are still cheap to fix.

Summary

- Security is a whole-system property, so every engineer shares responsibility rather than delegating it to a separate team at the end.
- Shifting security left catches flaws when they are cheapest to fix and reduces the risk of costly production breaches.
- Secure-by-design principles include least privilege, defense in depth, failing securely, and minimizing the attack surface.
- Threat modeling uses trust boundaries and frameworks like STRIDE to identify likely attacks during design.

10.2 Authentication, Authorization, and Data Protection

Almost every application needs to answer two questions about the people using it: who are you, and what are you allowed to do? Getting these answers right is central to security. Alongside them sits the equally important job of protecting the data your application handles, both the input flowing in and the sensitive information you store.

In this section, you will learn the difference between authentication and authorization, how to validate untrusted input, and how to protect sensitive data both at rest and in transit. You will also learn how to keep secrets like passwords and API keys out of your source code, a mistake that continues to expose countless systems.

Authentication

Authentication is the process of verifying that users are who they claim to be. The most common form is a username and password, but authentication also includes multi-factor methods, tokens, and biometrics. The critical rule of authentication is that you must never store passwords in plain text. If your database is ever stolen, plaintext passwords hand attackers the keys to every account instantly.

Instead, you store a **hash** of the password, a one-way transformation that cannot be reversed. When a user logs in, you hash the password they submit and compare it to the stored hash.

You should use a slow, purpose-built password hashing algorithm such as bcrypt, scrypt, or Argon2, which are designed to resist brute-force attacks.

```
import bcrypt

def hash_password(plain_password: str) -> bytes:
    salt = bcrypt.gensalt()
    return bcrypt.hashpw(plain_password.encode("utf-8"), salt)

def verify_password(plain_password: str, stored_hash: bytes) -> bool:
    return bcrypt.checkpw(plain_password.encode("utf-8"), stored_hash)

# Registering a new user
hashed = hash_password("correct horse battery staple")

# Later, during login
if verify_password("correct horse battery staple", hashed):
    print("Login successful")
```

This code uses bcrypt to hash and verify passwords safely. The `gensalt` function generates a random **salt**, a unique value mixed into each password before hashing so that two users with the same password produce different hashes. This defeats precomputed lookup tables. Notice that you never compare passwords directly; `checkpw` handles the comparison in a way that also resists timing attacks. You never need to store or even see the salt separately, because bcrypt embeds it inside the resulting hash.

Authorization

Once you know who a user is, **authorization** determines what that user is allowed to do. Authentication and authorization are frequently confused, but they are distinct. Authentication is proving identity; authorization is granting permissions based on that identity. A logged-in user is authenticated, but they should still be blocked from viewing another user's private data.

A common and dangerous mistake is checking authorization only in the user interface. If your web page simply hides a delete button from ordinary users, an attacker can still send the delete request directly to your server. Authorization must be enforced on the server for every sensitive operation.

```
def delete_document(current_user, document_id):
    document = db.get_document(document_id)

    # Enforce authorization on the server, not just in the UI
    if document.owner_id != current_user.id and not current_user.is_admin:
        raise PermissionError("You are not allowed to delete this document")

    db.delete_document(document_id)
```

This function checks authorization before performing the delete. It confirms that the current user either owns the document or is an administrator. Because this check lives on the server, it cannot be bypassed by manipulating the browser or crafting a raw request. This illustrates the least-privilege principle in action: ordinary users can only act on resources they own.

Input Validation

Input validation is the practice of checking that data entering your system matches what you expect before you act on it. Never trust input from users, other services, files, or even your own database if it originally came from an untrusted source. Attackers deliberately craft malicious input to break out of the context you intended.

The safest approach is **allowlisting**, where you define exactly what is acceptable and reject everything else. This is far stronger than **denylisting**, where you try to block known-bad values, because attackers are endlessly creative in finding inputs you did not anticipate.

```
import re

ALLOWED_USERNAME = re.compile(r"^[a-zA-Z0-9_]{3,20}$")

def validate_username(username: str) -> str:
    if not ALLOWED_USERNAME.match(username):
        raise ValueError("Username must be 3-20 letters, digits, or underscores")
    return username

def validate_age(raw_value: str) -> int:
    age = int(raw_value)  # raises ValueError on non-numeric input
    if not 0 <= age <= 130:
        raise ValueError("Age is out of the acceptable range")
    return age
```

These validators apply allowlisting rather than trying to catch bad input. The username regex accepts only a specific set of characters and lengths, rejecting anything unusual such as spaces, punctuation, or control characters that might be used in an attack. The age validator both converts the type and enforces a sensible range. Validating at the boundary means the rest of your code can safely assume it is working with clean data.

Protecting Sensitive Data

Sensitive data must be protected both **at rest**, when stored on disk, and **in transit**, when moving across a network. For data in transit, you use **TLS** (Transport Layer Security), the protocol behind HTTPS, which encrypts communication so eavesdroppers cannot read it. Every application handling personal or confidential data should serve traffic exclusively over HTTPS.

For data at rest, encrypt sensitive fields in your database and storage. You should also collect only the data you actually need, a principle called **data minimization**. Data you never collect cannot be stolen. When you must store sensitive information, classify it so you know which controls apply, and delete it when it is no longer needed.

Secrets Management

Secrets are the credentials your application uses to access other systems: database passwords, API keys, encryption keys, and signing tokens. The single most common secrets mistake is hardcoding them into source code, where they end up committed to version control and exposed to anyone with repository access.

```
import os

# Insecure: secret is baked into the source and committed to git
# DATABASE_PASSWORD = "SuperSecret123!"

# Secure: read secrets from the environment at runtime
DATABASE_PASSWORD = os.environ["DATABASE_PASSWORD"]
API_KEY = os.environ["PAYMENT_API_KEY"]
```

This example reads secrets from environment variables rather than storing them in code. The application receives its secrets at runtime from its deployment environment, which might inject them from a dedicated secrets manager such as HashiCorp Vault or a cloud provider's secret store. Because the values never appear in source files, they cannot leak through your git history. Secrets managers add further benefits like access auditing and automatic rotation, so a leaked credential can be revoked and replaced quickly.

Summary

- Authentication verifies identity and requires storing salted hashes with slow algorithms like bcrypt, never plaintext passwords.
- Authorization controls what an authenticated user may do and must always be enforced on the server.
- Input validation should use allowlisting to accept only expected data and reject everything else.
- Sensitive data must be protected in transit with TLS and at rest with encryption, guided by data minimization.
- Secrets belong in environment variables or a dedicated secrets manager, never hardcoded in source control.

10.3 Dependency and Application Vulnerabilities

Modern applications are built largely from code you did not write. A typical project pulls in dozens or hundreds of open-source libraries, each of which may itself depend on many more. This ecosystem lets you build quickly, but it also means you inherit every vulnerability in every dependency. Meanwhile, your own code faces a well-documented set of recurring flaws that attackers exploit again and again.

In this section, you will learn to manage the risks in your dependencies, recognize the most common web application vulnerabilities, and apply secure coding practices that prevent entire classes of attacks. Understanding these patterns is one of the highest-value security skills you can develop.

Dependency Vulnerabilities

A **dependency** is external code your project relies on, usually installed through a package manager like pip. When a security researcher discovers a flaw in a popular library, it is assigned a public identifier called a **CVE** (Common Vulnerabilities and Exposures). If you are using the affected version, your application is vulnerable until you upgrade.

The problem compounds through **transitive dependencies**, the dependencies of your dependencies. You might never directly install a vulnerable library, yet still ship it because something you did install requires it. This is why you need automated tools to scan your full dependency tree.

```
# Scan installed packages for known vulnerabilities
pip install pip-audit
pip-audit

# Example output:
# Found 1 known vulnerability in 1 package
# Name     Version  ID             Fix Versions
# requests 2.19.0  CVE-2018-18074 2.20.0
```

The `pip-audit` tool compares your installed packages against public vulnerability databases and reports any matches. Here it has found that version 2.19.0 of `requests` contains a known vulnerability, and it tells you exactly which version fixes the problem. Running this scan regularly, ideally as an automated step in your pipeline, ensures you learn about vulnerable dependencies quickly rather than months after a fix was available. You should also pin your dependency versions so builds are reproducible and upgrades are deliberate.

Common Web Application Vulnerabilities

The security community maintains lists of the most frequent and dangerous flaws, the best known being the **OWASP Top Ten**. Learning these patterns lets you recognize and prevent the vast majority of real-world attacks. Two of the most important are injection and cross-site scripting.

SQL injection occurs when untrusted input is concatenated directly into a database query. The attacker supplies input containing SQL syntax that changes the meaning of the query, allowing them to read, modify, or delete data they should never touch.

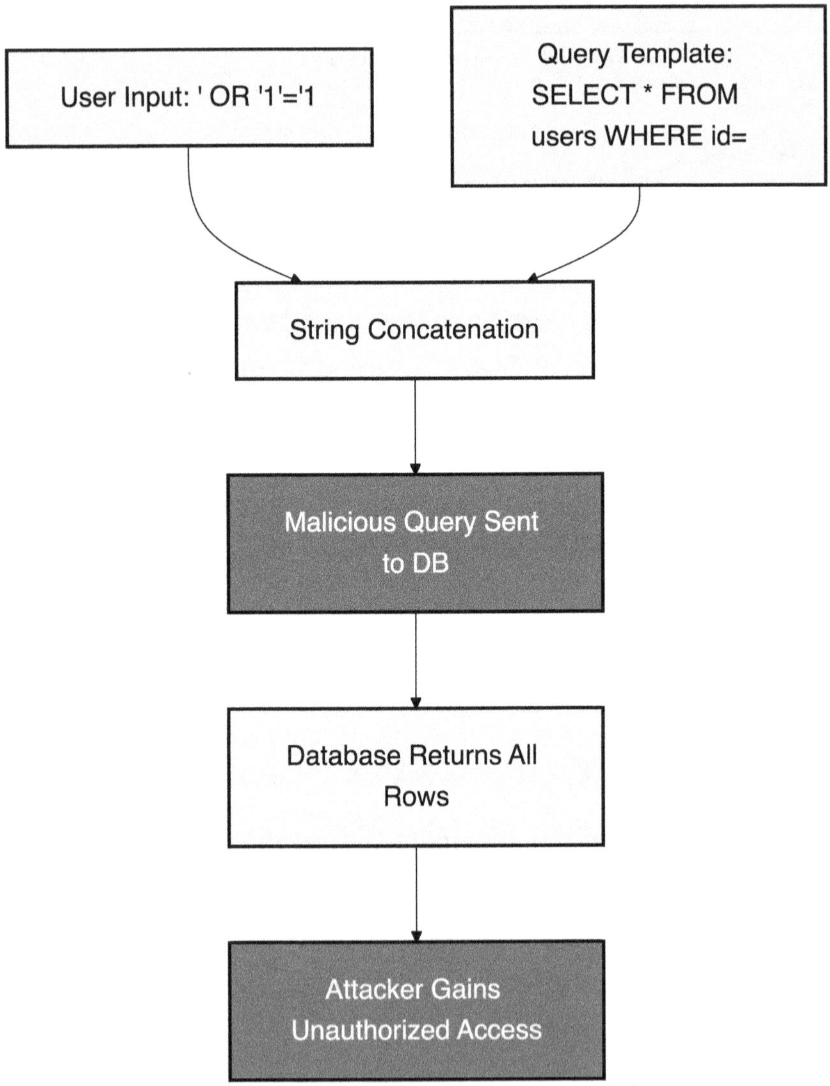

```python
# Vulnerable: user input is concatenated into the query
def get_user_insecure(username):
    query = "SELECT * FROM users WHERE username = '" + username + "'"
    return db.execute(query)

# An attacker supplies: ' OR '1'='1
# The query becomes: SELECT * FROM users WHERE username = '' OR '1'='1'
# which returns every user

# Secure: use parameterized queries
def get_user_secure(username):
    query = "SELECT * FROM users WHERE username = ?"
    return db.execute(query, (username,))
```

The insecure version builds its query by gluing strings together, so an attacker's input becomes part of the SQL command. The secure version uses a **parameterized query**, where the `?` placeholder tells the database to treat `username` strictly as data, never as executable SQL. This single practice eliminates SQL injection entirely, which is why you should use parameterized queries everywhere and never build queries through string concatenation.

Cross-site scripting, or **XSS**, is the injection equivalent for web pages. It happens when your application includes untrusted input in an HTML page without escaping it, letting an attacker inject malicious JavaScript that runs in other users' browsers. The defense is **output encoding**: converting characters like `<` and `>` into their safe HTML equivalents so the browser displays them as text rather than executing them. Most modern web frameworks and templating engines do this automatically, which is a strong reason to rely on them rather than assembling HTML by hand.

Secure Coding Practices

Beyond specific vulnerabilities, a handful of habits prevent whole categories of bugs. **Never trust input** applies everywhere, not just at login forms. **Encode output** based on the context where data will appear, whether HTML, a URL, or a shell command. **Handle errors carefully** so you do not leak internal details like stack traces or database structure to attackers, who use that information to plan further attacks.

```
def process_payment(request):
    try:
        charge_card(request.amount, request.token)
    except PaymentError as e:
        # Log full detail internally for debugging
        log.error("Payment failed: %s", e, exc_info=True)
        # Return a generic message to the user
        return {"error": "We could not process your payment. Please try again."}
```

This error handler logs the complete technical detail where your team can see it while returning a vague, harmless message to the user. An attacker learns nothing about your payment provider, internal exceptions, or code structure from the response. This balance, being verbose in private logs but terse in public responses, is a core secure coding habit.

Summary

- Dependencies, including transitive ones, carry inherited vulnerabilities that automated scanners like pip-audit help you find and fix.
- The OWASP Top Ten catalogs the most common web vulnerabilities, with injection and XSS among the most dangerous.
- Parameterized queries eliminate SQL injection by keeping user input strictly as data.
- Output encoding prevents cross-site scripting by rendering untrusted input as text rather than executable code.
- Careful error handling keeps internal details out of user-facing responses while preserving them in private logs.

10.4 Security Testing and the Software Supply Chain

Writing secure code is necessary but not sufficient. You also need to verify that your code stays secure over time, as features change and new vulnerabilities emerge. Just as automated tests catch functional regressions, automated security testing catches security regressions. And because so much of your software comes from outside your organization, you must extend your attention to the entire supply chain that produces and delivers your application.

In this section, you will learn the major categories of security testing, how to protect the software supply chain, and how the DevSecOps philosophy weaves security into the automated pipelines you studied in earlier chapters. These practices turn security from a periodic event into a continuous property of your delivery process.

Security Testing

Security testing comes in several complementary forms, each catching different kinds of problems. **Static Application Security Testing** (SAST) analyzes your source code without running it, looking for dangerous patterns like string-concatenated SQL queries or hardcoded secrets. Because it runs directly on code, it can point you to the exact line to fix and can run very early, even in your editor.

Dynamic Application Security Testing (DAST) tests a running application from the outside, sending malicious requests the way a real attacker would. It catches problems that only appear at runtime, such as misconfigured servers or authentication flaws, but it cannot tell you exactly where in the code the fault lies. **Software Composition Analysis** (SCA) is the dependency scanning you saw earlier, checking your libraries against vulnerability databases.

```
# A CI job that runs multiple security checks on every change
security-scan:
  script:
    - bandit -r ./src          # SAST: scan Python source for issues
    - pip-audit                # SCA: scan dependencies for CVEs
    - detect-secrets scan      # catch accidentally committed secrets
```

This continuous integration job runs three complementary scanners automatically on every change. `bandit` performs static analysis of Python source to find insecure patterns, `pip-audit` checks dependencies for known vulnerabilities, and `detect-secrets` searches for credentials that may have slipped into the code. Together they form a fast, automated safety net. No single tool catches everything, which is why layering multiple scan types reflects the same defense-in-depth principle you learned in the first lesson.

Software Supply Chain Security

The **software supply chain** is everything involved in producing and delivering your software: your source code, dependencies, build tools, container images, and deployment infrastructure. Attackers increasingly target the supply chain because compromising a single widely used component lets them reach thousands of downstream victims at once. High-profile incidents have shown that even build servers and popular open-source packages can be poisoned.

Protecting the supply chain involves several practices. You verify the integrity of dependencies using checksums or signatures so you know you received the genuine package. You produce a **Software Bill of Materials** (SBOM), a complete inventory of every component in your application, so that when a new vulnerability is announced you can instantly tell whether it affects you. You also secure your build pipeline itself, since a compromised build server can inject malicious code into otherwise clean source.

DevSecOps

DevSecOps extends the DevOps culture you studied earlier by integrating security into every stage of development and operations. Rather than treating security as a gate at the end, DevSecOps embeds automated security controls throughout the pipeline, giving developers fast feedback and making secure practices the path of least resistance.

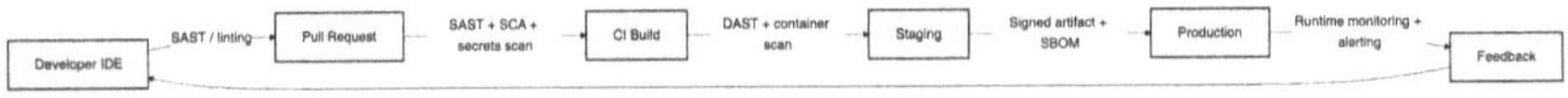

The key idea is that security controls appear at every stage. Developers get warnings in their editor as they type. Pull requests trigger SAST and dependency scans automatically. Builds produce an SBOM and verify signatures. Deployments run against hardened configurations, and running systems are monitored for suspicious behavior. Because these checks are automated and fast, they rarely slow developers down, and problems are caught close to the moment they are introduced.

DevSecOps also depends on culture, not just tooling. It works when developers, operations engineers, and security specialists share responsibility and collaborate rather than pointing fingers after an incident. This mirrors the collaborative spirit of DevOps in general: the goal is to make doing the secure thing also the easy and default thing.

Summary

- Security testing spans SAST for source code, DAST for running applications, and SCA for dependencies, each catching different flaws.
- Layering multiple automated scanners in CI applies defense in depth to your testing process.
- Supply chain security protects the whole production process through integrity checks, an SBOM, and hardened build pipelines.
- DevSecOps embeds automated security controls at every pipeline stage so feedback is fast and secure practices become the default.

Chapter Summary

This chapter reframed security from an afterthought into a core engineering discipline that runs through the entire software lifecycle. You began by seeing that security is a whole-system property owned by every engineer, and that designing with principles like least privilege and defense in depth prevents flaws before they are ever written. Threat modeling gave you a structured way to reason about attackers during design, when fixes are cheapest. These foundational ideas set the direction for everything that followed.

From there you moved into concrete mechanisms and patterns. You learned how to authenticate users with salted hashes, authorize actions on the server, validate untrusted input, and protect sensitive data and secrets. You studied the vulnerabilities that recur across real applications, from SQL injection and cross-site scripting to the risks hidden in your dependency tree, and you saw the specific coding practices that neutralize each one. The common thread is that most security defenses are not exotic; they are disciplined habits applied consistently.

Finally, you connected security to the automated engineering practices from earlier in the course. Security testing, supply chain protection, and DevSecOps turn security into a continuous, automated property of your pipeline rather than a manual gate at the end. You can now design safer systems, write code that resists common attacks, evaluate the risks in code you did not write, and build pipelines that enforce security automatically. These capabilities make you a more complete and trustworthy engineer, whatever kind of software you go on to build.

Chapter Lab: Identifying and Correcting Security Weaknesses in a Sample Application

In this lab, you will examine a small but realistic application that contains several deliberately planted security weaknesses, ranging from unsafe database queries and missing authorization checks to hardcoded secrets and unvalidated input. You will apply the threat modeling mindset and secure coding practices from this chapter to locate each weakness and rewrite the affected code so that it is safe. This exercise brings together authentication, authorization, input validation, secrets management, and vulnerability recognition into a single hands-on challenge that mirrors the kind of security review you will perform on real projects.

Chapter 11: DevOps, Continuous Delivery, and Software Maintenance

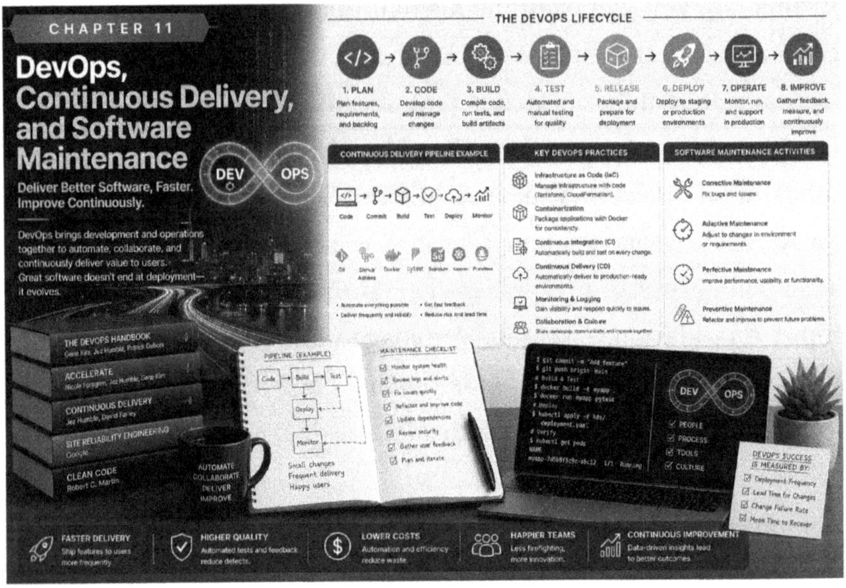

Building software is only half the story. In the earlier chapters, you learned how to design, write, and test code. But writing quality code means little if you cannot deliver it to users reliably, keep it running once it is live, and maintain it over the years that follow. Most of a software product's life is spent not in initial development but in the long stretch afterward — fixing bugs, adding features, and keeping the system healthy. This chapter is about that reality.

In this chapter, you will learn how modern teams bridge the gap between writing code and running it in production. You will explore **DevOps**, a culture and set of practices that unites developers and operations staff. You will see how continuous integration and continuous delivery automate the path from a code commit to a running application. You will learn about containers, infrastructure as code, and the deployment strategies teams use to release safely. Finally, you will study what happens after release: the software maintenance lifecycle, monitoring and observability, and the hard work of managing legacy systems.

By the end of this chapter, you will understand how software moves from a developer's machine to real users, and how to keep it working long after launch. These skills tie together everything you have learned about design, testing, and collaboration. They turn a working program into a dependable product.

11.1 What Is DevOps?

For decades, the people who wrote software and the people who ran it belonged to separate worlds. Developers built features and threw them "over the wall" to an operations team, who then struggled to deploy and support code they had never seen. When something broke, each side blamed the other. This friction slowed releases and frustrated everyone involved.

In this section, you will learn what DevOps is and why it emerged. You will see how it merges development and operations into a shared responsibility, and you will meet **continuous integration**, one of the foundational technical practices that makes DevOps work in daily life.

What Is DevOps?

DevOps is a culture and a set of practices that combine software development (Dev) and IT operations (Ops) to shorten the delivery cycle and improve software quality. It is less a specific tool than a way of working. The core idea is simple: the people who build software should also share responsibility for running it, and the whole delivery process should be automated as much as possible.

Think of a restaurant where the chefs never see the dining room. They cook dishes and hand them off, never learning which meals customers enjoyed or sent back. DevOps tears down that wall. The chefs and the servers work as one team, sharing feedback in real time and improving the experience together. In software terms, this means faster feedback, fewer surprises in production, and a culture where quality is everyone's job.

DevOps rests on a few key values: collaboration between teams, automation of repetitive tasks, continuous feedback from monitoring and users, and a willingness to improve the process itself over time. These values matter because software today changes constantly. A team that can safely release many times a day will outpace one that releases twice a year.

Development and Operations

To appreciate DevOps, you need to understand the two disciplines it unites. **Development** is the work of designing, coding, and testing software features. **Operations** is the work of deploying, running, scaling, and monitoring that software in production environments.

These two roles have naturally different incentives. Developers are rewarded for shipping change – new features, bug fixes, improvements. Operations staff are rewarded for stability – keeping systems up and avoiding outages. Left unchecked, these incentives pull in opposite directions. Developers want to release faster; operations wants to release less often because every change carries risk.

DevOps aligns these incentives by making both groups responsible for the same outcome: working software in the hands of users. When developers know they will help support what they build, they write more robust, observable code. When operations staff participate early in design, they catch deployment problems before they become emergencies. The wall comes down, and the whole system improves.

Continuous Integration

The first technical practice that makes DevOps real is **continuous integration** (CI). Continuous integration is the practice of merging every developer's code changes into a shared main branch frequently — often several times a day — and automatically building and testing the result each time.

Before CI, teams sometimes worked in isolation for weeks, then merged all their code together in a painful event known as "integration hell." Conflicts piled up, and bugs from combined changes were nearly impossible to trace. CI solves this by integrating small changes often. Each merge is small, so problems are small and easy to fix.

The heart of CI is automation. A **CI server** watches your shared repository. When a developer pushes new code, the server automatically pulls the changes, compiles the project, and runs the full test suite. If anything fails, the team is notified immediately.

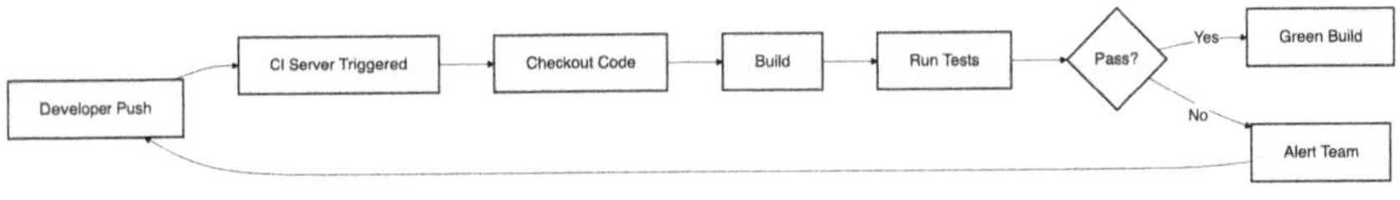

Here is a simple example of a test suite that a CI server would run automatically on every push:

```python
# calculator.py
def add(a, b):
    return a + b

def divide(a, b):
    if b == 0:
        raise ValueError("Cannot divide by zero")
    return a / b


# test_calculator.py
import pytest
from calculator import add, divide

def test_add_positive_numbers():
    assert add(2, 3) == 5

def test_divide_normal():
    assert divide(10, 2) == 5

def test_divide_by_zero_raises():
    with pytest.raises(ValueError):
        divide(10, 0)
```

This code defines two small functions and three tests that verify their behavior. In a CI setup, you would never run these tests only on your own machine. Instead, every time anyone pushes code, the CI server runs `pytest` and reports the results. If someone accidentally breaks the `divide` function, the `test_divide_by_zero_raises` test fails, and the team learns immediately — not weeks later when a customer hits the bug. This fast feedback loop is what makes CI so valuable.

Summary

- **DevOps** is a culture and set of practices that unite software development and operations to deliver software faster and more reliably.
- Development focuses on building change, while operations focuses on stability; DevOps aligns both around the shared goal of working software in production.
- **Continuous integration** means merging small code changes frequently and automatically building and testing each merge.
- A **CI server** watches the repository, runs the build and test suite on every push, and reports pass or fail immediately.
- Fast, automated feedback prevents "integration hell" and catches bugs early, when they are cheapest to fix.

11.2 Continuous Delivery and Deployment

Continuous integration gets your code merged and tested automatically, but it stops short of putting that code in front of users. The next step is to automate the delivery process itself. In this section, you will learn the difference between continuous delivery and continuous deployment — two terms that sound alike but mean importantly different things.

You will also see how build automation and automated testing pipelines form the backbone of these practices. By the end, you will understand how a single code commit can flow safely all the way to production with minimal human effort.

Continuous Delivery

Continuous delivery (CD) extends continuous integration by ensuring that your code is always in a deployable state. After the CI stage builds and tests the code, the delivery pipeline packages it and moves it through further automated checks so that it is ready to release at any moment. The key word is *ready*. With continuous delivery, releasing to production is a business decision made by a human clicking a button — not a technical scramble.

Imagine a delivery truck loaded, fueled, and parked at the loading dock. It can leave the instant someone gives the word. Continuous delivery keeps your software in that state permanently. The release itself might happen once a day or once a week, but the software is always prepared.

This matters because it removes fear from releasing. When deployment is fully automated and rehearsed on every change, the act of releasing becomes routine and low-risk. Teams practicing continuous delivery release far more often than those who treat deployment as a rare, manual event.

Continuous Deployment

Continuous deployment goes one step further than continuous delivery. In continuous deployment, every change that passes all automated stages is released to production automatically, with no human approval step at all. If the tests pass, the code goes live.

The difference is subtle but crucial. Continuous *delivery* keeps the software ready to release, but a person decides when. Continuous *deployment* removes even that decision — the pipeline is trusted to release on its own. This requires enormous confidence in your automated tests and monitoring, because there is no human safety net before code reaches users.

Continuous deployment suits products that release frequently and can tolerate a fast rollback if something goes wrong, such as web applications. Systems with strict regulatory approval or high consequences for failure often stop at continuous delivery, keeping a human in the loop.

Build Automation

Underneath both practices lies **build automation**: the use of scripts and tools to compile code, install dependencies, run tests, and package the application without manual steps. A build that requires a developer to remember a sequence of commands is fragile and error-prone. An automated build runs the same way every time.

Here is a small example of a build script expressed as a set of dependency-management and packaging commands you might automate:

```
# tasks.py — a simple automated build definition using invoke
from invoke import task

@task
def install(c):
    c.run("pip install -r requirements.txt")

@task
def test(c):
    c.run("pytest --verbose")

@task(pre=[install, test])
def build(c):
    c.run("python -m build")
    print("Build complete: package created in dist/")
```

This script defines three tasks. The `install` task installs dependencies, `test` runs the test suite, and `build` depends on both — meaning it automatically runs `install` and `test` before packaging the application. When you run `invoke build`, every step executes in the correct order automatically. Because the process is codified, it runs identically on your laptop, on a teammate's machine, and on the CI server. That consistency is the whole point of build automation.

Automated Testing Pipelines

An **automated testing pipeline** is a sequence of testing stages that a code change must pass through, each acting as a quality gate. Rather than running all tests at once, a pipeline organizes them into stages that grow more thorough and more expensive as the code advances.

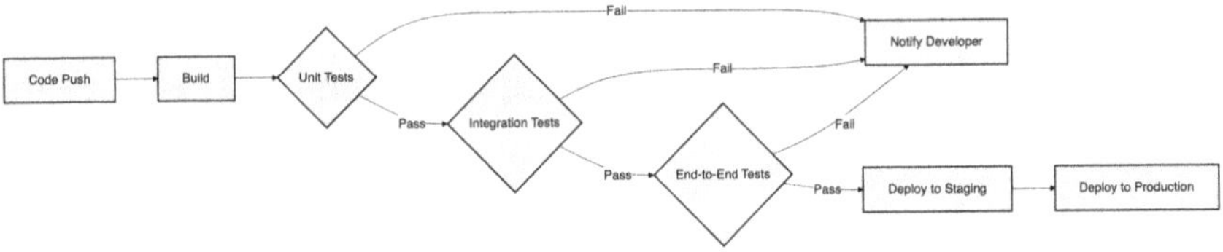

A typical pipeline runs fast unit tests first, because they give the quickest feedback. If those pass, it runs slower integration tests that check how components work together. Later stages might run end-to-end tests against a fully deployed copy of the application. Each stage must pass before the next begins, and a failure at any stage stops the pipeline immediately. This ordering saves time and resources — there is no point running a slow, expensive test suite on code that already failed a basic unit test.

Summary

- **Continuous delivery** keeps software always in a deployable state, with a human deciding when to release.
- **Continuous deployment** automatically releases every change that passes all stages, with no manual approval.
- **Build automation** uses scripts to compile, test, and package software consistently every time.
- An **automated testing pipeline** organizes tests into ordered quality gates, running fast checks before slow, expensive ones.
- A failure at any stage stops the pipeline, preventing broken code from advancing toward production.

11.3 CI/CD Pipelines and Containers

You now understand the ideas behind continuous integration and continuous delivery. This section shows how those ideas come together in a single, concrete structure: the **CI/CD pipeline**. You will also meet containers, a technology that solves one of the oldest problems in software deployment — the frustrating gap between "it works on my machine" and "it works in production."

By the end of this section, you will be able to read a basic pipeline configuration and write a simple container definition. These two tools work hand in hand, and together they form the practical foundation of modern software delivery.

CI/CD Pipelines

A **CI/CD pipeline** is an automated, end-to-end process that takes a code change from commit all the way to a deployable or deployed release, passing through a defined series of stages. It combines the continuous integration and continuous delivery practices you have already learned into one automated workflow.

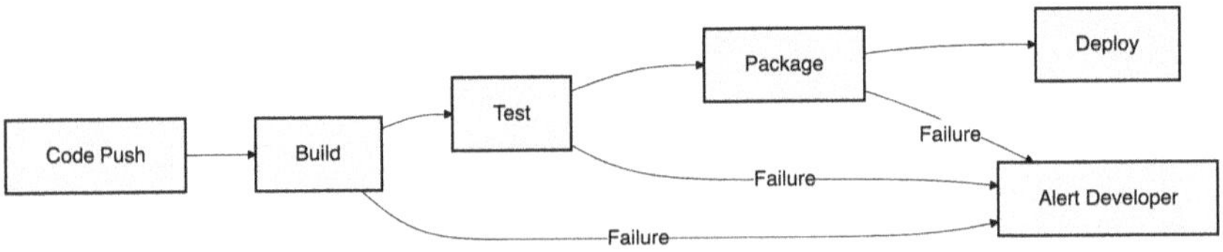

Most pipelines are defined as code, usually in a configuration file stored alongside your application. Here is a simplified pipeline definition in the YAML format used by many CI systems:

```yaml
# .github/workflows/ci.yml
name: CI Pipeline
on: [push]
jobs:
  build-and-test:
    runs-on: ubuntu-latest
    steps:
      - name: Check out code
        uses: actions/checkout@v4
      - name: Set up Python
        uses: actions/setup-python@v5
        with:
          python-version: "3.12"
      - name: Install dependencies
        run: pip install -r requirements.txt
      - name: Run tests
        run: pytest
```

This configuration tells the CI system to run a job every time code is pushed. The job checks out the code, sets up Python, installs dependencies, and runs the tests. Each step runs in order, and if any step fails, the pipeline stops and reports the failure. Because the pipeline lives in your repository as a file, it is versioned, reviewable, and reproducible just like your application code. Anyone on the team can see exactly how the software is built and tested.

Containers

A **container** is a lightweight, standalone package that bundles an application together with everything it needs to run — code, runtime, libraries, and system tools. The result runs the same way regardless of where you deploy it. Containers solve the notorious "it works on my machine" problem, where software runs on a developer's laptop but fails in production because of subtle environment differences.

Think of a shipping container in global trade. Before standardized containers, loading a ship meant handling countless odd-shaped crates and barrels, each requiring special care. The standard container changed everything: any container fits any ship, crane, or truck. Software containers bring that same standardization. Your application, packaged as a container, runs identically on any machine that can run containers.

Containers are more lightweight than traditional virtual machines because they share the host operating system's kernel rather than each running a full operating system of their own. This makes them fast to start and efficient to run, which is why teams often run many containers on a single server.

Introduction to Docker

Docker is the most widely used tool for building and running containers. With Docker, you describe your application's environment in a text file called a **Dockerfile**, and Docker uses that file to build a container image.

Here is a Dockerfile for a simple Python web application:

```
# Dockerfile
FROM python:3.12-slim

WORKDIR /app

COPY requirements.txt .
RUN pip install --no-cache-dir -r requirements.txt

COPY . .

EXPOSE 8000

CMD ["python", "app.py"]
```

This Dockerfile builds a container step by step. The `FROM` line starts from an official slim Python image, giving you a known, consistent base. `WORKDIR` sets the working directory inside the container. Copying `requirements.txt` and running `pip install` as separate steps lets Docker cache the dependency layer, so rebuilds are faster when only your code changes. The final `COPY . .` brings in your application code, `EXPOSE` documents the port the app uses, and `CMD` specifies the command that runs when the container starts. Once built, this image runs identically on any machine with Docker installed — your laptop, a teammate's computer, or a production server.

Summary

- A **CI/CD pipeline** automates the entire path from code commit to release, combining integration and delivery into one workflow.
- Pipelines are defined as code in configuration files, making them versioned, reviewable, and reproducible.
- A **container** bundles an application with all its dependencies so it runs identically everywhere.
- Containers are lighter than virtual machines because they share the host operating system's kernel.
- **Docker** builds containers from a **Dockerfile**, a text file describing the application's environment step by step.

11.4 Infrastructure and Deployment Strategies

Once your application is packaged and your pipeline is running, you face a new set of questions. How do you set up the servers and networks it runs on? How do you keep separate environments for testing and production? And how do you release updates without breaking things for users? This section answers those questions.

You will learn about infrastructure as code, the practice of managing servers with scripts instead of manual clicks. You will explore the standard environments that code passes through on its way to users, and you will study the deployment strategies teams use to release safely. Finally, you will see how security fits into the picture through **DevSecOps**.

Infrastructure as Code

Infrastructure as code (IaC) is the practice of defining and managing your servers, networks, and other infrastructure using machine-readable configuration files rather than manual setup. Instead of logging into a cloud console and clicking buttons to create a server, you write a file describing the server you want, and a tool creates it for you.

The benefits are significant. Because your infrastructure is defined in code, it is versioned in source control, reviewable by teammates, and repeatable. If a server is destroyed, you can recreate it exactly from the file. If you need ten identical servers, you run the same definition ten times. Manual setup, by contrast, is slow, error-prone, and nearly impossible to reproduce exactly.

Here is a simplified example of infrastructure defined declaratively:

```yaml
# infrastructure.yml - a declarative infrastructure definition
web_server:
  image: "ubuntu-22.04"
  size: "medium"
  count: 3
  region: "us-east-1"
  tags:
    role: "web"
    environment: "production"

database:
  engine: "postgresql"
  version: "15"
  storage_gb: 100
  backup_enabled: true
```

This file describes the desired state of your infrastructure: three medium web servers in one region and a PostgreSQL database with backups enabled. You do not write step-by-step instructions for creating these resources; you simply declare what you want, and the IaC tool figures out how to make reality match. This declarative approach means you can read the file and instantly understand your entire infrastructure — a huge advantage over infrastructure that exists only as a series of forgotten manual actions.

Development, Test, and Production Environments

Software does not go straight from a developer's machine to users. It passes through a series of **environments**, each a separate, isolated copy of the system used for a different purpose. The three standard environments are development, test, and production.

The **development environment** is where programmers write and try out code, often on their own machines. The **test environment** (sometimes called staging) closely mirrors production and is used to run automated tests and manual checks against realistic conditions. The **production environment** is the live system that real users interact with. Keeping these separate is essential. It means you can experiment freely in development, verify thoroughly in test, and protect the stability of production.

Using containers and infrastructure as code makes these environments consistent with one another. When each environment is built from the same definitions, a bug that only appears "in production" becomes far less likely, because production is no longer a mysterious special case.

Deployment Strategies

A **deployment strategy** is a technique for releasing a new version of your software while minimizing risk and downtime. The naive approach — shutting down the old version and starting the new one — causes downtime and offers no easy way back if the new version is broken. Better strategies avoid these problems.

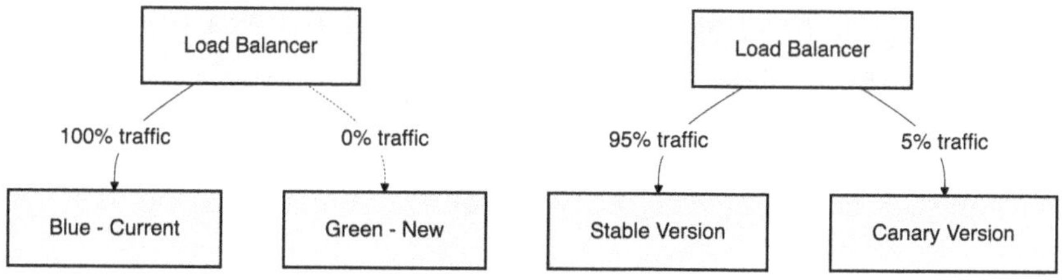

Two of the most common strategies are blue-green and canary deployment. In a **blue-green deployment**, you run two identical production environments, called blue and green. One serves live traffic while the other is idle. You deploy the new version to the idle environment, test it, then switch all traffic to it at once. If something goes wrong, you switch back instantly — a one-step rollback. In a **canary deployment**, you release the new version to a small slice of users first, watch how it behaves, and gradually increase the share of traffic if all looks well. The name comes from the "canary in a coal mine," an early warning of trouble. Canary deployments limit the blast radius of a bad release, because only a few users are exposed before problems are caught.

DevSecOps

DevSecOps extends DevOps by building security into every stage of the pipeline rather than treating it as a final checkpoint. The name adds "Sec" for security in the middle of "DevOps," reflecting that security should live at the heart of the process.

Traditionally, security reviews happened at the very end, right before release. This created a bottleneck and often surfaced serious problems too late to fix cheaply. DevSecOps "shifts security left," meaning it moves security checks earlier in the pipeline. Automated tools scan code for vulnerabilities on every commit, check dependencies for known security flaws, and enforce secure configurations. By catching security issues early and automatically, teams fix them when they are small, and security becomes a shared responsibility rather than a gate at the end.

Summary

- **Infrastructure as code** defines servers and networks in versioned configuration files, making infrastructure repeatable and reviewable.
- Software passes through separate **development**, **test**, and **production** environments, each isolated for its own purpose.
- A **deployment strategy** releases new versions while minimizing risk and downtime.
- **Blue-green deployment** switches all traffic between two environments for instant rollback; **canary deployment** exposes a small slice of users first.
- **DevSecOps** builds automated security checks into every pipeline stage, shifting security earlier in the process.

11.5 The Software Maintenance Lifecycle

A common misconception is that software is "finished" when it launches. In reality, launch is the beginning of the longest phase of a system's life. Studies have consistently shown that the majority of a software product's total cost is spent after its first release, on maintenance. Understanding this phase is essential to being a professional engineer.

In this section, you will learn about the software maintenance lifecycle and the four recognized categories of maintenance work. Knowing these categories helps you plan, communicate about, and budget for the ongoing work that keeps software useful and healthy over its lifetime.

The Software Maintenance Lifecycle

The **software maintenance lifecycle** is the ongoing, repeating process of modifying software after it has been deployed. Unlike initial development, which has a beginning and an end, maintenance is a continuous cycle that lasts as long as the software is in use.

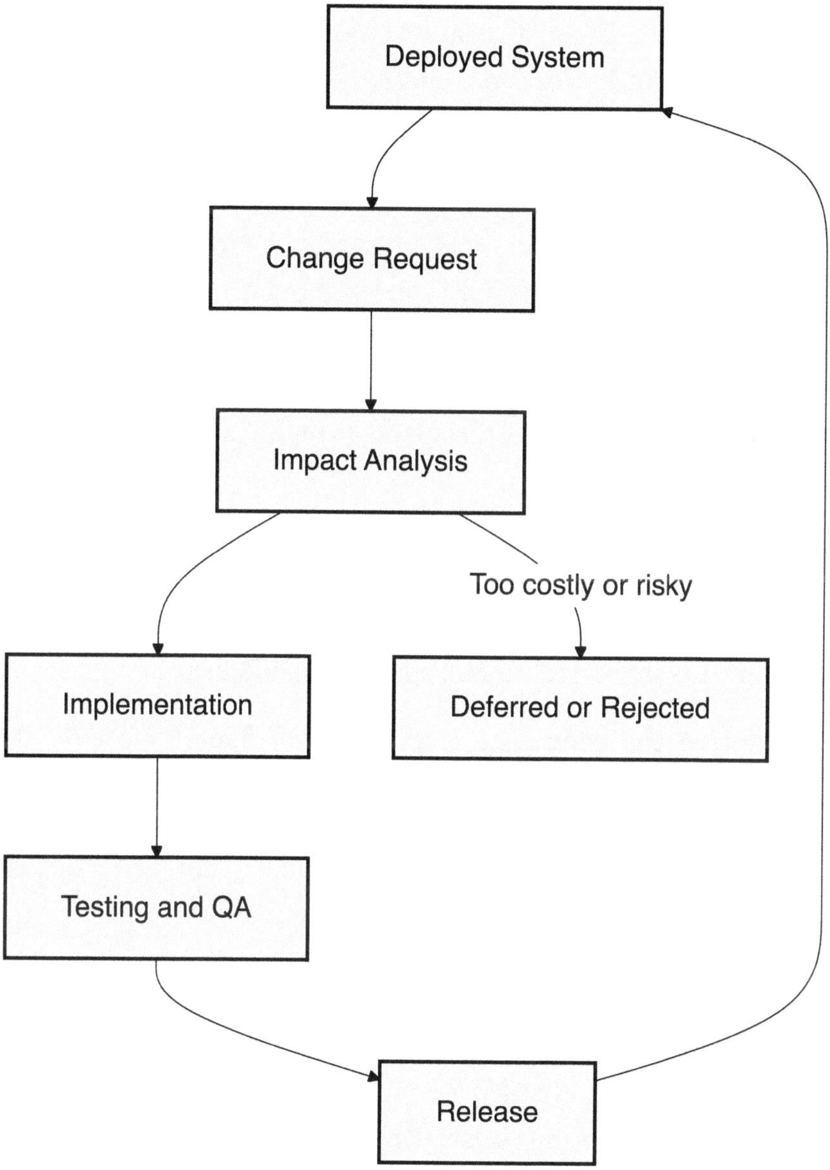

The cycle typically flows through several repeating steps. A change is requested — perhaps a bug report from a user or a new requirement from the business. The team analyzes the request to understand its impact and cost. They implement the change, test it thoroughly, and release it. That release, in turn, often triggers new requests, and the cycle continues. This loop mirrors the development practices you have already learned; maintenance is simply development that continues over a product's whole life.

Understanding maintenance as a lifecycle changes how you think about your work. Every feature you write today will be maintained by someone — possibly you — for years. This is why the earlier chapters emphasized clean design, tests, and documentation. Those investments pay off repeatedly throughout the maintenance lifecycle.

Corrective and Adaptive Maintenance

Software maintenance is traditionally divided into four categories. The first two are corrective and adaptive maintenance.

Corrective maintenance is the work of fixing defects — the bugs discovered after release. When a user reports that a feature crashes or produces the wrong result, the work to diagnose and fix it is corrective maintenance. This is what most people picture when they think of maintenance, but it is only one part of the whole.

Adaptive maintenance is the work of keeping software running as its environment changes around it, even when the software's own behavior stays the same. Operating systems get upgraded, third-party libraries release new versions, browsers change how they work, and legal regulations shift. Adaptive maintenance updates your software to stay compatible with this changing world. For example, when a payment provider deprecates an old

API version, you must update your integration even though your feature works exactly as before.

Perfective and Preventive Maintenance

The remaining two categories are perfective and preventive maintenance. These are proactive rather than reactive, and they are easy to neglect under deadline pressure.

Perfective maintenance improves the software based on evolving needs — adding new features, enhancing existing ones, or improving performance and usability. Much of what teams call "new development" on an existing product is actually perfective maintenance. When users request a report feature or ask that a slow page load faster, satisfying those requests is perfective work.

Preventive maintenance is work done to prevent future problems, improving the software's internal quality so it stays maintainable. This includes refactoring messy code, updating outdated dependencies before they cause trouble, and improving tests and documentation. Preventive maintenance rarely produces a visible feature, which is why it is often skipped — but neglecting it leads directly to the technical debt and legacy problems you will study later in this chapter.

Summary

- The **software maintenance lifecycle** is a continuous, repeating process of modifying software after deployment, not a one-time handoff.
- Most of a software product's total cost is spent on maintenance, making it a central concern for engineers.
- **Corrective maintenance** fixes defects, while **adaptive maintenance** keeps software compatible with a changing environment.
- **Perfective maintenance** adds and improves features based on evolving needs.
- **Preventive maintenance** improves internal quality to avoid future problems and is often neglected despite its long-term value.

11.6 Monitoring and Observability

You cannot maintain what you cannot see. Once software is running in production, you need to know how it is behaving – whether it is healthy, how fast it responds, and what happens when something goes wrong. This is the domain of monitoring and observability, and it is where operations work becomes concrete.

In this section, you will learn about logging, monitoring, and observability, and how they differ. You will explore application metrics and learn the basics of troubleshooting live systems and managing incidents. These skills let you understand your running software and respond calmly when problems arise.

Logging

Logging is the practice of recording events that happen while your software runs, writing them to a durable record you can review later. A **log** is a timestamped message describing something that occurred – a request received, an error raised, a task completed. Logs are your software's diary, and they are often the first thing you reach for when something goes wrong.

Here is an example of logging in Python:

```python
import logging

logging.basicConfig(
    level=logging.INFO,
    format="%(asctime)s %(levelname)s %(message)s"
)
logger = logging.getLogger(__name__)

def process_order(order_id, amount):
    logger.info("Processing order %s for $%.2f", order_id, amount)
    if amount <= 0:
        logger.error("Invalid amount for order %s: %.2f", order_id, amount)
        raise ValueError("Amount must be positive")
    logger.info("Order %s processed successfully", order_id)
    return True
```

This code configures Python's built-in `logging` module and uses it to record what happens during order processing. The `logger.info` calls record normal events, while `logger.error` records a problem. Notice the use of **log levels** — `INFO` for routine events and `ERROR` for serious issues. Log levels let you filter messages, showing only errors in a busy production system or all detail when debugging. Good logging like this turns an opaque running system into one you can inspect after the fact.

Monitoring

Monitoring is the practice of continuously collecting and checking data about a running system to confirm it is healthy and to alert you when it is not. Where logs record individual events, monitoring watches overall trends and thresholds. A monitoring system might track the rate of errors and automatically alert the on-call engineer if it spikes.

Monitoring answers questions you already know to ask: Is the server up? Is response time within acceptable limits? Is disk space running low? You define these checks in advance and set thresholds that trigger alerts. Effective monitoring means you learn about problems from your tools, not from angry users — a crucial difference in maintaining a professional service.

Observability

Observability is the broader ability to understand a system's internal state from the data it produces, including situations you did not anticipate in advance. Monitoring tells you *that* something is wrong; observability helps you understand *why*. The distinction matters as systems grow complex, because you cannot predict every failure mode in advance.

Observability is often described as resting on three pillars: **logs** (records of events), **metrics** (numeric measurements over time), and **traces** (records of how a single request flows through the system). Together, these let you explore an unexpected problem, asking new questions of your data without having to add new instrumentation first. A highly observable system is one where you can debug novel issues from the information it already emits.

Application Metrics

Application metrics are numeric measurements of your software's behavior collected over time. Common metrics include request rate, error rate, response latency, and resource usage such as memory and CPU. Metrics are compact and efficient, making them ideal for spotting trends and triggering alerts.

Here is a simple example of tracking a metric in application code:

```python
import time

class MetricsTracker:
    def __init__(self):
        self.request_count = 0
        self.error_count = 0
        self.total_latency = 0.0

    def record_request(self, duration, failed=False):
        self.request_count += 1
        self.total_latency += duration
        if failed:
            self.error_count += 1

    def average_latency(self):
        if self.request_count == 0:
            return 0.0
        return self.total_latency / self.request_count

    def error_rate(self):
        if self.request_count == 0:
            return 0.0
        return self.error_count / self.request_count
```

This class accumulates metrics as requests are handled. Each call to `record_request` updates the counts and total latency, and the helper methods compute averages on demand. In a real system, these numbers would be sent to a dedicated metrics platform that stores them over time and graphs them. The value is in the trend: a slowly rising `average_latency` or a climbing `error_rate` warns you of a developing problem long before it becomes an outage.

Troubleshooting Production Systems and Incident Management

When something does go wrong in production, you need a calm, structured approach. **Troubleshooting** is the process of diagnosing and resolving a problem in a live system, and **incident**

management is the organized practice of responding to service disruptions.

A good incident response follows a clear sequence:

1. **Detect** the incident, ideally through monitoring rather than user reports.
2. **Assess** its severity and impact on users.
3. **Mitigate** the immediate damage, often by rolling back a recent deployment or restoring service quickly, even before the root cause is known.
4. **Resolve** the underlying problem once service is stable.
5. **Review** the incident afterward in a blameless post-mortem to learn from it.

The most important principle here is to restore service first and investigate later. Users care that the system works, not why it broke. The **blameless post-mortem** — a review focused on improving the system rather than blaming individuals — turns each incident into a lesson that makes the system more resilient. This mindset closes the DevOps loop, feeding what you learn in production back into how you build software.

Summary

- **Logging** records timestamped events, using **log levels** to distinguish routine information from serious errors.
- **Monitoring** continuously checks known health indicators and alerts you when thresholds are crossed.
- **Observability** is the broader ability to understand *why* a system misbehaves, resting on logs, metrics, and traces.
- **Application metrics** are numeric measurements over time that reveal trends and trigger early warnings.
- Effective **incident management** restores service first, investigates later, and learns through blameless post-mortems.

11.7 Managing Legacy Systems

Every successful piece of software eventually becomes old. The code that once seemed clean grows tangled as requirements change and shortcuts accumulate. The technologies it depends on age. Yet these systems often run critical business operations and cannot simply be thrown away. Managing them is one of the most common and important challenges in a professional engineer's career.

In this section, you will learn how to think about technical debt, how to refactor legacy code safely, and how to modernize old systems using the strangler pattern. You will also learn how to plan the responsible retirement of software through deprecation and end-of-life planning. These skills will serve you throughout your career, because you will spend far more time working with existing software than building from scratch.

Managing Technical Debt

Technical debt is the implied future cost of choosing an easy or quick solution now instead of a better one that would take longer. The metaphor is financial: like monetary debt, technical debt lets you move faster in the short term but accrues "interest" – the extra effort every future change requires because of the shortcut you took.

Not all technical debt is bad. Sometimes taking on debt deliberately, to meet an important deadline, is the right business decision. The danger lies in debt that is invisible, unmanaged, and never repaid. When debt accumulates unchecked, the system becomes brittle, changes grow risky, and development slows to a crawl.

Managing technical debt means making it visible and deliberate. Teams track known debt, discuss its cost openly, and pay it down through the preventive maintenance you learned about earlier. The goal is not zero debt, which is unrealistic, but a healthy balance where debt is understood and kept under control.

Refactoring Legacy Systems

A **legacy system** is old software that remains in use and often lacks the tests, documentation, or clean structure that make code safe to change. **Refactoring** is the process of improving the internal structure of code without changing its external behavior. Refactoring legacy systems is delicate work, because the very qualities that make a system "legacy" also make it risky to modify.

The safest approach is to add tests before you change anything. If a legacy system lacks tests, you write **characterization tests** – tests that capture the system's current behavior, whatever it is, so you have a safety net. Only then do you make small, incremental improvements, running the tests after each change to confirm you have not broken anything.

```python
# A characterization test captures existing behavior as-is
def calculate_discount(customer_type, amount):
    # Legacy code with unclear original intent
    if customer_type == "premium" and amount > 100:
        return amount * 0.8
    elif customer_type == "premium":
        return amount * 0.9
    return amount

def test_premium_large_order_gets_20_percent_off():
    # We are documenting what the code DOES, not what it should do
    assert calculate_discount("premium", 200) == 160

def test_premium_small_order_gets_10_percent_off():
    assert calculate_discount("premium", 50) == 45

def test_regular_customer_gets_no_discount():
    assert calculate_discount("regular", 200) == 200
```

These tests do not judge whether the discount logic is correct; they simply record what the existing code does for various inputs. That is the point of a characterization test. Once these tests pass, you can safely refactor `calculate_discount` — renaming variables, extracting functions, or simplifying the logic — confident that the tests will catch any accidental change in behavior. This safety net is what makes refactoring legacy code possible rather than reckless.

Software Modernization and the Strangler Pattern

Sometimes a legacy system is too large or risky to refactor in place, yet too important to rewrite all at once. A full rewrite is one of the most dangerous projects a team can attempt, because it must reproduce years of accumulated behavior perfectly while the old system keeps changing. The **strangler pattern** offers a safer path.

The **strangler pattern** modernizes a system gradually by building new functionality around the old system and slowly redirecting work to the new code, until the old system can be safely retired. The name comes from the strangler fig, a plant that grows around a host tree and eventually replaces it. A routing layer sits in front of both the old and new systems, sending some requests to the new service and the rest to the legacy system.

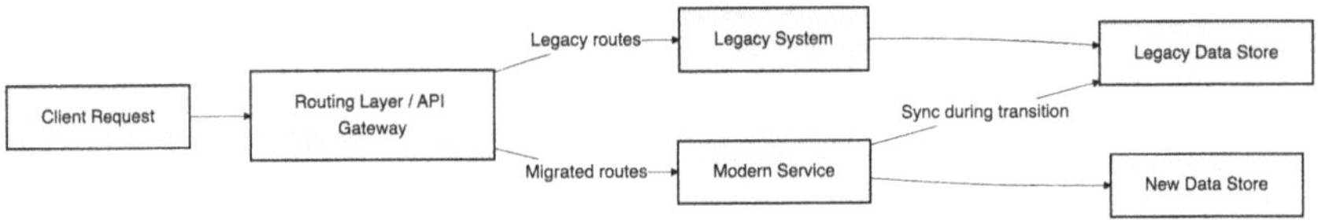

The great advantage of this approach is that it delivers value incrementally and reduces risk. Instead of a single terrifying cutover, you migrate one piece at a time, verifying each step in production before moving on. If a new piece has problems, only that slice of functionality is affected, and you can route back to the legacy system. Over time, more and more traffic flows to the new system until the old one handles nothing and can be shut off.

Deprecation and End-of-Life Planning

Eventually, some software or features must be retired. **Deprecation** is the process of formally marking a feature, API, or system as obsolete and discouraging its use, while still supporting it for a transition period. Deprecation is a courtesy to your users: it warns them that something will go away and gives them time to adapt before it does.

End-of-life planning is the process of managing the complete retirement of software, including migrating users off it, preserving any needed data, and finally shutting it down. Responsible end-of-life planning communicates timelines clearly, provides migration paths, and avoids sudden disruptions. A well-managed retirement is a sign of engineering maturity, closing the loop on the full lifecycle you have studied — from a code commit, through delivery and monitoring, all the way to a dignified end.

Summary

- **Technical debt** is the future cost of quick solutions; the goal is to keep it visible and managed, not to eliminate it entirely.
- Refactoring a **legacy system** safely requires adding **characterization tests** first to protect existing behavior.
- The **strangler pattern** modernizes systems incrementally by routing work to new code until the old system can be retired.
- **Deprecation** formally marks features as obsolete while supporting them during a transition period.
- **End-of-life planning** manages the complete, orderly retirement of software, including data preservation and user migration.

Chapter Summary

This chapter followed software through the second half of its life – the journey from a finished feature to a running, maintained product. You began with DevOps, the culture that unites development and operations, and saw how continuous integration turns frequent, small merges into a source of fast feedback. From there, continuous delivery and deployment automated the path to release, and CI/CD pipelines, containers, and Docker gave that path a concrete shape. Each of these ideas builds on the last: integration makes delivery possible, delivery makes safe deployment possible, and containers make it all reproducible across environments.

The second half of the chapter shifted from delivering software to keeping it alive. Infrastructure as code and deployment strategies let you release safely, while the software maintenance lifecycle reframed launch as a beginning rather than an end. Monitoring and observability gave you the eyes to understand a running system, and the study of legacy systems gave you tools – managing technical debt, refactoring with characterization tests, and the strangler pattern – to keep aging software valuable. You can now reason about not just how to write code, but how to deliver it, run it, and care for it over years.

These skills complete the picture that the earlier chapters began. Clean design, thorough testing, and clear documentation are not academic ideals; they are what make delivery smooth, maintenance affordable, and modernization possible. Together, they let you build software that not only works today but keeps working, and keeps improving, long into the future.

Chapter Lab: Containerizing the Project and Modernizing a Legacy Application

In these labs, you will put the chapter's practices into action. In Lab 11.1, you will containerize a project with Docker and build a simple continuous integration workflow that automatically builds and tests your code on every change. In Lab 11.2, you will apply refactoring, characterization tests, and the strangler pattern to modernize a small legacy application. Together, these labs exercise the delivery and maintenance skills at the heart of this chapter.

Chapter 12: Cloud-Native and Distributed Software

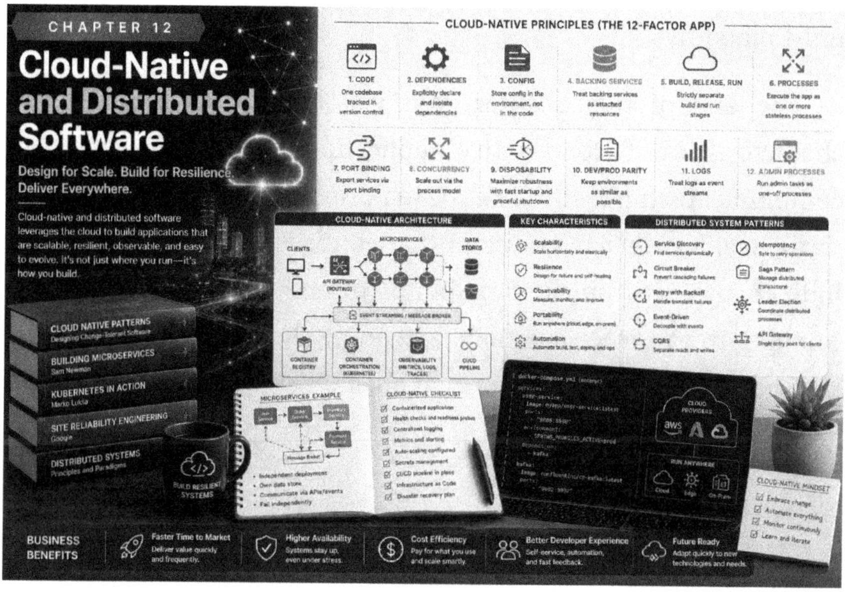

Software no longer lives on a single machine tucked away in a server closet. Today, the applications you build are far more likely to run across dozens of servers spread across the globe, scaling up and down as demand rises and falls. This shift toward the cloud has fundamentally changed how software engineers design, build, and operate systems. Understanding these changes is no longer optional — it is a core part of modern software engineering.

In this chapter, you will learn what it means for an application to be **cloud-native** and why that term describes far more than "software that happens to run on a cloud server." You will explore the design principles that make applications resilient and easy to scale, including stateless design, service-based architectures, containers, and microservices. You will also learn how distributed systems handle failure gracefully — because in a system made of many moving parts, failure is not a rare event but a certainty you must plan for.

By the end of this chapter, you will be able to describe the characteristics of cloud-native applications, explain how services communicate in a distributed system, reason about scalability and resilience, and design a system that continues to work even when individual pieces break. This builds directly on the architectural thinking from earlier chapters, extending those ideas into systems that run at scale across many machines.

12.1 Cloud Computing and Cloud-Native Applications

For most of software history, running an application meant buying physical hardware, installing it in a data center, and maintaining it yourself. If you needed more capacity, you bought more servers — a process that could take weeks. Cloud computing changed this equation entirely. This section introduces cloud computing from a software engineering perspective and explains what makes an application truly *cloud-native*.

Understanding these concepts matters because the way you design an application determines whether it can take advantage of the cloud at all. Simply moving old software onto a cloud server does not make it cloud-native, and it often leaves most of the cloud's benefits unused. In this section, you will learn how the cloud changes engineering decisions and what principles guide well-designed cloud applications.

Cloud Computing and Software Engineering

Cloud computing is the delivery of computing resources — servers, storage, databases, and networking — over the internet, on demand, and paid for as you use them. Instead of owning hardware, you rent it from a provider such as Amazon Web Services, Microsoft Azure, or Google Cloud. This turns a large upfront hardware purchase into a flexible operating expense.

The most important shift for engineers is **elasticity**: the ability to acquire and release resources almost instantly. If your application suddenly gets a million visitors, you can add servers in minutes and remove them just as quickly when traffic drops. This changes how you think about capacity. You no longer design for the peak load you *might* someday reach — you design for the load you have right now and let the system grow as needed.

Cloud providers organize their services into broad categories. **Infrastructure as a Service (IaaS)** gives you raw virtual machines and storage. **Platform as a Service (PaaS)** provides a managed environment where you deploy code without managing servers. **Software as a Service (SaaS)** delivers complete applications over the web. As an engineer, your architectural choices determine how much of this you manage yourself versus how much you delegate to the provider.

Cloud-Native Applications

A **cloud-native application** is one designed specifically to run in a dynamic, distributed cloud environment. It expects that servers may appear and disappear, that it will run as many identical copies, and that any single instance may fail at any moment. Cloud-native software embraces these realities rather than fighting them.

Consider the difference with a traditional application. A traditional app might store user session data in the memory of the single server handling a request. If that server disappears, the session is lost. A cloud-native app avoids this by keeping such state elsewhere, so any server can handle any request. This is the mindset that runs through everything in this chapter: build software that assumes change and failure are normal.

Cloud-native applications are typically composed of small, independent pieces that can be deployed, scaled, and updated separately. They rely heavily on automation for deployment and recovery. They are also built to be portable, running consistently whether on a developer's laptop or across thousands of servers in production.

Twelve-Factor Applications

The **Twelve-Factor App** methodology is a widely respected set of principles for building cloud-native software. Created by engineers at Heroku, it distills hard-won lessons into twelve guidelines. You do not need to memorize all twelve, but several are foundational to everything that follows.

- **Configuration in the environment:** Store settings like database URLs and API keys in environment variables, not in code. This lets the same build run in development, testing, and production.
- **Stateless processes:** The application should store no important data in local memory or disk between requests. Any state that must persist belongs in a backing service like a database.
- **Backing services as attached resources:** Treat databases, message queues, and caches as swappable resources connected through configuration.
- **Disposability:** Processes should start quickly and shut down gracefully, so the system can scale and recover fast.

The following example shows the difference between hard-coded configuration and the twelve-factor approach.

```python
import os

# Twelve-factor style: configuration comes from the environment
DATABASE_URL = os.environ.get("DATABASE_URL", "postgresql://localhost/dev")
CACHE_URL = os.environ.get("CACHE_URL", "redis://localhost:6379")
DEBUG_MODE = os.environ.get("DEBUG", "false").lower() == "true"

def start_app():
    print(f"Connecting to database at {DATABASE_URL}")
    print(f"Using cache at {CACHE_URL}")
    print(f"Debug mode: {DEBUG_MODE}")

start_app()
```

This code reads its configuration from environment variables using `os.environ.get`, falling back to sensible defaults for local development. Because the connection details are never written into the source code, the exact same program can run against a local database on your laptop and a production database in the cloud simply by changing the environment. This separation of configuration from code is one of the most practical habits you can adopt when building cloud software.

Summary

- **Cloud computing** delivers computing resources on demand, replacing upfront hardware purchases with elastic, pay-as-you-go capacity.
- **Elasticity** lets you add and remove resources in minutes, changing how you plan for load.
- A **cloud-native application** is designed to run in a distributed environment where servers come and go and failure is expected.
- The **Twelve-Factor App** methodology provides practical principles, including storing configuration in the environment and keeping processes stateless.

12.2 Designing Stateless, Service-Based Systems

Now that you understand what makes an application cloud-native, we can look at how to actually design one. The single most important design decision is how you handle **state** — the data your application remembers between requests. Getting this right unlocks the ability to scale, while getting it wrong creates systems that cannot grow.

In this section, you will learn why stateless design matters, how applications communicate through APIs and services, and how containers and orchestration platforms package and run those services reliably. These are the building blocks of nearly every modern cloud system, and they work together to create software that scales cleanly.

Stateless Application Design

A **stateless application** does not store client-specific data in its own memory between requests. Each request contains all the information needed to process it, or the application fetches that information from a shared external store. The application instance handling your request holds nothing important that would be lost if it disappeared.

Think of a stateless service like a fast-food counter where any cashier can serve any customer, because all the order information is written on the receipt rather than remembered in a single cashier's head. If one cashier leaves, another steps in without missing a beat. This is exactly what lets cloud systems run many identical copies of a service and route requests to whichever copy is available.

Where does the state go instead? Into **backing services** – external systems designed to hold state reliably. Session data might go into a shared cache like Redis. Persistent data goes into a database. The example below contrasts a stateful counter with a stateless one.

```
from flask import Flask, request
import redis

app = Flask(__name__)
cache = redis.Redis(host="cache", port=6379)

# Stateless: the count lives in an external store, not in memory
@app.route("/visit")
def record_visit():
    user_id = request.args.get("user_id")
    count = cache.incr(f"visits:{user_id}")
    return {"user_id": user_id, "visits": count}
```

In this example, the visit count is stored in Redis, not in a Python variable inside the process. Because the state lives outside the application, you can run ten copies of this service behind a load balancer and every copy will report the correct count. If any single instance crashes, no data is lost, because the instance was never the source of truth. This is the essence of stateless design.

APIs and Services

A **service** is a self-contained unit of software that performs a specific job and exposes it over the network. Other parts of the system talk to it through an **API** (Application Programming

Interface) — a well-defined contract describing what requests the service accepts and what responses it returns. The most common style is a **REST API**, which uses standard HTTP methods to operate on resources.

In a real system, clients rarely talk to internal services directly. Instead, requests pass through an **API Gateway**, a single entry point that handles cross-cutting concerns like authentication, rate limiting, and routing. This keeps individual services simpler, because they can focus on their core job rather than repeating security logic.

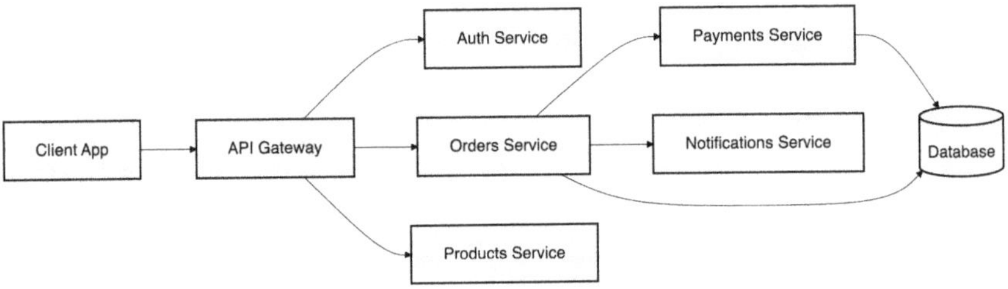

The diagram shows how a request travels from the client through the gateway and on to the correct internal service. Designing clear, stable APIs is critical, because services depend on each other's contracts. If you change an API carelessly, you can break every service that calls it. This is why APIs are usually versioned and evolved carefully over time.

Containers

A **container** packages an application together with everything it needs to run — code, libraries, and system tools — into a single, portable unit. The most popular container technology is **Docker**. A container runs identically on any machine that supports it, which solves the classic problem of "it works on my machine but not in production."

Containers are lightweight because they share the host operating system's kernel rather than including a full operating system like a traditional virtual machine. This means they start in seconds and use far fewer resources, so you can run many of them on a single server. A container is defined by a **Dockerfile**, a text file describing how to build the image.

```
# A simple Dockerfile for a Python service
FROM python:3.11-slim

WORKDIR /app
COPY requirements.txt .
RUN pip install --no-cache-dir -r requirements.txt

COPY . .

EXPOSE 8080
CMD ["python", "app.py"]
```

This Dockerfile starts from a slim Python base image, sets a working directory, installs dependencies, and copies the application code. The `CMD` line defines the command that runs when the container starts. Because everything the app needs is captured here, anyone can build this image and get an identical running environment. Containers pair perfectly with stateless design: since each container holds no important state, you can start and stop them freely.

Container Orchestration

Running one container is easy. Running hundreds of them across many servers — restarting the ones that crash, scaling them up under load, and connecting them together — is hard. **Container orchestration** automates this work. The dominant orchestration platform is **Kubernetes**, often abbreviated as K8s.

Kubernetes lets you declare the desired state of your system — for example, "always keep five copies of the payment service running" — and then continuously works to make reality match that declaration. If a container dies, Kubernetes starts a replacement automatically. If a whole server fails, it reschedules the affected containers onto healthy servers.

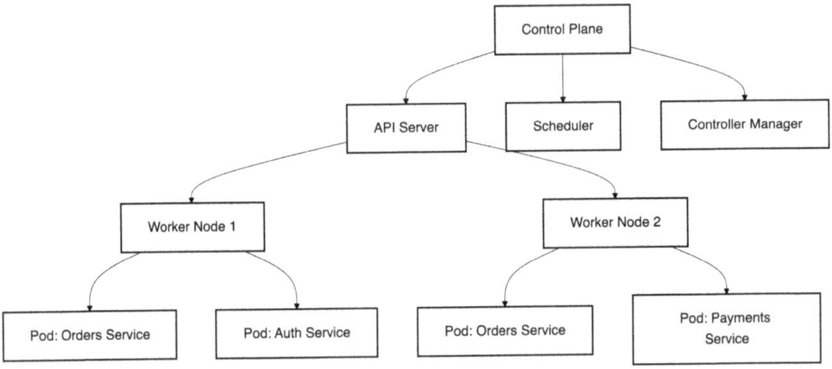

As the diagram illustrates, a Kubernetes cluster separates the **control plane**, which makes scheduling decisions, from the **worker nodes**, which run your actual containers. You interact mostly with the control plane, describing what you want, and Kubernetes handles the details of where and how to run it. This declarative model is a major reason cloud-native systems can be so resilient with relatively little manual intervention.

Summary

- A **stateless application** stores no client-specific data in local memory, allowing many identical copies to serve any request.
- **Backing services** like caches and databases hold state externally so instances remain disposable.
- Services expose their functionality through **APIs**, often behind an **API Gateway** that handles authentication and routing.
- **Containers** package an application with its dependencies into a portable, lightweight unit.
- **Container orchestration** with tools like **Kubernetes** automates deploying, scaling, and recovering containers across many servers.

12.3 Microservices and Event-Driven Systems

So far you have learned to build individual services and run them at scale. But how many services should an application have, and how should they be organized? This question leads to one of the most influential architectural styles in modern software: **microservices**. Alongside it, you will learn how services can communicate not just by calling each other directly, but by reacting to events.

This section matters because architecture shapes everything about how a system grows and how teams work. A well-chosen structure lets many teams build and deploy independently, while a poor one creates a tangled mess where every change risks breaking something else. You will learn what microservices are, how messaging connects them, and how event-driven design creates loosely coupled systems.

Microservices

A **microservice architecture** structures an application as a collection of small, independent services, each responsible for a single business capability. One service might handle orders, another inventory, another billing. Each service owns its own data and can be developed, deployed, and scaled independently of the others.

Contrast this with a **monolith**, where all functionality lives in one large codebase deployed as a single unit. Monoliths are simpler to start with, but as they grow, a small change in one area can require rebuilding and redeploying the entire application. With microservices, teams can update the billing service without touching the inventory service at all. This independence is the primary benefit.

Microservices are not free, however. They introduce the complexity of a distributed system: network calls can fail, data is spread across many services, and testing the whole system becomes harder. A common piece of advice is to start with a well-organized monolith and split it into services only when the benefits clearly outweigh these costs. The key skill is drawing service boundaries around genuine business capabilities so each service is truly independent.

Messaging

When services need to communicate without waiting on each other, they use **messaging**. A service sends a **message** to a **message broker** – software such as RabbitMQ or Apache Kafka that reliably stores and delivers messages. The receiving service processes the message when it is ready. This is called **asynchronous communication**, because the sender does not block waiting for a response.

Messaging decouples services in time. The sending service does not need the receiver to be available at that exact moment; the broker holds the message until the receiver is ready. This makes the overall system more resilient, because a temporary outage in one service does not immediately break the services that talk to it.

```python
import pika
import json

# Publishing a message to a broker (RabbitMQ)
connection = pika.BlockingConnection(pika.ConnectionParameters("broker"))
channel = connection.channel()
channel.queue_declare(queue="orders", durable=True)

order = {"order_id": 4821, "customer": "alice", "total": 59.90}
channel.basic_publish(
    exchange="",
    routing_key="orders",
    body=json.dumps(order),
)
print("Order message published")
connection.close()
```

This code connects to a message broker, declares a durable queue named `orders`, and publishes an order as a JSON message. The publishing service does not know or care which service will consume the message, or when. It simply hands the message to the broker and moves on. This loose coupling is what makes messaging so valuable in distributed systems.

Event-Driven Systems

An **event-driven system** takes messaging one step further. Instead of sending commands that tell a specific service to do something, services publish **events** — factual statements about something that has already happened, such as "order placed" or "payment received." Other services **subscribe** to the events they care about and react independently.

The power of this approach is that the service publishing an event does not need to know who is listening. When an order is placed, the order service publishes a single "order placed" event. Several other services can each subscribe and react in their own way, all without the order service being aware of them.

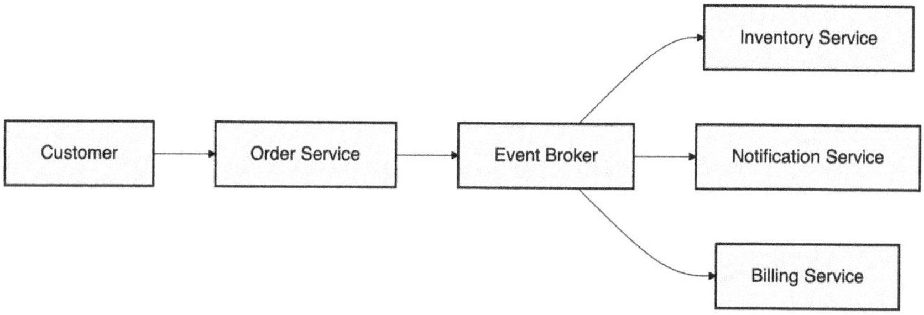

As the diagram shows, one published event can trigger the inventory, notification, and billing services simultaneously, each acting independently. This makes the system easy to extend: to add a new behavior when an order is placed — say, a loyalty-points service — you simply create a new subscriber. You never touch the order service at all. This is a profound shift from tightly coupled designs where every new feature requires editing existing code.

The trade-off is that event-driven systems can be harder to reason about, because the flow of logic is spread across many independent subscribers rather than written in one place. Good documentation and observability, which you will meet in the next section, become essential for understanding how the system behaves as a whole.

Summary

- A **microservice architecture** splits an application into small, independent services, each owning a single business capability and its own data.
- Microservices trade the simplicity of a monolith for independence, at the cost of distributed-system complexity.
- **Messaging** through a **message broker** lets services communicate asynchronously, decoupling them in time.
- In an **event-driven system**, services publish **events** about what has happened, and independent subscribers react without the publisher knowing about them.
- Event-driven design makes systems easy to extend but harder to trace, raising the importance of observability.

12.4 Scalability, Resilience, and Distributed Data

You have now assembled the pieces of a distributed cloud-native system. The final and perhaps most important topic is how to make such a system perform well under load and keep working when things go wrong. In a system with many services, servers, and network connections, something is almost always failing somewhere. Great engineers design for this reality rather than hoping it away.

In this section, you will learn how systems scale to handle more work, how they stay resilient in the face of failure, how data is managed when it is spread across many places, and how observability lets you understand what your system is actually doing. Together, these ideas separate systems that merely run from systems that run reliably at scale.

Scalability

Scalability is a system's ability to handle increasing load by adding resources. There are two fundamental approaches. **Vertical scaling** means making a single server more powerful — more CPU, more memory. **Horizontal scaling** means adding more servers and spreading the work across them. Cloud-native systems favor horizontal scaling because it has no hard ceiling and fits naturally with stateless, containerized services.

Horizontal scaling only works if your services are stateless, which is why that principle from earlier is so important. When any instance can handle any request, you can add instances freely. Modern orchestrators can even do this automatically through **auto-scaling**, adding instances when demand rises and removing them when it falls.

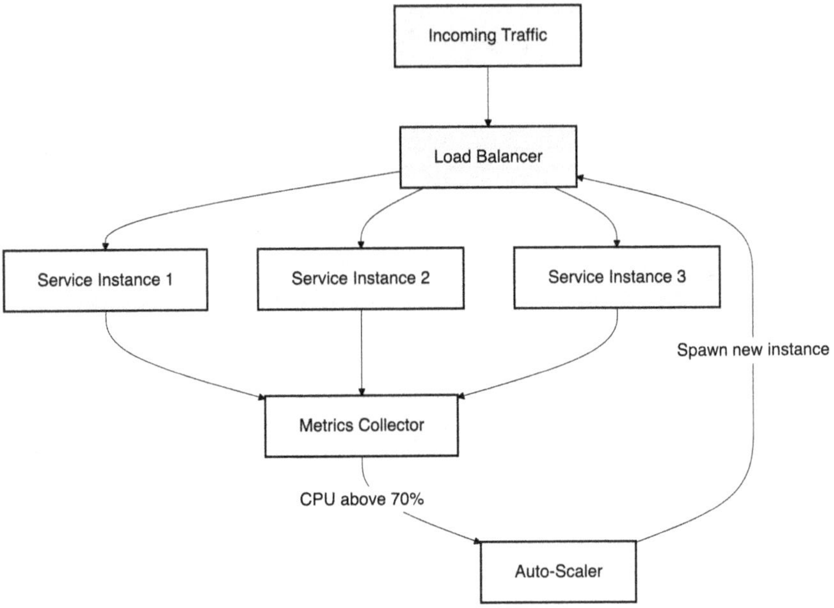

As the diagram shows, the orchestrator watches metrics like CPU utilization or request queue depth and adjusts the number of instances to match demand. This means you pay for capacity only when you need it, and users experience consistent performance even during traffic spikes. Auto-scaling is one of the clearest payoffs of designing your system to be stateless and containerized from the start.

Resilience

Resilience is a system's ability to keep functioning, perhaps in a degraded way, when parts of it fail. Because distributed systems have so many components, you cannot prevent all failures. Instead, you contain them so that one failure does not cascade into a total outage.

A key resilience pattern is the **circuit breaker**. When one service repeatedly fails to respond, a circuit breaker "trips" and stops sending requests to it for a while, giving it time to recover and preventing the caller from wasting resources on doomed requests. Other patterns include **retries** with backoff for transient errors and **timeouts** to avoid waiting forever on a stuck dependency.

```
import time

class CircuitBreaker:
    def __init__(self, failure_threshold=3, reset_seconds=30):
        self.failure_threshold = failure_threshold
        self.reset_seconds = reset_seconds
        self.failures = 0
        self.opened_at = None

    def call(self, func):
        if self.opened_at and time.time() - self.opened_at < self.reset_seconds:
            raise RuntimeError("Circuit is open; skipping call")
        try:
            result = func()
            self.failures = 0          # success resets the count
            return result
        except Exception:
            self.failures += 1
            if self.failures >= self.failure_threshold:
                self.opened_at = time.time()
            raise
```

This simplified circuit breaker tracks consecutive failures. Once failures reach the threshold, it records the time and "opens," rejecting calls immediately until the reset period passes. A successful call resets the failure count. In a real system, this prevents a struggling service from being overwhelmed by requests and stops the failure from spreading to callers. Patterns like this are how resilient systems fail gracefully instead of collapsing all at once.

Distributed Data

In a microservice system, data is spread across many services, each owning its own database. This solves the coupling problem but creates a new challenge: keeping data consistent across services. You can no longer wrap a change to several tables in a single database transaction, because the data lives in different places entirely.

This leads to the idea of **eventual consistency**. Rather than every part of the system seeing the same data at the exact same instant, the system guarantees that all copies will *become* consistent shortly after a change. For example, when an order is placed, the inventory service may take a moment to reflect the reduced stock. For many business problems this is perfectly acceptable, and it is often the only practical option at large scale.

A related concept is the **CAP theorem**, which states that a distributed data store cannot simultaneously guarantee **consistency**, **availability**, and **partition tolerance** — you must trade off between them when the network fails. Because network partitions are unavoidable in distributed systems, engineers usually choose between favoring consistency or availability. Understanding this trade-off helps you set realistic expectations for how distributed data behaves.

Observability

Observability is the ability to understand what is happening inside your system from the outside, based on the data it produces. In a monolith you might just read a log file, but in a distributed system a single user request may pass through a dozen services. You need better tools to see the whole picture. Observability rests on three types of telemetry, often called the three pillars.

- **Logs** are timestamped records of discrete events, useful for understanding what happened at a specific moment.
- **Metrics** are numeric measurements over time, such as request rate or error percentage, useful for spotting trends.
- **Traces** follow a single request as it travels across services, showing where time was spent and where it failed.

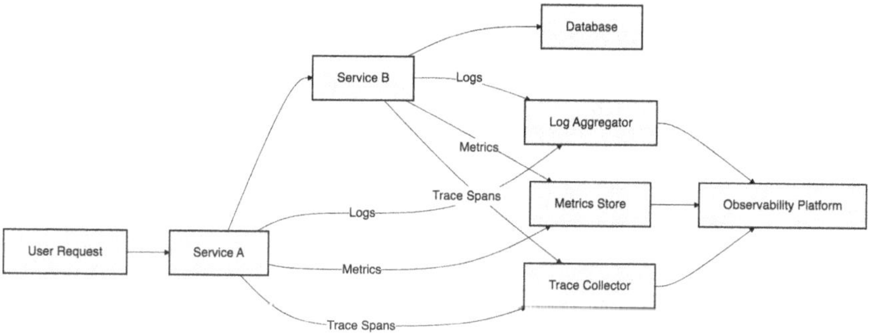

As the diagram shows, a single request produces all three signals, which are collected by an observability platform such as one built on OpenTelemetry. Together they let you answer not just *whether* something is broken, but *where* and *why*. Without observability, operating a distributed system is like flying blind, so investing in it early pays off enormously.

Designing for Failure

The theme running through this entire section is a single mindset: **design for failure**. In a distributed system, failures are not exceptional events to be surprised by — they are a constant background condition you plan for from the beginning. Every network call might fail, every server might vanish, every dependency might slow down.

Designing for failure means asking, for every interaction, "What happens if this goes wrong?" It means adding timeouts so you never wait forever, retries for transient glitches, and circuit breakers to contain cascading failures. It means running multiple instances so no single crash takes you down, and using health checks so the orchestrator can detect and replace unhealthy instances automatically.

Some organizations even practice **chaos engineering**, deliberately injecting failures into production to verify their systems recover as expected. Whether or not you go that far, the underlying principle applies to every cloud-native system you build: assume things will break, and make sure your system keeps serving users when they do. A system that expects failure is far more reliable than one that merely hopes to avoid it.

Summary

- **Scalability** comes primarily from **horizontal scaling** – adding more instances – which depends on stateless design and can be automated with auto-scaling.
- **Resilience** patterns such as **circuit breakers**, retries, and timeouts contain failures so they do not cascade across the system.
- **Distributed data** trades strict consistency for availability and scale, often relying on **eventual consistency** and shaped by the **CAP theorem**.
- **Observability** through logs, metrics, and traces lets you understand a distributed system's behavior from the outside.
- **Designing for failure** means treating failure as normal and building in timeouts, redundancy, and health checks from the start.

Chapter Summary

This chapter took you from the idea of the cloud as rented hardware to the full discipline of building software that thrives in a distributed, ever-changing environment. The concepts build on one another in a clear chain. Cloud computing gives you elastic resources, but you can only exploit that elasticity if your applications are stateless, which is why the Twelve-Factor principles and stateless design come first. Statelessness in turn makes containers and orchestration practical, because instances become disposable and interchangeable. Those disposable services can then be organized into microservices that communicate through APIs, messaging, and events.

With that architecture in place, the final concepts fall naturally into position. Horizontal scaling works precisely because your services are stateless and containerized. Resilience patterns matter precisely because a system of many independent services has many points of failure. Distributed data is a direct consequence of giving each microservice its own database, and observability becomes essential because a request now travels across many services rather than living inside one program. Each idea in this chapter exists to support the others.

You are now able to reason about software the way modern engineering teams do: as systems of cooperating services that scale on demand and expect failure as a normal condition. You can explain why an application should be stateless, describe how containers and orchestration run it, choose between direct API calls and event-driven messaging, and apply patterns that keep a system running when parts of it break. These are the foundations on which nearly all large-scale software is built today, and they connect directly to the architecture and design principles you studied in earlier chapters.

Chapter Lab: Designing a Cloud-Native Version of the Course Application

In this lab, you will take the course application you have worked with throughout the book and redesign it as a cloud-native, distributed system. You will apply the skills from this chapter by identifying stateless service boundaries, choosing how services communicate, and planning for scalability, resilience, and observability. The goal is to produce a clear design that demonstrates how the principles of cloud-native software come together in a real application.

Chapter 13: AI-Assisted Software Engineering

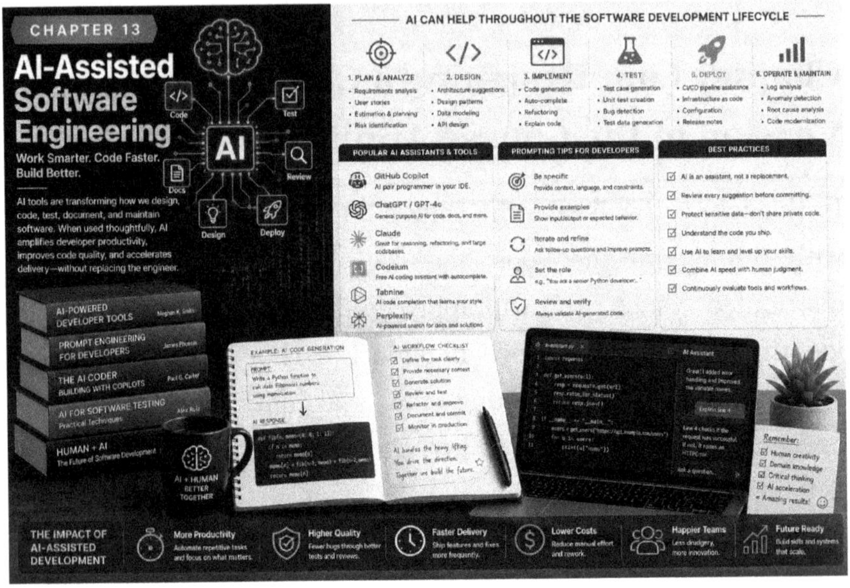

Over the past several chapters, you have built a solid foundation in the discipline of software engineering. You have learned how to gather requirements, design systems, write clean code, test thoroughly, and collaborate effectively with a team. Now a new force is reshaping every one of those activities. Artificial intelligence has moved from research labs into the daily toolkit of working developers, and it is changing how software gets built.

This chapter introduces you to **AI-assisted software engineering**, the practice of using artificial intelligence tools to help perform engineering tasks across the entire software development lifecycle. You will learn where AI fits into the work you already know how to do, how to use AI coding assistants to generate and explain code, and how AI can support requirements, design, testing, debugging, and refactoring. Just as importantly, you will learn about the real risks of relying on AI-generated code and the responsibilities that come with using these powerful tools.

By the end of this chapter, you will understand how to integrate AI into your workflow responsibly. You will be able to recognize where AI adds value and where it introduces danger. You will also understand how the role of the software engineer is evolving, and why the human skills you have developed throughout this course matter more than ever, not less.

13.1 AI in the Software Development Lifecycle

You already know the software development lifecycle, or **SDLC**, from earlier chapters. It describes the phases software passes through, from gathering requirements to design, implementation, testing, deployment, and maintenance. For most of computing history, every one of these phases depended almost entirely on human effort. AI is changing that.

In this section, you will learn where AI tools fit into the SDLC, what an AI coding assistant actually is, and how these tools can generate and explain code. Understanding the big picture first will help you use AI deliberately rather than reaching for it randomly.

Where AI Fits in the Lifecycle

It is tempting to think of AI as simply a tool for writing code faster. That view is far too narrow. Modern AI tools now participate in nearly every phase of the SDLC. They help analysts clarify requirements, suggest architectural patterns during design, autocomplete functions during implementation, generate test cases, explain confusing error messages, and even summarize changes for code review.

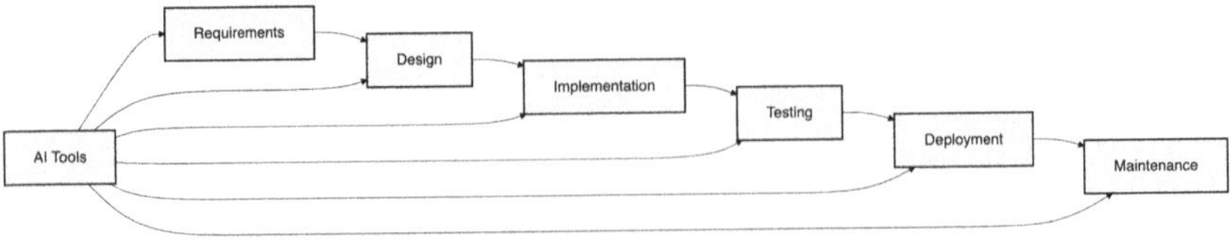

The real benefit of this broad reach is that problems get caught earlier. In traditional development, a misunderstanding in the requirements phase might not surface until testing, where it is expensive to fix. When AI assists across the whole lifecycle, it can flag inconsistencies and surface questions sooner. This does not remove the need for human judgment. It simply gives you more chances to notice trouble before it becomes costly.

AI Coding Assistants

An **AI coding assistant** is a software tool, usually built on a large language model, that helps you write, understand, and modify code through natural language and code context. You interact with it by describing what you want in plain English, by writing partial code that it completes, or by asking questions about existing code.

A **large language model**, often abbreviated as **LLM**, is a type of AI trained on enormous amounts of text and code. It predicts likely sequences of words or tokens based on patterns it learned during training. This is a crucial detail to remember: the model is predicting plausible output, not retrieving guaranteed-correct answers. That distinction explains both the power and the danger of these tools, a theme we will return to throughout this chapter.

Popular assistants integrate directly into your code editor. They watch what you type and offer suggestions inline. Others work as chat interfaces where you hold a conversation about a problem. Both styles share the same underlying idea: you provide context, and the assistant proposes text.

Generating and Explaining Code

One of the most immediate uses of an AI assistant is generating code from a description. Suppose you need a function that validates an email address. Instead of writing it from scratch, you can describe the goal and let the assistant draft it.

```
def is_valid_email(address):
    """Return True if address looks like a valid email."""
    import re
    pattern = r"^[a-zA-Z0-9._%+-]+@[a-zA-Z0-9.-]+\.[a-zA-Z]{2,}$"
    return re.match(pattern, address) is not None

# Example usage
print(is_valid_email("dev@destinlearning.com"))  # True
print(is_valid_email("not-an-email"))            # False
```

This code uses a regular expression to check whether the input matches a common email pattern. The function returns `True` when `re.match` finds a match and `False` otherwise. Notice that this validation is basic. It catches obvious mistakes but does not guarantee the address actually exists or fully complies with the email specification. An AI assistant will happily generate this for you, but you must still evaluate whether it meets your real needs.

Just as useful is the reverse task: asking an assistant to explain code you do not understand. Imagine you inherit the function above with no comments. You can paste it into an assistant and ask what it does. A good explanation would tell you that the pattern requires characters before an `@`, a domain in the middle, and a top-level suffix of at least two letters. This makes AI a powerful learning companion when you encounter unfamiliar code in a real project.

Summary

- AI tools now participate across the entire SDLC, not just the coding phase, which helps catch problems earlier.
- An **AI coding assistant** is a tool built on a **large language model** that helps you write, understand, and modify code.
- LLMs predict plausible output based on training patterns, so their answers are likely rather than guaranteed correct.
- AI can generate code from natural-language descriptions and explain unfamiliar code, making it useful for both productivity and learning.

13.2 AI-Assisted Requirements and Design

Before a single line of code is written, a great deal of thinking has to happen. What problem are we solving? Who are the users? What should the system do, and how should it be structured? In earlier chapters you learned that mistakes made during requirements and design are among the most expensive to fix later. AI can help you do this early work more thoroughly.

In this section, you will learn how AI supports requirements development and how it can accelerate software design. The key theme is that AI is a thinking partner here, not a decision maker. It helps you explore options and spot gaps, but the responsibility for the final requirements and architecture remains yours.

AI-Assisted Requirements Development

Gathering requirements means figuring out what a system must do. This work is full of ambiguity. Stakeholders describe what they want in vague terms, and it is your job to turn those descriptions into clear, testable statements. AI assistants are surprisingly good at helping with this translation.

You can give an assistant a rough description of a feature and ask it to produce structured requirements. For example, you might paste a stakeholder note that says "users should be able to reset their password if they forget it." An assistant can expand this into a list of specific requirements: the user requests a reset, the system sends a secure time-limited link, the link allows setting a new password, and the old password stops working immediately.

AI is also useful for finding gaps. You can ask, "What edge cases am I missing for this password reset feature?" The assistant might point out questions you had not considered. What happens if the email does not exist? How many reset attempts are allowed? Should the reset link expire? These prompts do not replace conversations with real stakeholders, but they help you arrive at those conversations better prepared.

AI-Assisted Software Design

Once requirements are clearer, you move into design. **Software design** is the process of deciding how a system will be structured to meet its requirements, including its components, their responsibilities, and how they interact. AI can propose an initial design that you then refine.

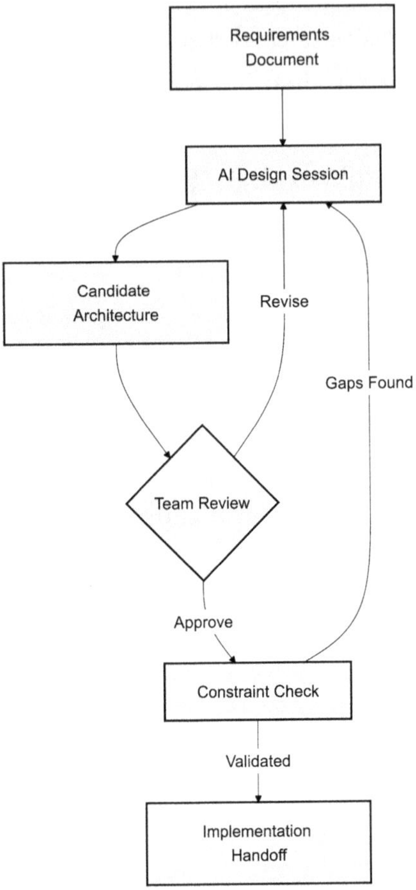

The workflow shown above is important because it captures the right relationship between engineer and AI. You feed in requirements. The AI proposes an architecture. Then, critically, you and your team review and challenge that proposal. The AI iterates based on your feedback, and you settle on a design you understand and can defend. The AI never has the final say.

Consider a simple example. Suppose you ask an assistant to sketch a design for a small task-tracking application. It might propose separating the code into clear layers.

```
# A simple layered design suggested by an AI assistant

# Data layer: responsible for storage
class TaskRepository:
    def __init__(self):
        self._tasks = []

    def add(self, task):
        self._tasks.append(task)

    def all(self):
        return list(self._tasks)

# Service layer: business logic
class TaskService:
    def __init__(self, repository):
        self.repository = repository

    def create_task(self, title):
        if not title.strip():
            raise ValueError("Task title cannot be empty")
        self.repository.add({"title": title, "done": False})

# Usage
service = TaskService(TaskRepository())
service.create_task("Write chapter 13")
```

This design separates concerns into two layers. The `TaskRepository` handles storage, while the `TaskService` handles business rules, such as rejecting empty titles. The service receives its repository through its constructor, a pattern called **dependency injection** that makes the code easier to test. An AI assistant can produce this structure quickly, but you must decide whether this layering is appropriate for your project's size and complexity. For a tiny script, it may be overkill. For a growing application, it may be exactly right.

Summary

- AI can translate vague stakeholder descriptions into clear, structured, testable requirements.
- Asking AI to identify edge cases and gaps helps you prepare for stakeholder conversations, though it does not replace them.
- In design, AI proposes an initial architecture that you and your team must review, challenge, and refine.
- AI can quickly sketch structural patterns like layered designs, but you decide whether the proposed structure fits your project.

13.3 AI-Assisted Testing, Debugging, and Refactoring

In earlier chapters you learned that writing code is only part of the job. Software must be tested, debugged when it breaks, and refactored to stay maintainable. These tasks are often tedious and time-consuming, which makes them ideal candidates for AI assistance. Used well, AI can dramatically reduce the friction of these activities so you spend more time on the parts that require real judgment.

In this section, you will learn how AI helps generate tests, debug failing code, refactor for clarity, and produce documentation and code reviews. Throughout, remember that AI accelerates the work but does not absolve you of responsibility for its correctness.

Generating Tests

Writing tests is essential, but many developers find it tedious. AI assistants can generate test cases from your code or from a description of expected behavior. This lowers the barrier to good testing.

```python
import unittest

def divide(a, b):
    if b == 0:
        raise ValueError("Cannot divide by zero")
    return a / b

class TestDivide(unittest.TestCase):
    def test_normal_division(self):
        self.assertEqual(divide(10, 2), 5)

    def test_division_by_zero(self):
        with self.assertRaises(ValueError):
            divide(10, 0)

    def test_negative_numbers(self):
        self.assertEqual(divide(-6, 2), -3)

if __name__ == "__main__":
    unittest.main()
```

This test suite covers three scenarios for the `divide` function: normal division, division by zero, and negative numbers. An AI assistant can generate all three cases in seconds from the function alone. However, you should always check whether the generated tests cover the cases that actually matter. AI tends to test obvious paths and may miss the subtle edge cases specific to your domain. Treat generated tests as a starting point, then add the scenarios you know are important.

Debugging with AI

Debugging is detective work. You gather evidence, form a hypothesis, test it, and repeat. AI can speed up this loop by helping interpret error messages and suggesting likely causes. The most effective way to use AI here is to follow a disciplined loop.

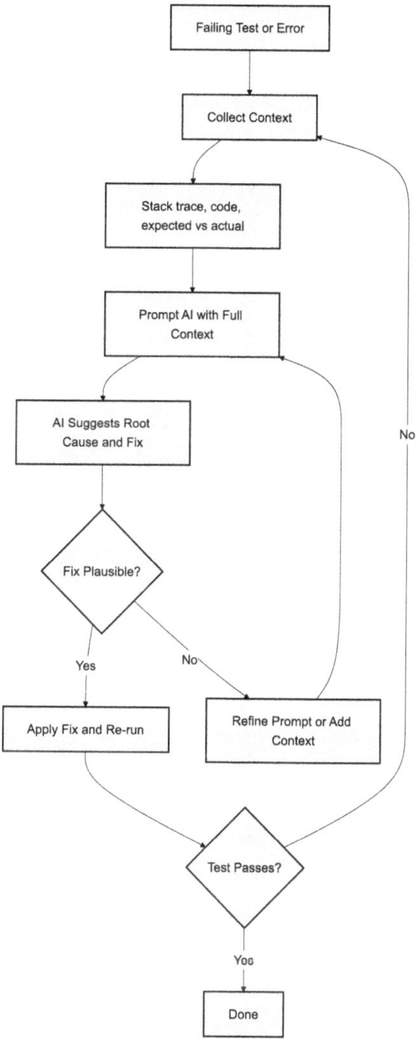

The loop begins by gathering evidence: the error message, the stack trace, and the code involved. You then give the AI full context, not just the error line. The more relevant information you provide, the better its suggestion. You evaluate that suggestion critically, apply a fix, and re-run to confirm. If it did not work, you gather new evidence and go around again.

Context matters enormously. If you paste only an error message with no surrounding code, the AI must guess. If you include the failing function, the input that triggered the failure, and the full traceback, the assistant can reason far more accurately. This is why skilled engineers get better results from AI than beginners do: they know what evidence to provide.

Refactoring with AI

Refactoring means improving the internal structure of code without changing its external behavior. AI is well suited to this because refactoring often follows recognizable patterns, such as extracting repeated logic into a function or renaming variables for clarity.

```
# Before: repetitive and unclear
def process(orders):
    total = 0
    for o in orders:
        if o["status"] == "paid":
            total = total + o["amount"] * 1.08
    return total

# After: clearer, with the tax rate named and logic extracted
TAX_RATE = 0.08

def order_total_with_tax(order):
    return order["amount"] * (1 + TAX_RATE)

def total_paid_revenue(orders):
    return sum(
        order_total_with_tax(order)
        for order in orders
        if order["status"] == "paid"
    )
```

The refactored version improves readability without changing what the code computes. The magic number `1.08` becomes a named constant, `TAX_RATE`, so its meaning is obvious. The tax calculation moves into its own function, `order_total_with_tax`, which can now be tested independently. An AI assistant can suggest exactly this kind of transformation, but you must verify that behavior is truly unchanged, ideally by running your tests before and after.

Documentation Generation and Code Review

AI can also generate documentation from code, producing docstrings, README sections, and usage examples. This helps address one of the most neglected tasks in software: keeping documentation current. You can ask an assistant to write a docstring for a function, then edit it for accuracy.

AI can assist with code review as well. It can flag potential bugs, style inconsistencies, and missing error handling before a human reviewer even sees the code. Think of this as a first pass that catches routine issues, freeing your human reviewers to focus on higher-level concerns like design and correctness. The AI review supplements human review; it does not replace it.

Summary

- AI can quickly generate test cases, but you must add the domain-specific edge cases it tends to miss.
- Effective AI debugging follows a tight loop of gathering evidence, providing full context, evaluating suggestions, and re-running.
- Providing rich context to the AI produces far better debugging results than pasting an error message alone.
- AI excels at pattern-based refactoring, though you must confirm that external behavior stays unchanged.
- AI can generate documentation and perform a first-pass code review that supplements, but never replaces, human review.

13.4 Risks of AI-Generated Code

So far this chapter has emphasized what AI can do for you. Now we must be equally honest about what can go wrong. AI-generated code carries real risks, and engineers who ignore them cause serious harm. The convenience of AI can lull you into a false sense of trust, and that trust is exactly where danger lives.

In this section, you will learn about three major categories of risk: security vulnerabilities, hallucinations and incorrect code, and intellectual property concerns. Understanding these risks is not about avoiding AI. It is about using it with your eyes open.

Security and AI-Generated Code

AI assistants learn from vast amounts of public code, including code that contains security flaws. As a result, they sometimes reproduce insecure patterns. A common example is code that builds database queries by directly inserting user input.

```
# DANGEROUS: vulnerable to SQL injection
def find_user(username, cursor):
    query = "SELECT * FROM users WHERE name = '" + username + "'"
    cursor.execute(query)
    return cursor.fetchall()

# SAFE: uses a parameterized query
def find_user_safe(username, cursor):
    query = "SELECT * FROM users WHERE name = ?"
    cursor.execute(query, (username,))
    return cursor.fetchall()
```

The first function is vulnerable to **SQL injection**, an attack where malicious input alters the meaning of a database query. If a user enters a specially crafted username, they could read or destroy data they should never access. The second function fixes this by using a **parameterized query**, where the database treats the input strictly as a value, never as part of the command. An AI assistant might generate either version. It is your job to recognize the dangerous one and reject it. This is why security knowledge remains essential even when AI writes the code.

Hallucinations and Incorrect Code

Because LLMs predict plausible text, they sometimes produce output that looks correct but is not. This is called **hallucination**, where the model generates confident, well-formatted content that is factually wrong or does not work. AI might invent a function that does not exist in a library, cite a nonexistent configuration option, or write logic that is subtly incorrect.

The danger of hallucination is that it looks authoritative. The code compiles, the explanation sounds reasonable, and the variable names are sensible. A beginner may accept it without question. This is precisely why you must test and verify AI output rather than trusting it. Never assume that fluent, confident-looking code is correct code.

A practical safeguard is to treat every AI suggestion as a hypothesis to be checked. Run it. Test it against known inputs. Look up any function or option you do not recognize. If the AI claims a library behaves a certain way, confirm it in the official documentation. These habits protect you from the most damaging mistakes.

Intellectual Property Considerations

There are also legal and ethical questions around AI-generated code. Because these models were trained on large bodies of existing code, some of which was under restrictive licenses, questions arise about who owns AI-generated output and whether it might reproduce someone else's protected work.

Intellectual property, often abbreviated **IP**, refers to legal rights over creations of the mind, including source code. When you accept AI-generated code into your project, you should consider whether it might closely match licensed code, whether your organization's policies permit AI-generated contributions, and whether the code you ship can be legally used and distributed. Many companies now have explicit policies governing AI tool use for exactly these reasons. As a professional, you are responsible for knowing and following those policies.

Summary

- AI can reproduce insecure patterns like SQL injection, so you must review generated code for security flaws.
- **Hallucination** occurs when AI produces confident, plausible-looking output that is actually wrong or nonexistent.
- Treat every AI suggestion as a hypothesis to be tested and verified, never as guaranteed-correct code.
- AI-generated code raises **intellectual property** questions, and you must follow your organization's policies on AI use.

13.5 Responsible and Human-Guided AI Use

The previous section made the risks clear. This final section turns those warnings into positive practice. How do you use AI in a way that captures its benefits while protecting against its dangers? The answer centers on human oversight, responsible habits, and a clear understanding of how your role as an engineer is changing.

In this section, you will learn why human oversight is non-negotiable, what responsible AI use looks like in practice, and how the profession of software engineering is evolving. These lessons tie together everything you have learned in this chapter and, in many ways, this entire course.

Human Oversight

The single most important principle in AI-assisted engineering is that a human remains accountable. **Human oversight** means that a qualified person reviews, understands, and takes responsibility for AI-generated output before it is used. AI can suggest, draft, and accelerate, but it cannot be held responsible when something goes wrong. You can.

This principle has a practical consequence: you should never commit code you do not understand. If an AI produces a solution you cannot explain, that is a signal to slow down. Ask the assistant to explain it. Break it into smaller pieces. Test each part. The moment you ship code you cannot reason about, you have surrendered the very judgment that makes you an engineer.

Human oversight also means knowing when not to use AI at all. For highly sensitive systems, for novel problems with no established patterns, or for situations where a mistake carries serious consequences, human reasoning must lead. AI is a powerful assistant, but assistance is not authority.

Responsible Use of AI

Responsible use builds on oversight with a set of everyday habits. First, verify before you trust. Run the code, test the edge cases, and check any facts the AI asserts. Second, protect confidential information. Do not paste secrets, proprietary code, or private customer data into tools that may store or train on it. Third, be transparent. If your team or client expects to know when AI contributed to work, tell them.

Responsible use also means using AI to strengthen your skills rather than replace them. If you always accept AI code without understanding it, your abilities will stagnate. If instead you use AI to explore alternatives, learn new patterns, and check your reasoning, you grow. The goal is to become a better engineer with AI, not a dependent one.

The Changing Role of the Software Engineer

As AI takes over more routine coding, you may wonder what remains for human engineers. The answer is a great deal, and arguably the most valuable parts. When AI handles boilerplate and repetitive tasks, your value shifts toward work that requires judgment, context, creativity, and accountability.

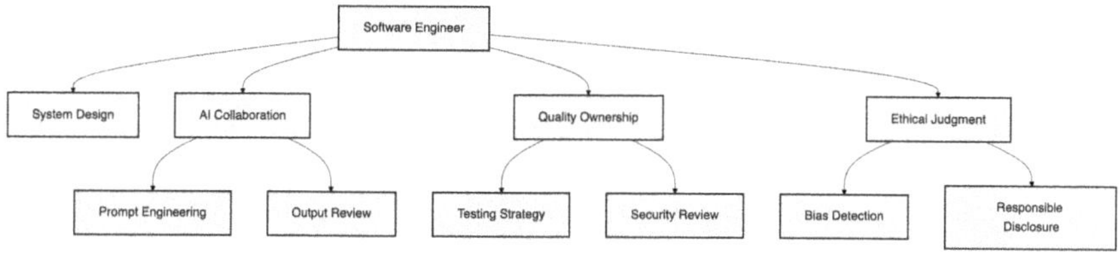

The activities that grow in importance are exactly the ones this course has emphasized. Understanding what users truly need. Making sound architectural trade-offs. Reasoning about security and ethics. Communicating with stakeholders. Deciding which problems are worth solving at all. AI cannot own these responsibilities because they require understanding real-world context and being accountable for outcomes.

This is why the fundamentals you have learned matter more, not less, in an age of AI. A strong engineer who understands requirements, design, testing, and security can direct AI tools effectively and catch their mistakes. An engineer who lacks those fundamentals cannot tell good AI output from dangerous output. The tools have changed, but the discipline of engineering, careful, accountable problem-solving in service of real human needs, remains firmly in your hands.

Summary

- **Human oversight** means a qualified person reviews, understands, and remains accountable for all AI-generated output.
- You should never commit code you cannot understand and explain.
- Responsible use means verifying before trusting, protecting confidential data, being transparent, and using AI to grow rather than replace your skills.
- As AI handles routine coding, the engineer's value shifts toward judgment, design, ethics, and accountability, making core fundamentals more important than ever.

Chapter Summary

This chapter brought together everything you have learned across the course and placed it in the context of a rapidly changing profession. You began by seeing how AI reaches into every phase of the software development lifecycle, from requirements through maintenance, and how coding assistants generate and explain code. From there you explored how AI supports the early, high-stakes work of requirements and design, always as a partner that proposes options for a human to refine. You then saw how AI accelerates the often tedious tasks of testing, debugging, and refactoring, turning slow chores into faster feedback loops.

Crucially, this chapter did not present AI as a magic solution. You learned that AI-generated code can be insecure, that models hallucinate confident but incorrect output, and that using AI raises real intellectual property questions. These risks are not reasons to avoid AI. They are reasons to use it with discipline. The response to every risk was the same underlying principle: verify, understand, and remain accountable.

That principle connects directly to the bigger picture of your career as a software engineer. AI changes the tools of the trade, but it does not change the trade itself. The judgment to know what to build, the design skill to structure it well, the security awareness to keep it safe, and the accountability to stand behind it all remain human responsibilities. Because you have built these fundamentals throughout this course, you are equipped not just to use AI, but to direct it wisely and catch it when it errs. That combination of strong fundamentals and skilled tool use is what defines an effective engineer in the age of AI.

Chapter Lab: Using an AI Assistant to Analyze, Test, and Refactor an Application

In this lab, you will work with an AI assistant to analyze an existing application, generate tests for its behavior, and refactor it for improved clarity and structure. You will apply the skills from this chapter by providing effective context to the assistant, critically evaluating its suggestions, and verifying that its output is correct and secure. The lab reinforces the central lesson of the chapter: AI accelerates the work, but human oversight and verification keep that work trustworthy.

Chapter 14: Software Engineering as a Profession

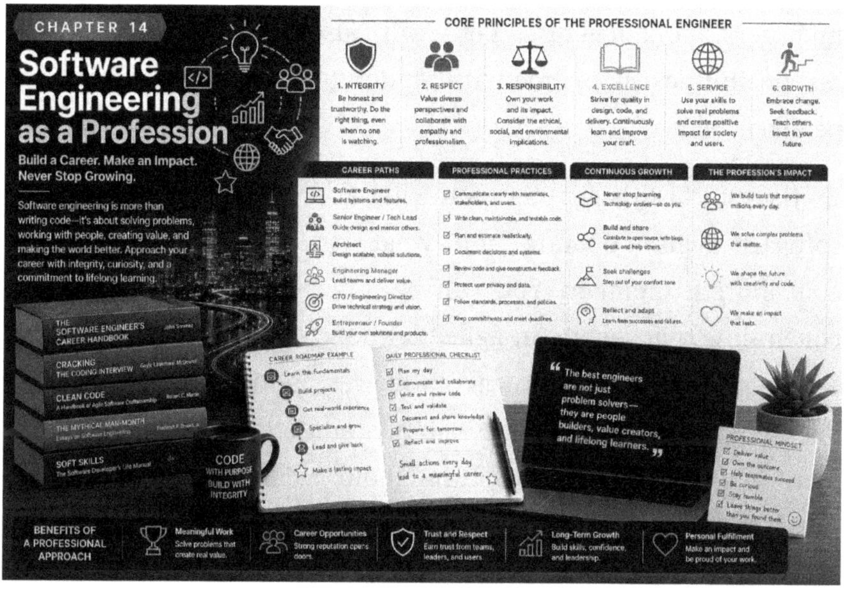

Up to this point, you have focused on the technical craft of building software: writing clean code, structuring programs, testing your work, and collaborating through version control. Those skills form the foundation of your career. But technical ability alone does not make someone a professional software engineer. Real projects have deadlines, budgets, stakeholders with competing priorities, and ethical implications that reach far beyond the code editor. Learning to navigate these realities is what separates a hobbyist from a working professional.

In this chapter, you will step back from the keyboard and look at software engineering as a profession. You will learn how software projects are planned, estimated, and scheduled, and how teams manage the risks and changes that inevitably arise. You will explore what it means to lead technically, communicate effectively, and work productively on a team alongside designers, product managers, and clients. You will also examine the ethical responsibilities that come with building software that affects real people.

By the end of this chapter, you will understand how professional software teams operate and what is expected of you as a contributing member. You will be able to reason about project constraints, participate in agile planning, communicate with both technical and non-technical audiences, and make responsible decisions about privacy, accessibility, and ethics. Finally, you will learn how to keep growing throughout a career that will change many times over. These are the skills that turn a competent coder into a trusted engineer.

14.1 Software Project Planning

Every meaningful piece of software begins not with code but with a plan. Before a single line is written, someone must decide what the software should do, how much effort it will take, and when it needs to be finished. **Software project planning** is the process of defining this work and mapping it onto time and resources. Without it, teams drift, deadlines slip, and stakeholders lose trust.

In this section, you will learn the core planning activities that shape every project: defining scope, estimating effort, building a schedule, and setting milestones. These activities matter because they turn a vague idea ("we want an app that helps people track expenses") into a concrete, achievable set of tasks. Whether you work at a large corporation or a two-person startup, some form of planning is happening around you, and understanding it makes you a far more effective contributor.

Software Project Planning

Planning answers three fundamental questions: *What are we building? How long will it take? Who does what, and when?* A plan is not a promise carved in stone. It is a shared understanding of the current best guess, meant to be revised as you learn more.

Good planning balances detail with flexibility. Plan too little, and the team has no direction. Plan too much, and you waste time predicting a future that will change anyway. The goal is to plan enough to coordinate work and manage expectations, then adapt as reality unfolds.

Consider how a small team might capture a plan in a simple structured form:

```
project_plan = {
    "name": "Expense Tracker",
    "goal": "Help users record and categorize daily expenses",
    "team": ["Ana", "Ben", "Chris"],
    "tasks": [
        {"id": 1, "title": "Design database schema", "owner": "Ana", "days": 3},
        {"id": 2, "title": "Build expense entry form", "owner": "Ben", "days": 5},
        {"id": 3, "title": "Add category reports", "owner": "Chris", "days": 4},
    ],
}

total_days = sum(task["days"] for task in project_plan["tasks"])
print(f"Estimated total effort: {total_days} developer-days")
```

This example represents a plan as data, which makes it easy to analyze. Each task has an owner and an estimate, and summing the `days` field gives a rough total effort of `12` developer-days. Representing plans this way is useful because it forces you to be explicit about who owns what and how long each piece will take. Real teams use dedicated tools for this, but the underlying idea is the same: break the work into named, owned, estimated pieces.

Scope, Estimation, and Scheduling

Three concepts work together to turn an idea into a schedule. **Scope** defines exactly what the project will and will not include. **Estimation** predicts how much effort each piece of scope requires. **Scheduling** places that estimated work onto a calendar, accounting for who is available and in what order tasks must happen.

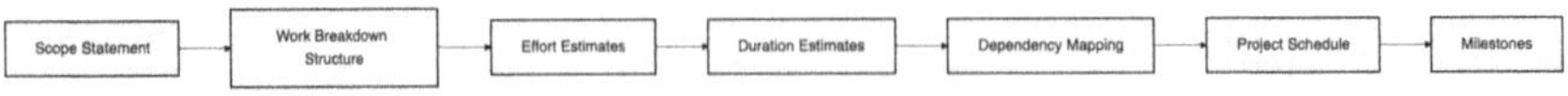

Scope is the foundation. If you do not know what you are building, you cannot estimate it. A common failure is **scope creep**, where new features quietly get added without adjusting the estimate or schedule. Defining scope clearly, and writing down what is explicitly *out* of scope, protects the project from slowly ballooning beyond its budget.

Estimation is notoriously difficult. Humans are optimistic and consistently underestimate how long work takes. A useful technique is to estimate in ranges rather than single numbers ("this will take 3 to 5 days") and to compare new tasks against similar past work. Another is to break large tasks into smaller ones, because small tasks are far easier to estimate accurately than large, fuzzy ones.

```
def schedule_tasks(tasks, start_day=1):
    schedule = []
    current_day = start_day
    for task in tasks:
        end_day = current_day + task["days"] - 1
        schedule.append({
            "title": task["title"],
            "start": current_day,
            "end": end_day,
        })
        current_day = end_day + 1
    return schedule

tasks = [
    {"title": "Design database schema", "days": 3},
    {"title": "Build expense entry form", "days": 5},
    {"title": "Add category reports", "days": 4},
]

for item in schedule_tasks(tasks):
    print(f"{item['title']}: day {item['start']} to day {item['end']}")
```

This function takes estimated tasks and lays them out sequentially on a calendar of "days." Each task starts the day after the previous one ends, producing a simple schedule. Real schedules are more complex because some tasks can run in parallel and some depend on others, but this shows the essential move from estimates to a timeline. Notice that the schedule is only as reliable as the estimates feeding it, which is why estimation quality matters so much.

Milestones

A **milestone** is a significant checkpoint in a project, usually marking the completion of a meaningful chunk of work. Unlike ordinary tasks, milestones represent moments where the team can pause, assess progress, and demonstrate results to stakeholders. Examples include "database design complete," "first working prototype," or "public launch."

Milestones serve two purposes. First, they give the team concrete targets to aim for, which keeps momentum high. Second, they create natural points to check whether the project is on track and to communicate progress to people outside the team. A project with no milestones is hard to steer, because there is no way to tell whether you are ahead or behind until the very end.

Summary

- Software project planning turns a vague idea into concrete, owned, estimated tasks and a shared understanding of the work.
- Scope defines what is and is not included; unmanaged scope creep is a common cause of project failure.
- Estimation is difficult, so estimate in ranges, break large tasks down, and compare against past work.
- Scheduling places estimated work onto a calendar and is only as reliable as the estimates behind it.
- Milestones mark significant checkpoints, giving the team targets and creating natural moments to assess and communicate progress.

14.2 Managing Risk and Agile Planning

No plan survives contact with reality. Requirements change, technical problems appear, and people leave the team. Professional engineers do not pretend that plans are perfect; instead, they build processes that expect and absorb change. This is the heart of both risk management and agile planning.

In this section, you will learn how to identify and respond to project risks before they become crises, and how agile methods replace rigid long-term plans with short, iterative cycles. These approaches matter because software projects are inherently uncertain. The teams that succeed are not the ones with perfect plans, but the ones that adapt fastest when the plan proves wrong.

Risk Management

A **risk** is any uncertain event that could negatively affect a project. Examples include a key library being deprecated, an estimate being wildly wrong, or a critical team member falling ill. **Risk management** is the practice of identifying these threats early, assessing how likely and how damaging each one is, and preparing responses.

The basic workflow is to list your risks, rate each one by probability and impact, and then decide on a response. You can *avoid* a risk by changing your approach, *mitigate* it by reducing its likelihood or impact, *transfer* it to someone else (such as through insurance or a vendor contract), or *accept* it and prepare a contingency plan. The riskiest projects are the ones where nobody has thought about what could go wrong.

```python
risks = [
    {"description": "Third-party payment API may change", "probability": 0.4, "impact": 8},
    {"description": "Lead developer might leave mid-project", "probability": 0.2, "impact": 9},
    {"description": "Estimates may be too optimistic", "probability": 0.7, "impact": 5},
]

for risk in risks:
    exposure = risk["probability"] * risk["impact"]
    risk["exposure"] = round(exposure, 2)

risks.sort(key=lambda r: r["exposure"], reverse=True)

for risk in risks:
    print(f"{risk['exposure']:>5}  {risk['description']}")
```

This code calculates a **risk exposure** score by multiplying each risk's probability (from 0 to 1) by its impact (on a scale of 1 to 10), then sorts the risks so the most dangerous appear first. Ranking risks this way helps a team focus its limited attention on the threats that matter most. Notice that a moderately likely but low-impact risk can score higher than a rare but catastrophic one, which is exactly the kind of trade-off that risk scoring makes visible.

Agile Planning and Backlogs

Traditional planning tries to define an entire project up front. **Agile planning** takes a different approach: it plans in short cycles, delivers working software frequently, and adjusts based on feedback. Rather than a fixed master plan, agile teams work from a **backlog**, which is a prioritized list of everything the team might build.

Each item in the backlog is typically written as a **user story**, a short description of a feature from the user's point of view, often in the form "As a [user], I want [goal] so that [benefit]." The backlog is continuously reordered so that the most valuable work sits at the top. This means the team is always working on what matters most right now, not what someone guessed would matter months ago.

```
backlog = [
    {"story": "As a user, I want to log in so my data is private", "priority": 1, "points": 5},
    {"story": "As a user, I want to export my expenses to CSV", "priority": 3, "points": 3},
    {"story": "As a user, I want to add an expense so I can track spending", "priority": 2, "points": 8},
]

backlog.sort(key=lambda item: item["priority"])

print("Prioritized backlog:")
for item in backlog:
    print(f"  [{item['points']} pts] {item['story']}")
```

Here the backlog is a list of user stories, each with a priority and an estimate measured in **story points**. Story points express relative effort rather than exact hours, which sidesteps the false precision of time estimates. Sorting by priority produces the ordered list the team will pull work from. The team always takes from the top, so keeping the backlog well ordered is one of the most important ongoing planning activities.

Sprint Planning and Tracking Progress

Most agile teams work in **sprints**, which are short fixed-length iterations, usually one to four weeks. At the start of each sprint, the team holds **sprint planning**, where they pull the highest-priority stories from the backlog into the sprint, committing only to what they can realistically finish.

To track progress during a sprint, teams often use a **burndown chart**, which plots the remaining work against time. As stories are completed, the remaining work "burns down" toward zero.

Comparing the actual progress line against the ideal straight line instantly reveals whether the team is ahead, behind, or on track.

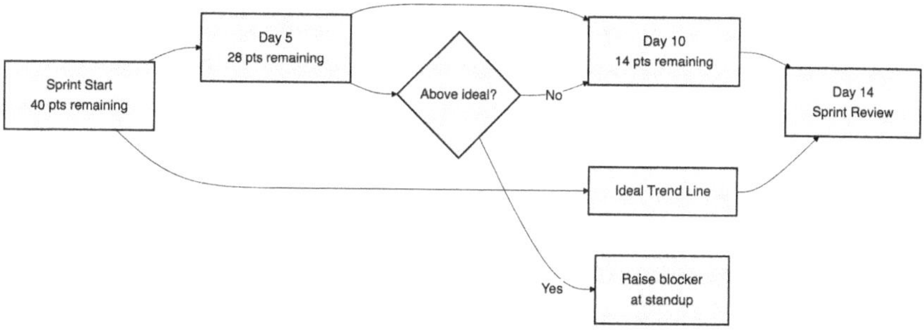

The value of this tracking is that problems become visible early. If the burndown line is flat halfway through the sprint, the team knows *now* that something is wrong, rather than discovering it on the final day. This early visibility is what allows agile teams to adjust before a small slippage becomes a missed deadline.

Summary

- A risk is an uncertain event that could harm a project; risk management means identifying, assessing, and preparing responses early.
- Ranking risks by exposure (probability times impact) helps a team focus attention on the most dangerous threats.
- Agile planning works in short cycles from a prioritized backlog of user stories rather than a fixed master plan.
- Story points express relative effort and avoid the false precision of hour-based estimates.
- Sprints and burndown charts make progress visible early, so teams can adjust before small problems become crises.

14.3 Leadership and Communication

As you gain experience, your influence will extend beyond the code you personally write. You will guide technical decisions, mentor newer developers, and help your team navigate difficult trade-offs. This is leadership, and it is a skill every senior engineer must develop, whether or not they hold a formal management title.

In this section, you will learn what technical leadership looks like in practice, why clear communication and documentation are among the most valuable skills an engineer can have, and how to manage the constant tension between time, cost, scope, and quality. These skills matter because software is built by people, and coordinating people well is often harder than solving the technical problems themselves.

Technical Leadership

Technical leadership is the ability to guide a team toward good technical outcomes through influence, expertise, and trust rather than authority alone. A technical leader sets direction on architecture and standards, unblocks teammates, and makes hard calls when the team is stuck. Crucially, leadership is not about being the smartest person in the room; it is about making the whole team more effective.

Great technical leaders mentor others generously, share context so that everyone can make good decisions independently, and take responsibility when things go wrong. They ask questions instead of dictating answers, because a team that understands *why* a decision was made will apply that reasoning to future problems.

Leadership is a multiplier: your impact grows when you make the people around you better.

Communication and Documentation

The best technical solution is worthless if you cannot explain it. **Communication** is the engineer's tool for aligning people, and it takes many forms: writing clear commit messages, explaining a design in a meeting, or answering a question in a chat channel. Strong communicators tailor their message to the audience, giving a project manager the business impact while giving a fellow engineer the technical detail.

Documentation is communication that outlives the conversation. Good documentation captures *why* decisions were made, not just what the code does, so that future developers (including your future self) can understand the reasoning. Undocumented systems become fragile, because the knowledge lives only in people's heads and disappears when they leave.

```python
def calculate_late_fee(days_overdue, daily_rate=0.50, max_fee=10.00):
    """Calculate the late fee for an overdue library book.

    We cap the fee at max_fee because library policy (see policy
    doc section 4.2) forbids fees exceeding the book's replacement
    cost. Returns 0 for books returned on time.

    Args:
        days_overdue: Whole days past the due date. Negative or
            zero means the book is not overdue.
        daily_rate: Fee charged per overdue day, in dollars.
        max_fee: Maximum total fee allowed by policy.

    Returns:
        The fee owed, as a float, never exceeding max_fee.
    """
    if days_overdue <= 0:
        return 0.0
    fee = days_overdue * daily_rate
    return min(fee, max_fee)
```

This function's **docstring** does far more than describe parameters. It explains *why* the fee is capped by referencing a specific policy, which is exactly the kind of context that would otherwise be lost. A future developer tempted to remove the cap would immediately understand the business reason it exists. This is the difference between documentation that merely repeats the code and documentation that preserves genuine knowledge.

Managing Change

Change is constant in software. Requirements shift, priorities move, and new information arrives daily. **Managing change** means having a process for evaluating proposed changes rather than either blindly accepting them all or rigidly refusing them.

When a change is requested, a good team asks what it costs, what it displaces, and whether its value justifies the disruption. Every accepted change has a ripple effect: it consumes time, may introduce new risks, and often forces trade-offs against other work. Communicating these trade-offs clearly to stakeholders is what keeps a project honest, because it prevents the illusion that new features are free.

Balancing Time, Cost, Scope, and Quality

Every project operates under four competing pressures: **time** (the schedule), **cost** (the budget and people), **scope** (the features), and **quality** (how well it works). These four cannot all be maximized at once. Pushing on one inevitably strains the others.

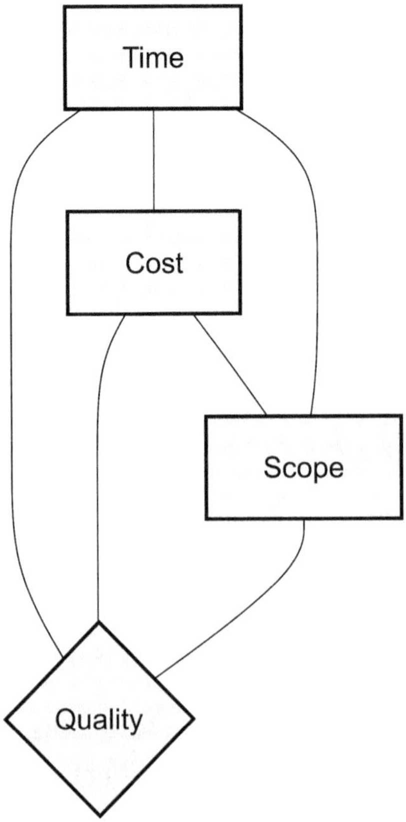

The classic mistake is to add scope while holding time and cost fixed, which forces quality to drop, usually in the form of bugs and technical debt. A professional engineer's job is to make these trade-offs visible and explicit. When a stakeholder asks for a new feature by the same deadline, you must be able to say clearly: "We can do that, but either something else drops out of scope, or we need more time." Making the invisible cost visible is one of the most valuable things you can do for a project.

Summary

- Technical leadership guides teams through influence, expertise, and trust, and multiplies impact by making others more effective.
- Communication aligns people and must be tailored to the audience's needs and level of technical detail.
- Good documentation captures *why* decisions were made, preserving knowledge that would otherwise vanish when people leave.
- Managing change means evaluating each request's cost and ripple effects rather than blindly accepting or refusing it.
- Time, cost, scope, and quality are competing constraints; a professional makes their trade-offs visible and explicit.

14.4 Working on Software Teams

Almost all professional software is built by teams, not lone individuals. This changes everything about how you work. Your code must be readable by others, your decisions must be discussed, and your success depends on how well the whole group functions. Learning to be an effective team member is just as important as learning to program.

In this section, you will learn what it means to treat software engineering as a profession, how development teams are structured and coordinated, which communication skills matter most day to day, and how to work productively with the stakeholders who define and depend on your work. These skills determine whether you are someone teams want to work with, which has an enormous effect on your career.

Software Engineering as a Profession

A **profession** is more than a job. It carries shared standards, ongoing responsibilities, and an expectation that practitioners act in the interest of those affected by their work. Doctors, lawyers, and civil engineers are held to professional standards, and software engineering is steadily maturing toward the same expectations, because software now controls cars, medical devices, and financial systems.

Treating your work as a profession means taking ownership of quality, being honest about what you know and do not know, and continually improving your craft. It means writing code that others can maintain, testing your work before shipping it, and speaking up when you see something that could harm users. Professionalism is a mindset as much as a set of skills.

Working on Development Teams

Modern development teams are usually **cross-functional**, meaning they combine people with different specialties: front-end and back-end developers, quality assurance testers, designers, and a product owner. Coordinating this mix requires shared conventions, so teams adopt agreed-upon coding standards, branching strategies, and review processes.

Code review is one of the most important team practices. When a teammate reviews your work before it merges, they catch bugs, share knowledge, and keep the codebase consistent. Reviewing well is a skill: focus on the code rather than the person, explain your reasoning, and distinguish between required fixes and personal preferences. Being gracious about receiving feedback matters just as much as giving it.

Communication Skills

Day-to-day teamwork runs on communication. Beyond writing and speaking clearly, effective communication includes **active listening**, which means genuinely understanding another person's point before responding. Misunderstandings, not technical difficulty, are the cause of many project failures.

Several small habits make a big difference. Ask clarifying questions instead of assuming. Summarize decisions in writing so everyone shares the same understanding. Give feedback kindly and specifically. When you disagree, argue the idea, not the person. These habits build the trust that lets a team move quickly, because people can rely on each other to raise concerns honestly and resolve them constructively.

Working with Stakeholders

A **stakeholder** is anyone with an interest in the project's outcome: users, clients, managers, and sometimes regulators. Stakeholders define what "success" means, and their needs are often unspoken or contradictory. Learning to elicit real requirements from them is a core professional skill.

The key is to translate between two worlds. Stakeholders speak in terms of goals and problems ("customers keep abandoning their carts"), while engineers think in terms of features and systems. Your job is to dig beneath a requested feature to find the underlying need, because the feature someone asks for is often not the one that best solves their problem. Asking "what are you trying to achieve?" frequently reveals a simpler, better solution than the one originally proposed.

Summary

- Treating software engineering as a profession means owning quality, being honest about your knowledge, and protecting the people affected by your work.
- Modern teams are cross-functional and rely on shared conventions and code review to stay coordinated and consistent.
- Effective communication depends heavily on active listening, clarifying questions, and written summaries of decisions.
- Stakeholders define success but express needs in terms of goals, so engineers must translate goals into features and dig beneath requests to find the real need.

14.5 Ethics and Responsibility

Software is not neutral. The systems you build shape how people communicate, whether they can access services, and what happens to their personal information. With this power comes responsibility. As a professional, you will sometimes face decisions where the technically easy path and the right path diverge.

In this section, you will learn to think through the ethical dimensions of your work, protect user privacy, build software that is accessible to everyone, and understand the role of open-source software in the wider ecosystem. These are not abstract concerns. They arise in ordinary projects all the time, and how you handle them defines what kind of engineer you become.

Ethics

Ethics in software engineering is the set of principles that guide you to build software responsibly, considering its effects on users and society. Professional bodies such as the ACM and IEEE publish codes of ethics, but ethics is ultimately about judgment, not rule-following. The core question is always: *who could be harmed by this, and how?*

Ethical issues appear in everyday work. A recommendation algorithm might maximize engagement by promoting outrage. A dark pattern in a checkout flow might trick users into subscriptions they did not want. A dataset used to train a model might encode discriminatory bias. In each case, the code works perfectly, yet the outcome is harmful. Recognizing these situations, and being willing to raise concerns even when it is uncomfortable, is what ethical practice demands.

Privacy

Privacy is the user's right to control their personal information. When your software collects data, you become a custodian of something that does not belong to you, and users trust you to protect it. Violating that trust, through carelessness or exploitation, causes real harm.

A practical principle is **data minimization**: collect only the data you actually need, keep it only as long as necessary, and protect it while you hold it. Many jurisdictions now enforce privacy through laws such as the GDPR, but the ethical obligation exists regardless of legal requirements.

```
import hashlib

def anonymize_email(email):
    """Return a one-way hash of an email for analytics.

    We store the hash instead of the raw email so we can count
    unique users without retaining personally identifiable
    information. The original email cannot be recovered.
    """
    normalized = email.strip().lower()
    return hashlib.sha256(normalized.encode("utf-8")).hexdigest()

hashed = anonymize_email("User@Example.com ")
print(hashed[:16], "...")
```

This function demonstrates privacy by design. Instead of storing raw email addresses for analytics, it stores a one-way **hash**, which lets the team count unique users without keeping data that could identify or harm them if leaked. The email is normalized first so that the same address always produces the same hash. Techniques like this let you achieve business goals while respecting the principle of collecting and retaining as little personal data as possible.

Accessibility

Accessibility means designing software that people with disabilities can use, including those who are blind, have low vision, are deaf, or have motor impairments. Roughly one in six people worldwide lives with a significant disability, so accessibility is not an edge case; it is a large population of real users.

Accessible software follows established guidelines such as the Web Content Accessibility Guidelines (WCAG). Practical steps include providing text alternatives for images, ensuring sufficient color contrast, making everything usable by keyboard alone, and structuring content so screen readers can interpret it. Building accessibility in from the start is far easier than retrofitting it later, and it often improves the experience for *everyone*, not only users with disabilities.

Open-Source Software

Open-source software is software whose source code is publicly available and licensed so that anyone can use, study, modify, and share it. It powers a vast portion of modern technology, from operating systems to the libraries you import in nearly every project.

Working with open source carries responsibilities. You must respect software **licenses**, which set the rules for how code can be used; ignoring them can create legal and ethical problems. Contributing back to open source, through code, documentation, or bug reports, strengthens the shared foundation that the whole industry relies on. Understanding this ecosystem, and participating in it responsibly, is part of being a professional engineer.

Summary

- Software is not neutral, and ethics requires you to ask who could be harmed by what you build and to raise concerns when needed.
- Privacy makes you a custodian of user data; practice data minimization and protect information regardless of legal requirements.
- Accessibility ensures people with disabilities can use your software and often improves the experience for all users.
- Open-source software underpins modern technology, and using it responsibly means respecting licenses and contributing back where you can.

14.6 Growing as a Software Engineer

Technology changes constantly. The languages, frameworks, and tools you learn today will look different in ten years, and some will disappear entirely. The one skill that never goes out of date is the ability to keep learning. A software career is a long journey of continuous growth, and this final section will help you navigate it.

In this section, you will learn how to keep your skills current, understand the common career paths open to you, build a portfolio that demonstrates your abilities, prepare effectively for technical interviews, and think about where the field is heading. These skills matter because your career will outlast any single technology, and the engineers who thrive are the ones who never stop growing.

Continuous Learning

Continuous learning is the ongoing practice of expanding your knowledge throughout your career. In a field that reinvents itself every few years, the developer who stops learning quickly falls behind. The good news is that learning is a skill you can develop deliberately.

Effective learning combines several habits: reading documentation and source code, building small side projects to try new ideas, following how experienced engineers work, and reflecting on your mistakes. Depth matters as much as breadth. Understanding *why* a technology works the way it does lets you transfer that knowledge when the specific tool inevitably changes. Focus on durable fundamentals, because they age far more slowly than any particular framework.

Software Engineering Career Paths

A software engineering career rarely follows a single straight line. Early on, you build broad foundations. As you gain experience, you typically reach a fork between two directions: the **individual contributor** track, where you deepen technical expertise and may become a senior engineer, architect, or specialist; and the **management** track, where you lead people and coordinate teams.

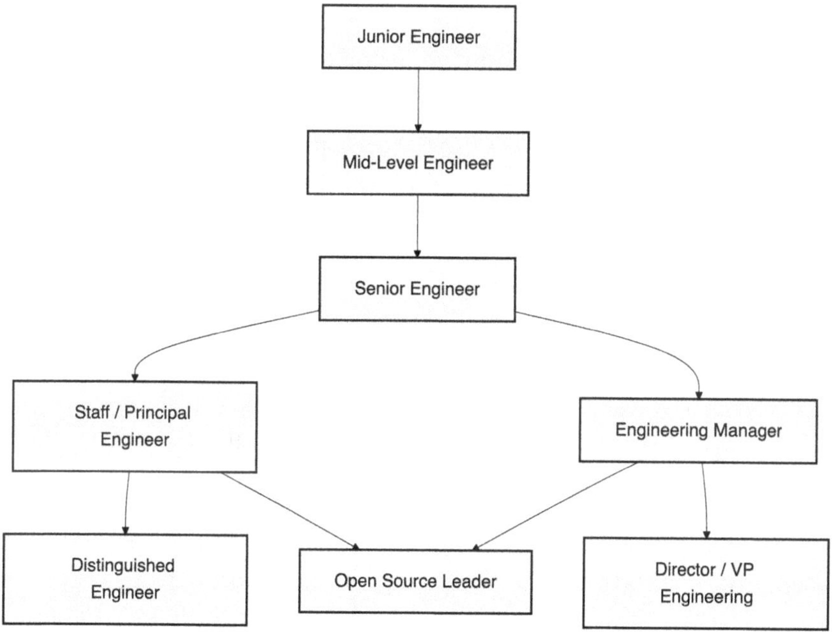

Neither path is superior, and many engineers move between them over time. Some specialize deeply in a domain such as security, machine learning, or embedded systems. Others become generalists who thrive on variety. The important thing is to make deliberate choices about which direction excites you, rather than drifting by default. Your career is long enough to change direction more than once.

Building a Professional Portfolio

A **portfolio** is a curated collection of work that demonstrates your skills to potential employers or collaborators. For a software engineer, this usually includes public code repositories, personal projects, and contributions to open source. A strong portfolio shows what you can actually do, which is far more convincing than a list of buzzwords on a résumé.

Quality beats quantity. A few well-documented, working projects say more than dozens of half-finished experiments. Include a clear README for each project explaining what it does, why you built it, and how to run it. Your portfolio is often the first real evidence an employer sees of how you think and write code, so treat it as a professional showcase.

Preparing for Technical Interviews

Technical interviews are how most software roles are filled, and they test a specific set of skills that overlap only partially with day-to-day work. You will typically be asked to solve coding problems, explain your reasoning aloud, and discuss system design and past projects. Preparation makes an enormous difference.

Practice solving problems while narrating your thought process, because interviewers care about *how* you reason, not just whether you reach the answer. Review core computer science fundamentals such as data structures, algorithms, and time complexity, since these appear constantly. Rehearse describing your past projects clearly, including the trade-offs you made. And remember that an interview is a two-way evaluation; you are also deciding whether the team and role are right for you.

The Future of Software Engineering

The field continues to evolve rapidly. Artificial intelligence tools are changing how code is written, cloud computing has reshaped how software is deployed, and new concerns around ethics, privacy, and sustainability are becoming central to the profession. Predicting specifics is impossible, but the direction is clear: software will grow more powerful and more deeply woven into daily life.

What this means for you is that adaptability is your most valuable trait. Tools that automate routine coding will raise the value of the skills machines cannot easily replicate: understanding real human problems, making sound judgment calls, designing systems thoughtfully, and communicating clearly. The engineers who succeed in the future will be those who combine strong fundamentals with the flexibility to keep learning as the ground shifts beneath them.

Summary

- Continuous learning is the one skill that never goes out of date; focus on durable fundamentals over specific tools.
- Careers commonly fork between the individual contributor and management tracks, and you can move between them over time.
- A strong portfolio of a few well-documented, working projects demonstrates your abilities better than any list of buzzwords.
- Technical interviews reward clear reasoning and solid fundamentals, and they are a two-way evaluation of fit.
- The future favors adaptability and the human skills, judgment, communication, and problem understanding, that automation cannot easily replace.

Chapter Summary

This chapter shifted your focus from the mechanics of writing code to the realities of building software as a professional. You began with planning, learning how scope, estimation, scheduling, and milestones turn an idea into an achievable project. From there you saw why no plan is perfect, and how risk management and agile practices let teams absorb the constant change that defines real software work. These ideas connect directly: planning gives you direction, and agile methods give you the flexibility to correct course when that direction proves wrong.

You then moved from process to people. Leadership, communication, and documentation are the skills that let a group of individuals function as a team, and the constraints of time, cost, scope, and quality frame nearly every decision a team makes. Working effectively with teammates and stakeholders, and holding yourself to ethical standards around privacy, accessibility, and responsible use of open source, is what earns the trust that a professional career depends on. These are not separate topics but facets of the same thing: engineering is a human activity with human consequences.

Before this chapter, you could build software. Now you understand how software is built by teams, for stakeholders, under real constraints, and with genuine responsibility to the people it affects. Finally, you looked ahead to your own growth, because a career in this field is a long process of continuous learning. The specific technologies will change many times, but the professional judgment, communication, and ethical grounding you have studied here will remain valuable for as long as you build software.

Chapter Lab: Planning and Reflecting on a Software Project

In this lab, you will apply the professional skills from this chapter by drafting a lightweight project plan and agile backlog for a small application, identifying its top risks, and writing a short reflection on the ethical and accessibility considerations it raises. You will practice defining scope, estimating and prioritizing work as user stories, ranking risks by exposure, and reasoning about your responsibilities to users. The lab brings together planning, risk management, agile thinking, and ethics so you can experience how a professional engineer approaches a project before writing any code.

Chapter 15: Appendix A: Accessing the Online Course

With the purchase of this book, you also receive access to the online labs and additional learning resources available through the Destin Learning Lab platform.

To access the labs for this course:

1. https://labs.destinlearning.com
2. Sign up for a free account
3. Open your account profile/settings page
4. Enter the course access code:

```
PRINCIPLES2026
```

1. Navigate to the **Courses** section to access the *Foundations of Java Programming* online labs and resources.

These hands-on labs are designed to reinforce the concepts covered throughout this book and provide practical Linux experience in a real lab environment.

If you experience any issues registering or accessing the course, please contact:

sales@destinlearning.com

www.ingramcontent.com/pod-product-compliance
Lightning Source LLC
LaVergne TN
LVHW050754061126
851857LV00012B/557
* 9 7 9 8 2 4 0 8 4 1 3 1 6 *